DUST BOWL
THE SOUTHERN PLAINS IN THE 1930s

DUST

The Southern Plains

Oxford New York

Toronto Melbourne

BOWL

in the 1930s

DONALD WORSTER

OXFORD UNIVERSITY PRESS

OXFORD UNIVERSITY PRESS
Oxford London Glasgow
New York Toronto Melbourne Auckland
Delhi Bombay Calcutta Madras Karachi
Kuala Lumpur Singapore Hong Kong Tokyo
Nairobi Dar es Salaam Cape Town

and associate companies in
Beirut Berlin Ibadan Mexico City Nicosia

Library of Congress Cataloging in Publication Data
Worster, Donald E   1941-
Dust Bowl.
Bibliography: p.
Includes index.
1. Southwestern States—History.   2.   Great Plains—History.
3. Agriculture—Southwestern States—History.
4. Agriculture—Great Plains—History.
5. Dust storms—Great Plains.   6. Dust storms—Southwestern States.
7. Depressions—1929—United States.
I. Title.   F786.W87   978   78-27018
ISBN 0-19-502550-4
ISBN 0-19-503212-8 (pbk.)

ACKNOWLEDGMENTS

Woody Guthrie: "The Great Dust Storm," words and music by Woody Guthrie, TRO ©
Copyright 1960 & 1963 Ludlow Music, Inc., New York, N.Y., used by permission; and
"Do Re Mi," words and music by Woody Guthrie, TRO Copyright © 1961 & 1963 Ludlow
Music, Inc., New York, N.Y. Used by permission.

Dorothea Lange and Paul Taylor, *An American Exodus,* Yale University Press, 1969 © Paul
Schuster Taylor. Used by permission.

Archibald MacLeish, *Land of the Free,* Harcourt Brace Jovanovich. Used by permission.

Carey McWilliams, *Ill Fares the Land,* 1942, Little, Brown & Co. Used by permission.

N. Scott Momaday, "A First American Views His Land," *National Geographic,* July 1976.
Used by permission.

John Steinbeck, *The Grapes of Wrath,* Copyright 1939 by John Steinbeck; renewed © 1967
by John Steinbeck. All rights reserved. Reprinted by permission of Viking Penguin, Inc.

17 19 20 18
Printed in the United States of America

For my parents,
Delbert and Bonnie Worster,
who went through it

PREFACE

This book was undertaken for a selfish and private reason: I wanted to see the plains again. After a decade and a half of living in other places, many of them exotic and distant, and of studying the ideas of a larger world, I thought it was time to come home for a while and take another look at the land and people who gave me so much to start with. Had I been a Wallace Stegner, I might have written a novel or an autobiography instead of a work of history. But in its own way, and despite the scholar's footnotes, this book is the result of my coming to grips with my own past. It is the product of twenty-odd impressionable years spent growing up on the plains—but also, necessarily, of that amount of time spent away. There were many in the 1930s generation who would have understood my situation and feelings exactly: the return of a native who has discovered that during his absence how much he loves the home country, but who cannot, for all that, view it without criticism. The argument of this book, I am aware, will not be acceptable to many plainsmen. It is, however, based not only on extensive library research, but on conversations with farmers, agronomists, and storekeepers; on travels back and forth across the region; on the indelible memories of blowing dust, and not least on a native son's affection.

The names of many plains residents who generously aided my research will appear later on in the text. But there were others who, though they are not quoted here, were also good enough to share their stories, perspectives, and even a meal or two: Miller and Ruby Easley, Elzy and Vivien Tanner, Lee Thaxton, George Twombley, Truman Tucker, and Norma Jean Young (all of Cimarron County, Oklahoma); Dale and Leona Blair, Erma Lea Henley, Albert Snellbacher, L. O. Stanley, Alta Weidner, and Everett Williams (all of Haskell County, Kansas). Many of these people invited me into their homes—or in one case a hospital room and in another a sheriff's office—and gave me an afternoon or evening of their time.

Quite as accommodating were the busy staffs of several county Soil Conservation Service and extension offices, as well as of many libraries and museums around the country. Among the latter I want to acknowledge especially George Griffin and his associates at the Spencer Research Library of the University of Kansas, Claire Kuehn of the Panhandle-Plains Historical Museum, Helen Ulibarri at the National Archives, and Robert Richmond (among many others) at the Kansas State Historical Society. It is still not a fully appreciated fact in this society that public employees such as these are almost always diligent, efficient, and helpful—not because they expect to gain something for themselves, but because they believe in their work.

The list of those who encouraged me to pursue my own work, and enabled it to reach completion, begins with the American Council of Learned Societies, who supplied an indispensable research fellowship. Sydney Ahlstrom, Lawrence Fuchs, David Hall, and Seymour Lutzky were instrumental in my obtaining that award; and my colleagues at the University of Hawaii granted me an untimely leave of absence to accept it. My agent, Gerard McCauley, and my publisher—in particular, Sheldon Meyer, Caroline Taylor, and Joseph Coghlan at Oxford—have done their part with skill and judgment. Among others who gave support, either by sending information or by listening to or reading parts of the manuscript, were Marjorie Guthrie, Alexandre Hogue, Guy Logsdon, Gil Pagel, Walter Orr Roberts, Peter Rollins, Paul Sears, Charles Stockton, and the American Studies faculty and students at the University of Iowa and of Kansas. Sharon Hagen worked up the maps with skill and insight. Beyond all these I owe a scholar's and a friend's debt to Daniel Rodgers, who gave each chapter a perceptive, tough-minded going over and improved the end product immeasurably. I can only hope at this point that the book is what he and all these supporters deserve and will find satisfying.

Coming home again has been worth all the trouble and dislocation it takes, if for nothing else to learn again the virtues and strengths of my family. Much of the burden in this project has been cheerfully borne by my wife, Beverly, and my children, William and Catherine; if they got as much out of the experience as I did then perhaps they are repaid for the heavy demands made on them. Among my family, however, it is my parents I most need to thank: my deceased mother and my father. They had nothing to do directly with the writing of this book—but everything, indirectly. In fact, this is really their story more than it is mine. They were among the last of the plains people to go west in the thirties, settling briefly in California's deserts, where I was born, and among the first to come back in the better years. To them, and, by extension, to all the dispossesed and uprooted and anonymous of that decade, I dedicate these pages.

Honolulu, Hawaii   D.W.
June 1979

CONTENTS

DUST BOWL
THE SOUTHERN PLAINS IN THE 1930s

INTRODUCTION

All progress in capitalistic agriculture
is a progress in the art, not only
of robbing the laborer, but of robbing
the soil.

Karl Marx, *Capital*

THE SOUTHERN PLAINS are a vast austerity. They sprawl over more than 100 million acres, including parts of five states—Kansas, Colorado, New Mexico, Oklahoma, and Texas. Nothing that lives finds life easy under their severe skies; the weather has a nasty habit of turning harsh and violent just when things are getting comfortable. Failure to adapt to these rigors has been a common experience for Americans, so that the plains have become our cultural boneyard, where the evidences of bad judgment and misplaced schemes lie strewn about like bleached skulls. Few of us want to live in the region now. There is too much wind, dirt, flatness, space, barbed wire, drought, uncertainty, hard work. Better to fly over it with the shades pulled down.

Yet the plains have had their place in American dreams, back when the West was new and the grasslands offered unexplored possibilities. In fact they were, for a while, at the front edge of our collective imagination. Walt Whitman called them "North America's characteristic landscape," suggesting that here would

be played out the true heroic drama of our history. Some time ago we spoiled that
hope and lost it. When we look at the plains today, we are amazed that previous
generations could have found so much excitement in so bare a country. The promise
of the land was real, personal, and extravagant to them. For us, however, promises
are harder to believe in, and the land is not where we would look, anyway.

But remote and unappealing as they may be, the plains are still important
to us all. They remain, after much abuse, one of our greatest agricultural treasures—
a crucial source of food, not only for ourselves but for an undernourished world.
They are also a land with which we have not fully learned to be at peace, where
our institutions, even after 100 years, do not fit in and belong. This failure of
adaptation may be the region's most important value—as a model from which we can
learn much about the ecological insensitivity of our culture. Out on the high tableland of the plains occurred one of the most tragic, revealing, and paradigmatic
chapters in our environmental history—one with increasing relevance to mankind's
future. And such matters are what this book is about. It will not offer new mythologies of the American West to replace those that have been discarded. Perhaps
it will not convince every reader that the plains can still be a place of overwhelming
grace and beauty. But I would like to succeed in making the region and its destiny
a part of the reader's concern, as it is of mine.

The Dust Bowl was the darkest moment in the twentieth-century life of
the southern plains. The name suggests a place—a region whose borders are as
inexact and shifting as a sand dune. But it was also an event of national, even plan-
etary, significance. A widely respected authority on world food problems, George
Borgstrom, has ranked the creation of the Dust Bowl as one of the three worst
ecological blunders in history.[1] The other two are the deforestation of China's up-
lands about 3000 B.C., which produced centuries of silting and flooding, and the
destruction of Mediterranean vegetation by livestock, which left once fertile lands
eroded and impoverished. Unlike either of those events, however, the Dust Bowl
took only 50 years to accomplish. It cannot be blamed on illiteracy or overpopulation
or social disorder. It came about because the culture was operating in precisely the
way it was supposed to. Americans blazed their way across a richly endowed continent with a ruthless, devastating efficiency unmatched by any people anywhere.
When the white men came to the plains, they talked expansively of "busting" and
"breaking" the land. And that is exactly what they did. Some environmental catas-
trophes are nature's work, others are the slowly accumulating effects of ignorance or
poverty. The Dust Bowl, in contrast, was the inevitable outcome of a culture that
deliberately, self-consciously, set itself that task of dominating and exploiting the
land for all it was worth.

The Dust Bowl came into being during the 1930s, as fulvous dirt began
to blow all the way from the plains to the East Coast and beyond. That was also

the age of the Great Depression. Coincidence, some might say, that the two traumas should come at the same time. Few who have written on either affair have noticed any connection between them. My argument, however, is that there was in fact a close link between the Dust Bowl and the Depression—that the same society produced them both, and for similar reasons. Both events revealed fundamental weaknesses in the traditional culture of America, the one in ecological terms, the other in economic. Both offered a reason, and an opportunity, for substantial reform of that culture.

That the thirties were a time of great crisis in American, indeed, in world, capitalism has long been an obvious fact. The Dust Bowl, I believe, was part of that same crisis. It came about because the expansionary energy of the United States had finally encountered a volatile, marginal land, destroying the delicate ecological balance that had evolved there. We speak of farmers and plows on the plains and the damage they did, but the language is inadequate. What brought them to the region was a social system, a set of values, an economic order. There is no word that so fully sums up those elements as "capitalism." It is of course a common epithet, often undefined and pejorative; but if the historian eschews the word, to paraphrase R. H. Tawney, he may also ignore the fact. That is what has usually happened in writings about Americans and the land, and, indeed, in much of our historical literature.[2] If I seem to exaggerate in this case, it is only because the arguments have been so gingerly stepped around by others. Capitalism, it is my contention, has been the decisive factor in this nation's use of nature. To understand that use more fully we must explain how and why the Dust Bowl happened, just as we have analyzed our financial and industrial development in the light of the 1929 stock market crash and the ensuing factory shutdowns.

There is no way to attach a neat, simple meaning to a phenomenon as large and changeable as capitalism. Even in the industrial period of the last 200 years it has worn many faces and forms. The words we associate with it are clues to its elusive breadth: private property, business, laissez-faire, profit motive, the pursuit of self-interest, free enterprise, an open marketplace, the bourgeoisie. For Adam Smith it was an economic system loosed from the shackles of feudalism—a "natural liberty" to make, buy, and sell things. For Karl Marx it was a vicious class order in which a few owned the means of production and the rest sold their labor to stay alive. For Max Weber capitalism was a "spirit" that emphasized hard work, accumulation, and economic rationality. America, the nation most thoroughly dominated by business institutions and drives, shows a similar diversity of meaning—a fur trapper going up the Missouri, a railroad executive selling stock, a wheat farmer buying more land, an archetypical factory owner hiring and firing workers. In the 1930s capitalism in Henry Ford's automobile empire meant one thing—a pattern of investment and credit, organization of people and resources—but on the Great

Plains it meant something slightly different, perhaps more primitive, albeit strongly influenced by Ford's machines and production methods. Capitalism is, in other words, a complex economic culture. It is a mode of production that is constantly evolving in many particulars and varying from country to country, from region to region, from decade to decade. But it maintains a recognizable identity all the same: a core of values and assumptions more permanent than these outer forms—an enduring ethos, we will call it here, that gives the economic culture continuity.

The land in this culture, as in any other, is perceived and used in certain, approved ways; there are, in other words, ecological values taught by the capitalist ethos. We may sum them up in three maxims.

1. *Nature must be seen as capital.* It is a set of economic assets that can become a source of profit or advantage, a means to make more wealth. Trees, wildlife, minerals, water, and the soil are all commodities than can either be developed or carried as they are to the marketplace. A business culture attaches no other values to nature than this; the nonhuman world is desanctified and demystified as a consequence. Its functional interdependencies are also discounted in the economic calculus.

2. *Man has a right, even an obligation, to use this capital for constant self-advancement.* Capitalism is an intensely maximizing culture, always seeking to get more out of the natural resources of the world than it did yesterday. The highest economic rewards go to those who have done the most to extract from nature all it can yield. Private acquisitiveness and accumulation are unlimited ideals, impossible to satisfy once and for all.

3. *The social order should permit and encourage this continual increase of personal wealth.* It should free individuals (and corporations as collective individuals) from encumbrances on their aggressive use of nature, teach young people the proper behavior, and protect the successful from losing what they have gained. In pure capitalism, the self as an economic being is not only all-important, but autonomous and irresponsible. The community exists to help individuals get ahead and to absorb the environmental costs.

Every society has within it, of course, contradictory values, and America has been no exception. The white pioneers who first came to the southern plains did bring with them religious ideas, family institutions, and other social traditions that opposed or moderated (or reinforced) this economic ethos. But in their behavior toward the land, capitalism was the major defining influence. From the beginning of settlement, the plainsman was intent on turning the land to more and more gainful use. Like American agriculturalists elsewhere, he increasingly came to view farming and ranching as businesses, the objects of which were not simply to make a living, but to make money.[3] The notion that nature puts restraints on what man can do in those businesses was as abhorrent to him as were social controls. During the laissez-faire, expansionist 1920s the plains were extensively plowed and put to wheat—

turned into highly mechanized factory farms that produced unprecedented harvests. Plains operators, however, ignored all environmental limits in this enterprise, just as Wall Street ignored sharp practices and a top-heavy economy. In a more stable natural region, this sort of farming could have gone on exploiting the land much longer with impunity. But on the plains the elements of risk were higher than they were anywhere else in the country, and the destructive effects of capitalism far more sudden and dramatic. There was nothing in the plains society to check the progress of commercial farming, nothing to prevent it from taking the risks it was willing to take for profit. That is how and why the Dust Bowl came about.

Other ages and cultures, as I have said, have created environmental disasters, though very few of them have been as terrible as that which took place on the plains in the 1930s. The United States has no absolute monopoly on growth-mania, acquisitiveness, ecological insensitivity, or dust bowls. In the 1954-65 period, for instance, the Soviet Union created a little publicized débacle of its own. Food production was not keeping pace with consumer demand, and Premier Nikita Khrushchev personally decided to have the state collective farms plow up 40 million hectares of the "virgin lands" in Kazakstan, Siberia, and Russia. Drought in the sixties led to wind erosion that damaged 17 million of those hectares, and helped depose Khrushchev from office. It is instructive, however, to follow Khrushchev's logic in this plow-up and observe its source. In defending his program against the views of a prominent scientist, he wrote:

> Put Comrade Barayev [the critic] into conditions of capitalist competition and his farm, with its present system of plantings, probably would not survive. Could he ever compete with a large capitalist farm if he keeps 32 percent of his plowed land in clean fallow?[4]

American agriculture has been powerfully persuasive in the world, even among those who profess to live by different principles. Its willingness to take risks for increased production has set a pace that other nations, such as the Soviet Union, feel constrained to follow—just as less aggressive plains farmers have been led to emulate their more affluent entrepreneurial neighbors. There may be many reasons why people misuse their land. But the American Dust Bowl of the thirties suggests that a capitalist-based society has a greater resource hunger than others, greater eagerness to take risks, and less capacity for restraint.

The implications of this should be obvious, though it is not my intention here to spell out detailed remedies or even dwell at length on the contemporary situation. Many have assumed that the New Deal found a sufficient cure for the excesses of free enterprise. From an ecological point of view that confidence seems grossly misplaced, if the evidence of the last several decades counts for anything.

America is still, at heart, a business-oriented society; its farming has evolved even further toward the Henry Ford example of using machinery and mass production to make more and more profits. We are still naïvely sure that science and technique will heal the wounds and sores we leave on the earth, when in fact those wounds are more numerous and more malignant than ever. Perhaps we will never be at perfect peace with the natural order of this continent, perhaps we would not be interesting if we were. But we could give it a better try.

Part I

A DARKLING PLAIN

It fell across our city like a curtain
    of black rolled down,
We thought it was our judgment, we thought
    it was our doom.

Woody Guthrie,
"The Great Dust Storm"

The Black

THE THIRTIES BEGAN in economic depression and in drought. The first of those disasters usually gets all the attention, although for the many Americans living on farms drought was the more serious problem. In the spring of 1930 over 3 million men and women were out of work. They had lost their jobs or had been laid off without pay in the aftermath of the stock market crash of the preceding fall. Another 12 million would suffer the same fate in the following two years. Many of the unemployed had no place to live, nor even the means to buy food. They slept in public toilets, under bridges, in shantytowns along the railroad tracks, or on doorsteps, and in the most wretched cases they scavenged from garbage cans—a Calcutta existence in the richest nation ever. The farmer, in contrast, was slower to feel the impact of the crash. He usually had his own independent food supply and stood a bit aloof from the ups and downs of the urban-industrial system. In the twenties that aloofness had meant that most farm families had not fully shared in the giddy burst of affluence—in new washing machines, silk stockings, and shiny roadsters. They had, in fact, spent much of the decade in economic doldrums. Now, as banks began to fail and soup lines formed, rural Americans went on as before, glad to be spared the latest reversal and just a little pleased to see their proud city cousins humbled. Then the droughts began, and they brought the farmers to their knees, too.[1]

During the spring and summer of 1930, little rain fell over a large part of the eastern United States. A horizontal band on the map, from Maryland and Vir-

Chapter One

Blizzards Roll In

ginia to Missouri and Arkansas, marked the hardest hit area of wilting crops, shrinking ground-water supplies, and uncertain income. Over the summer months in this drought band the rainfall shortage was 60,000 tons for each 100-acre farm, or 700 tons a day. Seventeen million people were affected. In twelve states the drought set record lows in precipitation, and among all the Eastern states only Florida was above normal. Three years earlier the Mississippi River had overflowed its banks and levees in one of the most destructive floods in American history. Now captains there wondered how long their barges would remain afloat as the river shrank to a fraction of its average height.[2]

During the thirties serious drought threatened a great part of the nation. The persistent center, however, shifted from the East to the Great Plains, beginning in 1931, when much of Montana and the Dakotas became almost as arid as the Sonoran Desert. Farmers there and almost everywhere else watched the scorched earth crack open, heard the gray grass crunch underfoot, and worried about how long they would be able to pay their bills. Around their dried-up ponds the willows and wild cherries were nearly leafless, and even the poison ivy drooped. Drought, of course, is a relative term: it depends upon one's concept of "normal." But following the lead of the climatologists of the time, we can use a precipitation deficiency of at least 15 per cent of the historical mean to qualify as drought. By that standard, of all the American states only Maine and Vermont escaped a drought year from 1930 to 1936. Twenty states set or equaled record lows for their entire span of official weather data. Over the nation as a whole, the 1930s drought was, in the words of a Weather Bureau scientist, "the worst in the climatological history of the country."[3]

Intense heat accompanied the drought, along with economic losses the nation could ill afford. In the summer of 1934, Nebraska reached 118 degrees, Iowa, 115. In Illinois thermometers stuck at over 100 degrees for so long that 370 people died— and one man, who had been living in a refrigerator to keep cool, was treated for frostbite. Two years later, when the country was described by *Newsweek* as "a vast simmering caldron," more than 4500 died from excessive heat, water was shipped into the West by diverted tank-cars and oil pipelines, and clouds of grasshoppers ate what little remained of many farmers' wheat and corn—along with their fence-posts and the washing on their clotheslines. The financial cost of the 1934 drought alone amounted to one-half the money the United States had put into World War I. By 1936, farm losses had reached $25 million a day, and more than 2 million farmers were drawing relief checks. Rexford Tugwell, head of the Resettlement Administration, who toured the burning plains that year, saw "a picture of complete destruction"—"one of the most serious peacetime problems in the nation's history."[4]

As the decade reached its midpoint, it was the southern plains that experienced the most severe conditions. During some growing seasons there was no soil moisture down to three feet over large parts of the region. By 1939, near Hays, Kansas, the accumulated rainfall deficiency was more than 34 inches—almost a two-year supply in arrears. Continued long enough in such a marginal, semiarid land, a drought of that magnitude would produce a desert. Weathermen pointed out that there had been worse single years, as in 1910 and 1917, or back in the 1890s, and they repeatedly assured the people of the region that their records did not show any modern drought lasting more than five years, nor did they suggest any long-range adverse climatic shift.[5] But farmers and ranchers did not find much comfort in statistical charts; their cattle were bawling for feed, and their bank credit was drying up along with the soil. Not until after 1941 did the rains return in abundance and the burden of anxiety lift.

Droughts are an inevitable fact of life on the plains, an extreme one occurring roughly every twenty years, and milder ones every three or four. They have always brought with them blowing dust where the ground was bare of crops or native grass. Dust was so familiar an event that no one was surprised to see it appear when the dry weather began in 1931. But no one was prepared for what came later: dust storms of such violence that they made the drought only a secondary problem— storms of such destructive force that they left the region reeling in confusion and fear.

"Earth" is the word we use when it is there in place, growing the food we eat, giving us a place to stand and build on. "Dust" is what we say when it is loose and blowing on the wind. Nature encompasses both—the good and the bad from our perspective, and from that of all living things. We need the earth to stay alive, but dust is a nuisance, or, worse, a killer. On a planet such as ours, where there is much wind, where there are frequent dry spells, and where we encounter vast expanses of bare soil, dust is a constant presence. It rises from the hooves of animals, from a wagon's wheels, from a dry riverbed, from the deserts. If all the continents were an English greensward, there would be no dust. But nature has not made things so. Nor has man, in many times and places.

Dust in the air is one phenomenon. However, dust storms are quite another. The story of the southern plains in the 1930s is essentially about dust storms, when the earth ran amok. And not once or twice, but over and over for the better part of a decade: day after day, year after year, of sand rattling against the window, of fine powder caking one's lips, of springtime turned to despair, of poverty eating into self-confidence.

Explaining why those storms occurred requires an excursion into the history of the plains and an understanding of the agriculture that evolved there. For the "dirty thirties," as they were called, were primarily the work of man, not nature. Admittedly, nature had something to do with this disaster too. Without winds the soil would have stayed put, no matter how bare it was. Without drought, farmers would have had strong, healthy crops capable of checking the wind. But natural factors did not make the storms—they merely made them possible. The storms were mainly the result of stripping the landscape of its natural vegetation to such an extent that there was no defense against the dry winds, no sod to hold the sandy or powdery dirt. The sod had been destroyed to make farms to grow wheat to get cash. But more of that later on. It is the storms themselves we must first comprehend: their magnitude, their effect, even their taste and smell. What was it like to be caught in one of them? How much did the people suffer, and how did they cope?

Weather bureau stations on the plains reported a few small dust storms throughout 1932, as many as 179 in April 1933, and in November of that year a large one that carried all the way to Georgia and New York. But it was the May 1934 blow that swept in a new dark age. On 9 May, brown earth from Montana and Wyoming swirled up from the ground, was captured by extremely high-level winds, and was blown eastward toward the Dakotas. More dirt was sucked into the airstream, until 350 million tons were riding toward urban America. By late afternoon the storm had reached Dubuque and Madison, and by evening 12 million tons of dust were falling like snow over Chicago—4 pounds for each person in the city. Midday at Buffalo on 10 May was darkened by dust, and the advancing gloom stretched south from there over several states, moving as fast as 100 miles an hour. The dawn of 11 May found the dust settling over Boston, New York, Washington, and Atlanta, and then the storm moved out to sea. Savannah's skies were hazy all

A black blizzard advancing over Prowers County, Colorado, 1937. It came from the north and lasted almost three hours. (*Western History Collection, University of Oklahoma Library*)

day 12 May; it was the last city to report dust conditions. But there were still ships in the Atlantic, some of them 300 miles off the coast, that found dust on their decks during the next day or two.[6]

"Kansas dirt," the New York press called it, though it actually came from farther north. More would come that year and after, and some of it was indeed from Kansas—or Nebraska or New Mexico. In a later spring, New Hampshire farmers, out to tap their maples, discovered a fresh brown snow on the ground, discoloration from transported Western soil.[7] Along the Gulf Coast, at Houston and Corpus Christi, dirt from the Llano Estacado collected now and then on windowsills and sidewalks. But after May 1934 most of the worst dust storms were confined to the southern plains region; less frequently were they carried by those high-altitude currents moving east or southeast. Two types of dusters became common then: the dramatic "black blizzards" and the more frequent "sand blows." The first came with a rolling turbulence, rising like a long wall of muddy water as high as 7000 or 8000 feet. Like the winter blizzards to which they were compared, these dusters were caused by the arrival of a polar continental air mass, and the atmospheric electricity it generated helped lift the dirt higher and higher in a cold boil, sometimes accompanied by thunder and lightning, other times by an eerie silence. Such storms were not only terrifying to observers, but immensely destructive to the region's fine, dark

Standing in its path—same place, same storm. (*Western History Collection, University of Oklahoma Library*)

soils, rich in nutrients. The second kind of duster was a more constant event, created by the low sirocco-like winds that blew out of the southwest and left the sandier soils drifted into dunes along fence rows and ditches.[8] Long after New York and Philadelphia had forgotten their taste of the plains, the people out there ate their own dirt again and again.

In the 1930s the Soil Conservation Service compiled a frequency chart of all dust storms of regional extent, when visibility was cut to less than a mile. In 1932 there were 14; in 1933, 38; 1934, 22; 1935, 40; 1936, 68; 1937, 72; 1938, 61—dropping as the drought relented a bit—1939, 30; 1940, 17; 1941, 17. Another measure of severity was made by calculating the total number of hours the dust storms lasted during a year. By that criterion 1937 was again the worst: at Guymon, in the panhandle of Oklahoma, the total number of hours that year climbed to 550, mostly concentrated in the first six months of the year. In Amarillo the worst year was 1935, with a total of 908 hours. Seven times, from January to March, the visibility there reached zero—all complete blackouts, one of them lasting eleven hours. A single storm might rage for one hour or three and a half days. Most of the winds came from the southwest, but they also came from the west, north, and northeast, and they could slam against windows and walls with 60 miles-per-hour force.[9] The dirt left behind on the front lawn might be brown, black, yellow, ashy gray, or, more rarely, red, depending upon its source. And each color had its own peculiar aroma, from a sharp peppery smell that burned the nostrils to a heavy greasiness that nauseated.

Dodge City, Kansas, at ten a.m., 30 March 1935. (*Kansas State Historical Society*)

In the memory of older plains residents, the blackest year was 1935, particularly the early spring weeks from 1 March to mid-April, when the Dust Bowl made its full-blown debut. Springtime in western Kansas can be a Willa Cather world of meadowlarks on the wing, clean white curtains dancing in the breeze, anemones and wild verbena in bloom, lilacs by the porch, a windmill spinning briskly, and cold fresh water in the bucket—but not in 1935. After a February heat wave (it reached 75 degrees in Topeka that month), the dust began moving across Kansas, Oklahoma, and Texas, and for the next six weeks it was unusual to see a clear sky from dawn until sundown. On 15 March, Denver reported that a serious dust storm was speeding eastward. Kansans ignored the radio warnings, went about their business as usual, and later wondered what had hit them. Small-town printer Nate White was at the picture show when the dust reached Smith Center: as he walked out the exit, it was as if someone had put a blindfold over his eyes; he bumped into telephone poles, skinned his shins on boxes and cans in an alleyway, fell to his hands and knees, and crawled along the curbing to a dim houselight. A seven-year-old boy wandered away and was lost in the gloom; the search party found him later, suffocated in a drift. A more fortunate child was found alive, tangled in a barbed wire fence. Near Colby, a train was derailed by dirt on the tracks, and the passengers spent twelve dreary hours in the coaches. The Lora-Locke Hotel in Dodge City overflowed with more than two hundred stranded travelers; many of them bedded down on cots in the lobby and ballroom. In the following days, as the dust kept falling, electric lights burned continuously, cars left tracks in the dirt-covered streets, and schools and offices stayed closed. A reporter at Great Bend remarked on the bizarre scene: "Uncorked jug placed on sidewalk two hours, found to be half filled

Western Kansas, 14 April 1935—Black Sunday. (*Kansas State Historical Society*)

with dust. Picture wires giving way due to excessive weight of dust on frames. Irreparable loss in portraits anticipated. Lady Godiva could ride thru streets without even the horse seeing her."[10]

The novelty of this duster, so like a coffee-colored winter snow, made it hard for most people to take it seriously. But William Allen White, the Emporia editor, called it "the greatest show" since Pompeii was buried in ashes. And a Garden City woman described her experience for the *Kansas City Times:*

> All we could do about it was just sit in our dusty chairs, gaze at each other through the fog that filled the room and watch that fog settle slowly and silently, covering everything—including ourselves—in a thick, brownish gray blanket. When we opened the door swirling whirlwinds of soil beat against us unmercifully. . . . The door and windows were all shut tightly, yet those tiny particles seemed to seep through the very walls. It got into cupboards and clothes closets; our faces were as dirty as if we had rolled in the dirt; our hair was gray and stiff and we ground dirt between our teeth.

By the end of the month conditions had become so unrelenting that many Kansans had begun to chew their nails. "Watch for the Second Coming of Christ," warned one of Topeka's unhinged, "God is wrathful." Street-corner sects in Hill City and other towns warned pedestrians to heed the signs of the times. A slightly less frenetic Concordian jotted in her log: "This is ultimate darkness. So must come the end of the world."[11] The mood of the people had begun to change, if not to apocalyptic dread in every case, at least to a fear that this was a nightmare that might never end.

By 24 March southeastern Colorado and western Kansas had seen twelve consecutive days of dust storms, but there was worse to come. Near the end of March a new duster swept across the southern plains, destroying one-half the wheat crop in Kansas, one-quarter of it in Oklahoma, and all of it in Nebraska—5 million acres blown out. The storm carried away from the plains twice as much earth as men and machines had scooped out to make the Panama Canal, depositing it once again over the East Coast states and the Atlantic Ocean.[12] Then the wind slackened off a bit, gathering strength, as it were, for the spectacular finale of that unusual spring season—Black Sunday, 14 April.

Dawn came clear and rosy all across the plains that day. By noon the skies were so fresh and blue that people could not remain indoors; they remembered how many jobs they had been postponing, and with a revived spirit they rushed outside to get them done. They went on picnics, planted gardens, repaired henhouses, attended funerals, drove to the neighbors for a visit. In midafternoon the summery air rapidly turned colder, falling as many as 50 degrees in a few hours, and the people noticed then that the yards were full of birds nervously fluttering and chattering—and more were arriving every moment, as though fleeing from some unseen enemy. Suddenly there appeared on the northern horizon a black blizzard, moving toward them; there was no sound, no wind, nothing but an immense "boogery" cloud. The storm struck Dodge City at 2:40 p.m. Not far from there John Garretson, a farmer in Haskell County, Kansas, who was on the road with his wife, Louise, saw it coming, but he was sure that he could beat it home. They had almost made it when they were engulfed; abandoning the car, they groped for the fencewire and, hand over hand, followed it to their door. Down in the panhandle Ed and Ada Phillips of Boise City, with their six-year-old daughter, were on their way home too, after an outing to Texline in their Model A Ford. It was about five o'clock when the black wall appeared, and they still had fifteen miles to go. Seeing an old adobe house ahead, Ed realized that they had to take shelter, and quickly. By the time they were out of the car the dust was upon them, making it so dark that they nearly missed the door. Inside they found ten other people, stranded, like themselves, in a two-room hut, all fearing that they might be smothered, all unable to see their companions' faces. For four hours they sat there, until the storm let up enough for them to follow the roadside ditch back to town. By then the ugly pall was moving south across the high plains of Texas and New Mexico.[13]

Older residents still remember Black Sunday in all its details—where they were when the storm hit, what they did then. Helen Wells was the wife of the Reverend Rolley Wells, the Methodist minister in Guymon. Early that morning she had helped clean the accumulated dust from the church pews, working until she was choking and exhausted. Back in the parsonage she switched on the radio for some inspiring music, and what she heard was the hymn "We'll Work Till Jesus Comes."

Liberal, Kansas, 14 April 1935. (*Kansas State Historical Society*)

"I just had to sit down and laugh," she recalls; she had worn out her sweeper but still had a broom if that was needed. Later that day her husband, partly to please two visiting *Saturday Evening Post* reporters, held a special "rain service," which concluded in time for the congregation to get home before the dust arrived.[14]

A Kansas cattle dealer, Raymond Ellsaesser, almost lost his wife that day. She had gone into Sublette with her young daughter for a Rebekah lodge meeting. On the way home she stopped along the highway, unable to see even the winged hood ornament on her car. The static electricity in the storm then shorted out her ignition, and, foolishly, she determined to walk the three-quarters of a mile home. Her daughter plunged ahead to get Raymond's help, and he quickly piled into a truck and drove back down the road, hallooing out the window. Back and forth he passed, but his wife had disappeared into the fog-like dust, wandering straight away from the car into the field, where she stumbled about with absolutely no sense of direction. Each time she saw the truck's headlights she moved that way, not re-

Red Cross volunteers wearing dust masks, Liberal, Kansas. (*Kansas State Historical Society*)

alizing her husband was in motion too. It was only by sheer luck that she found herself at last standing in the truck's beams, gasping for air and near collapse.[15]

The last of the major dust storms that year was on 14 April, and it was months before the damages could be fully calculated. Those who had been caught outside in one of the spring dusters were, understandably, most worried about their lungs. An epidemic of respiratory infections and something called "dust pneumonia" broke out across the plains. The four small hospitals in Meade County, Kansas, found that 52 per cent of their April admissions were acute respiratory cases—thirty-three patients died.[16] Many dust victims would arrive at a hospital almost dead, after driving long distances in a storm. They spat up clods of dirt, washed the mud out of their mouths, swabbed their nostrils with Vaseline, and rinsed their bloodshot eyes with boric acid water. Old people and babies were the most vulnerable to the dusters, as were those who had chronic asthma, bronchitis, or tuberculosis, some of whom had moved to the plains so they might breathe the high, dry air.

Doctors could not agree on whether the dust caused a new kind of pneumonia, and some even denied that there were any unusual health problems in their communities. But the Red Cross thought the situation was so serious that it set up six emergency hospitals in Kansas, Colorado, and Texas, and it staffed them with its own nurses. In Topeka and Wichita volunteers worked in high school sewing rooms to make dust masks of cheesecloth; over 17,000 of those masks were sent to the plains, especially to towns where goggles had been sold out.[17] Chewing tobacco was a better remedy, snorted some farmers, who thought it was too much of a bother to wear such gadgets when driving their tractors. But enough wore the Red Cross masks or some other protection to make the plains look like a World War I battlefield, with dust instead of mustard gas coming out of the trenches.

On 29 April the Red Cross sponsored a conference of health officers from several states. Afterward the representatives of the Kansas Board of Health went to work on the medical problem in more detail, and eventually they produced a definitive study on the physiological impact of the dust storms. From 21 February to 30 April they counted 28 days of "dense" dust at Dodge City and only 13 days that were "dust free." Dirt deposited in bakepans during the five biggest storms gave an estimated 4.7 tons of total fallout per acre. Agar plate cultures showed "no pathogenic organisms" in the accumulation, only harmless soil bacteria, plant hair, and microfungus spores. But the inorganic content of the dust was mainly fine silicon particles, along with bits of feldspar, volcanic ash, and calcite; and "silica," they warned, "is as much a body poison as is lead"—"probably the most widespread and insidious of all hazards in the environment of mankind," producing, after sufficient contact, silicosis of the lungs. These scientists also found that a measles outbreak had come with the black blizzards, though why that happened was not clear; in only five months there were twice as many cases as in any previous twelve-month period. The death rate from acute respiratory infections in the 45 western counties of Kansas, where the dust was most intense, was 99 per 100,000, compared with the statewide average of 70; and the infant mortality was 80.5, compared with the state's 62.3.[18]

The medical remedies for the dust were at best primitive and makeshift. In addition to wearing light gauze masks, health officials recommended attaching translucent glasscloth to the inside frames of windows, although people also used cardboard, canvas, or blankets. Hospitals covered some of their patients with wet sheets, and housewives flapped the air with wet dish towels to collect dust. One of the most common tactics was to stick masking tape, felt strips, or paraffin-soaked rags around the windows and door cracks. The typical plains house was loosely constructed and without insulation, but sometimes those methods proved so effective that there was not enough air circulation inside to replenish the oxygen supply. Warren Moore of southwestern Kansas remembers watching, during a storm, the gas flame on the range steadily turn orange and the coal-oil lamp dim until the people simply had to open the window, dust or no dust.[19] But most often there was no way to seal out the fine, blowing dirt: it blackened the pillow around one's head, the dinner plates on the table, the bread dough on the back of the stove. It became a steady part of one's diet and breathing. "We thrived on it," claim some residents today; it was their "vitamin K." But all the same they prayed that they would not

Sand blowing at ground level, sunshine overhead. (*National Archives*)

ingest so much it would maim them for life, or finish them off, as it had a neighbor or two.

Livestock and wildlife did not have even those crude defenses. "In a rising sand storm," wrote Margaret Bourke-White, "cattle quickly become blinded. They run around in circles until they fall and breathe so much dust that they die. Autopsies show their lungs caked with dust and mud." Newborn calves could suffocate in a matter of hours, and the older cattle ground their teeth down to the gums trying to eat the dirt-covered grass. As the dust buried the fences, horses and cattle climbed over and wandered away. Where there was still water in rivers, the dust coated the surface and the fish died too. The carcasses of jackrabbits, small birds, and field mice lay along roadsides by the hundreds after a severe duster; and those that survived were in such shock that they could be picked up and their nostrils and eyes wiped clean.[20] In a lighter vein, it was said that prairie dogs were now able to tunnel upward several feet from the ground.

Cleaning up houses, farm lots, and city stores after the 1935 blow season was an expensive matter. People literally shoveled the dirt from their front yards and swept up bushel-basketfuls inside. One man's ceiling collapsed from the silt that had collected in the attic. Carpets, draperies, and tapestries were so dust-laden that their patterns were indiscernible. Painted surfaces had been sandblasted bare. Automobile and tractor engines operated in dust storms without oil-bath air cleaners were ruined by grit, and the repair shops had plenty of business. During March alone, Tucumcari, New Mexico, reported over $288,000 in property damage, although most towns' estimates were more conservative than that: Liberal, Kansas, $150,000; Randall County, Texas, $10,000; Lamar, Colorado, $3800. The merchants of Amarillo calculated from 3 to 15 per cent damage to their merchandise, not to mention the loss of shoppers during the storms. In Dodge City a men's clothing store advertised a "dust sale," knocking shirts down to 75 cents. But the heaviest burdens lay on city work crews, who had to sweep dirt from the gutters and municipal swimming pools, and on housewives, who struggled after each blow to get their houses clean.[21]

The emotional expense was the hardest to accept, however. All day you could sit with your hands folded on the oilcloth-covered table, the wind moaning around the eaves, the fine, soft, talc sifting in the keyholes, the sky a coppery gloom; and when you went to bed the acrid dust crept into your dreams. Avis Carlson told what it was like at night:

A trip for water to rinse the grit from our lips. And then back to bed with washcloths over our noses. We try to lie still, because every turn stirs the dust on the blankets. After a while, if we are good sleepers, we forget.

After 1935 the storms lost much of their drama; for most people they were simply a burden to be endured, and sometimes that burden was too heavy. Druggists sold out their supplies of sedatives quickly. An Oklahoman took down his shotgun, ready to kill his entire family and himself—"we're all better off dead," he despaired.[22] That, to be sure, was an extreme instance, but there were indeed men and women who turned distraught, wept, and then, listless, gave up caring.

The plains people, however, then as now, were a tough-minded, leather-skinned folk, not easily discouraged. Even in 1935 they managed to laugh a bit at their misfortunes. They told about the farmer who fainted when a drop of water struck him in the face and had to be revived by having three buckets of sand thrown over him. They also passed around the one about the motorist who came upon a ten-gallon hat resting on a dust drift. Under it he found a head looking at him. "Can I help you some way?" the motorist asked, "Give you a ride into town maybe?" "Thanks, but I'll make it on my own," was the reply, "I'm on a horse."

Street scene in Amarillo, Texas, 1936. (*Arthur Rothstein, Library of Congress*)

They laughed with Will Rogers when he pointed out that only highly advanced civilizations—like ancient Mesopotamia—were ever covered over by dirt, and that California would never qualify. Newspaper editors could still find something to joke about, too: "When better dust storms are made," the *Dodge City Globe* boasted, "the Southwest will make them." Children were especially hard to keep down; for them the storms always meant adventure, happy chaos, a breakdown of their teachers' authority, and perhaps a holiday.[23] When darkness descends, as it did that April, humor, bravado, or a childlike irresponsibility may have as much value as a storm cellar.

Whether they brought laughter or tears, the dust storms that swept across the southern plains in the 1930s created the most severe environmental catastrophe in the entire history of the white man on this continent. In no other instance was there greater or more sustained damage to the American land, and there have been few times when so much tragedy was visited on its inhabitants. Not even the Depression was more devastating, economically. And in ecological terms we have nothing in the nation's past, nothing even in the polluted present, that compares. Suffice it to conclude here that in the decade of the 1930s the dust storms of the plains were an unqualified disaster.

At such dark times the mettle of a people is thoroughly and severely tested, revealing whether they have the will to go on. By this test the men and women of the plains were impressive, enduring, as most of them did, discouragements the like of which more recent generations have never had to face. But equally important, disasters of this kind challenge a society's capacity to think—require it to analyze and explain and learn from misfortune. Societies that fail this test are sitting ducks for more of the same. Those that pass, on the other hand, have attained through suffering and hardship a more mature, self-appraising character, so that they are more aware than before of their vulnerabilities and weaknesses. They are stronger because they have been made sensitive to their deficiencies. Whether the dust storms had this enlarging, critical effect on the minds of southern plainsmen remains to be seen.

THE AMERICAN PLAINS are a "next year" country. This season the crops may wither and die, the winds may pile up dirt against the barn, but next time we will do better—we will strike a bonanza. If we are poor today, we will be rich tomorrow. If there is drought, it will rain soon. In the dirty thirties that quality of hope was strained to the breaking point. But for every discouraged resident who wanted to leave, or did so, there were two more who were determined to stick it out, hang on, stay with it. Some remained out of sheer inertia or bewilderment over what else to do, or because they had the economic means to stay where others did not. Whatever the reasons people had for not moving away, hope was commonly a part of them. The people were optimists, unwilling to believe that the dust storms would last or that their damage would be very severe. That attitude was not so much a matter of cold reason as it was of faith that the future must be better. Optimism may be an essential response for survival in this sometimes treacherous world; it certainly brought many Western farmers through to greener days. But it also can be a form of lunancy. There is about the perennial optimist a dangerous naïveté, a refusal to face the grim truths about oneself or others or nature. Optimism can also divert our attention from critical self-appraisal and substantive reforms, which is exactly what happened on the plains.

Optimism may rest either on a confidence in one's ability to affect the course of events or, paradoxically, on a happy, fatalistic belief that the world is preordained to promote one's welfare. Plainsmen in the 1930s went both ways. They were sure that they could manage the land and bring it under control, especially if Franklin Roosevelt's New Deal would give them a bit of help. Hard work and determination

Chapter Two

Rains

would pay off in the end. They were even surer that the laws of nature were on their side. A perceptual geographer, Thomas Saarinen, has concluded that Great Plains farmers consistently and habitually underrate the possibility of drought—that they minimize the risks involved in their way of life. When drought occurs, they insist that it cannot last long. Consequently, although they may become unhappy or upset by crop failures, they feel no need to seek out logical solutions or change their practices. They are prouder of their ability to tough it out than to analyze their situation rationally, because they expect nature to be good to them and make them prosper.[1] It is an optimism at heart fatalistic—and potentially fatal in a landscape as volatile as that of the plains.

The source of that optimism is cultural: it is the ethos of an upwardly mobile society. When a people emphasize, as much as Americans do, the need to get ahead in the world, they must have a corresponding faith in the benignity of nature and the future. If they are farmers on the Western plains, they must believe that rain is on its way, that dust storms are a temporary aberration, and that one had better plant wheat again even if there is absolutely no moisture in the soil. The black blizzards said, however, that there was something seriously amiss in the plainsmen's thinking—that nature would not yield so easily, so reliably, all the riches expected, and that the future would not necessarily bring higher and higher levels of prosperity. Blowing dirt challenged the most cherished assumptions of middle-class farmers and merchants about the inevitability of progress; therefore the dirt had to be minimized, discounted, evaded, even ignored. The bedrock plainsmen's response was to shout down nature's message with a defense of the old assumptions. Changes in attitudes did occur, to be sure, but the most incredible fact of the dirty thirties was the tenacity of bourgeois optimism and its imperviousness to all warnings.

The pattern of reaction among plainsmen went something like this: fail to anticipate drought, underestimate its duration when it comes, expect rain momentarily, deny that they are as hard hit as outsiders believe, defend the region against critics, admit that *some* help would be useful, demand that the government act and act quickly, insist that federal aid be given without strings and when and where local residents want it, vote for those politicians who confirm the people's optimism and pooh-pooh the need for major reform, resent interference by the bureaucrats, eagerly await the return of "normalcy" when the plains will once more proceed along the road of steady progress. Accepting the coming of the New Deal fit into that pattern more or less easily. The region received more federal dollars than any other, along with reassurance, solicitation, and encouragement. But whenever the New Deal really tried to become new and innovative, plainsmen turned hostile. The fate of the plains lay in the hands of Providence, and Providence, not Washington, would see them come out all right.

The day after Black Sunday the Dust Bowl got its name. Robert Geiger, an Associated Press reporter from Denver, traveled through the worst-hit part of the plains, and he sent a dispatch to the *Washington Evening Star,* which carried it on 15 April 1935: "Three little words," it began, "achingly familiar on a Western farmer's tongue, rule life in the dust bowl of the continent—if it rains." That Geiger meant nothing special by the label was apparent two days later, when in another dispatch he called the blow area the "dust belt." But, inexplicably, it was "bowl" that stuck, passing quickly into the vernacular, its author soon forgotten and never really sure himself where it all began. Some liked the name as a satire on college football—first the Rose Bowl and the Orange Bowl, now the Dust Bowl—or they thought it described nicely what happened to the sugar bowl on the table. Geiger more likely had recalled the geographical image of the plains pushed forward by another Denver man, William Gilpin. In the 1850s, the continent, Gilpin had thought, was a great fertile bowl rimmed by mountains, its concave interior destined one day to become the seat of empire. If that was the unconscious precedent, then Geiger's "dust bowl" was more ironic than anyone realized.[2]

Within weeks the southern plains had a new identity, one that they would never be able to shake off. The label came spontaneously into the speeches of the region's governors, into the pressrooms of city newspapers, and into the private letters of local residents to their distant friends—for all of them it was a handle to put on this peculiar problem. When the Soil Conservation Service capitalized it and began using it on their maps, even setting up a special office in the area, "Dust Bowl" became official. The SCS followed Geiger's own delineation rather closely: "the

western third of Kansas, Southeastern Colorado, the Oklahoma Panhandle, the
northern two-thirds of the Texas Panhandle, and Northeastern New Mexico." But
the SCS's Region VI also covered an extensive fringe that made a total of almost
100 million acres, stretching 500 miles from north to south, 300 from east to west—
about one-third of the entire Great Plains. A serious blowing hazard existed on a
shifting 50 million of those acres from 1935 to 1938. In 1935 the Dust Bowl
reached well down into the cotton belt of west Texas, but three years later it had
moved northeastward, making Kansas the most extensively affected state. By 1939
the serious blow area within the Bowl had shrunk to about one-fifth its original size;
it increased again to 22 million acres in 1940, then in the forties it disappeared.[3]

The difficulty in making the Dust Bowl more fixed and precise was that it
roamed around a good deal—it was an event as well as a locality. A puzzled tourist
stopped George Taton, a Kansas wheat farmer, in Garden City one day: "Can you
tell me where this Dust Bowl is?" "Stay where you are," Taton told him, "and it'll
come to you." Even locals could not always discover the exact boundaries, wondering
exasperatedly, "Are we in it or ain't we?"[4] In a sense, wherever there were recurring
dust storms and soil erosion there was a dust bowl, and by that test most of the
Great Plains was "in it" during a part of the 1930s, some of the most severe conditions occurring as far north as Nebraska and the Dakotas. But SCS officials, surveying the entire plains, placed their Dust Bowl perimeters around the most persistent
problem area, and there was no doubt which counties were at the heart of this
Bowl: Morton in Kansas, Baca in Colorado, Texas and Cimarron in Oklahoma,
Dallam in Texas, and Union in New Mexico.

By 1935 the landscape in those and surrounding counties had become, in
Geiger's words, "a vast desert, with miniature shifting dunes of sand." The fences,
piled high with tumbleweeds and drifted over with dirt, looked like giant backbones
of ancient reptiles. Elsewhere the underlying hardpan was laid bare, as sterile and
unyielding as a city pavement. The winds exposed long-buried Indian campgrounds,
as well as arrowheads, pioneer wagon wheels, Spanish stirrups, branding irons, tractor wrenches, the chain someone had dropped in the furrow the previous year. By
1938, the peak year for wind erosion, 10 million acres had lost at least the upper
five inches of topsoil; another 13.5 million acres had lost at least two and a half
inches. Over all the cultivated land in the region, there were 408 tons of dirt blown
away from the average acre, in some cases only to the next farm, in others to the
next state or beyond. According to Roy Kimmel, the special federal coordinator assigned to the Dust Bowl, in 1938 they were still losing 850 million tons of earth a
year to erosion, far more than was washed down the Mississippi. The dirt that blew
away, one Iowa-deposited sample revealed, contained ten times as much organic
matter and nitrogen—the basics of fertility—as did the sand dunes left behind in
Dallam County, Texas.[5]

EXTENT OF AREA SUBJECT TO SEVERE WIND EROSION

1935-1940

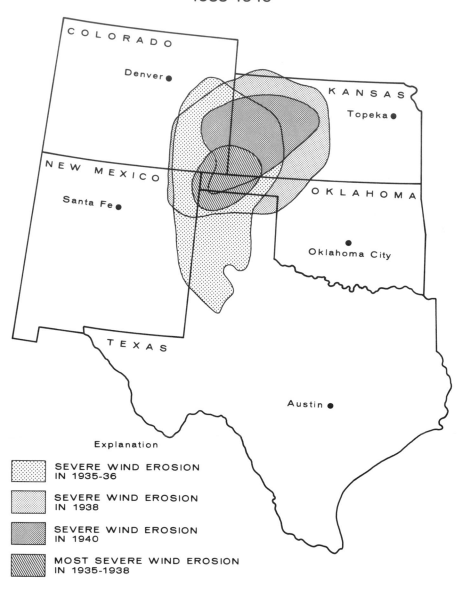

COLORADO

Denver ●

KANSAS

Topeka ●

NEW MEXICO

Santa Fe ●

OKLAHOMA

Oklahoma City ●

TEXAS

Austin ●

Explanation

SEVERE WIND EROSION
IN 1935-36

SEVERE WIND EROSION
IN 1938

SEVERE WIND EROSION
IN 1940

MOST SEVERE WIND EROSION
IN 1935-1938

(Sharon Hagen)

After Geiger, other journalists came to the Dust Bowl, and they described the scene to urban Americans. They usually carried with them a license for hyperbole and a capacity for shock. George Greenfield of the *New York Times,* passing through Kansas on the Union Pacific, was the most funereal: "Today I have seen the cold hand of death on what was one of the great breadbaskets of the nation . . . a lost people living in a lost land." But more cutting was the 1937 *Collier's* article by Walter Davenport, "Land Where Our Children Die," which found in the Dust Bowl only "famine, violent death, private and public futility, insanity, and lost generations." For Davenport the source of the devastation lay in its Dogpatch residents—its Willie Mae Somethings, Jere Hullomons, Twell Murficks, all too stupid or greedy to be trusted with the land. Then there were the newsreel photographers from the *March of Time,* who had heard about Texas crows being forced to build their nests out of barbed wire and, of course, hurriedly came to exploit the rumor rather than examine it.[6] In theaters, newspapers, and magazines, Americans began to see more of the southern plains, a place remote from their experience and heretofore ignored, but invariably what they saw was the same extreme slice of reality, the most sensationally barren parts of that land.

These outside reports, however, were not total fabrications, as many local residents admitted in their own descriptions of what they saw. Albert Law of the *Dalhart Texan* published this frank account in 1933, well before the peak years:

Not a blade of wheat in Cimarron County, Oklahoma; cattle dying there on the range; a few bushels of wheat in the Perryton area against an average yield of from four to six million bushels; with all the stored surplus not more than fifty per cent of the seeding needs will be met—ninety per cent of the poultry dead because of the sand storms; sixty cattle dying Friday afternoon between Guymon and Liberal from some disease induced by dust —humans suffering from dust fever—milk cows going dry, turned into pasture to starve, hogs in such pitiable shape that buyers will not have them; cattle being moved from Dallam and other counties to grass; no wheat in Hartley County; new crops a remote possibility, cattle facing starvation; Potter, Seward and other Panhandle counties with one-third of their population on charity or relief work; ninety per cent of the farmers in most counties have had to have crop loans, and continued drouth forcing many of them to use the money for food, clothes, medicine, shelter.

Confirmation of those details came from all over. In Moore County, Texas, for example, the welfare director, on behalf of the Dumas Chamber of Commerce, reported to federal officials in March 1935 that it was "an impossible task to describe the utter destruction": roads obliterated, the crops all gone, "no hope or ambition left," and many farmers "near starvation."[7] Today, more than forty years later, old-timers often point out that outsiders never knew what the dirty part of the thirties was really like, never appreciated how severe the problem was.

But at the same time there were many on the plains, especially businessmen in the towns, who bitterly resented their "Dust Bowl" reputation, so much so that they formed truth squads to get the straight facts to the rest of the nation. Usually "straight" meant "most flattering," and those who did not conform, who saw things differently, could be in for trouble. Albert Law's paper lost more than $1000 in advertising after his frank article appeared, and in later years he learned to speak more carefully, even to join the truth-squad vigilantes. In 1936 he referred to that "harebrained individual" who "in an abortive fit" misnamed the plains "Dust Bowl." Leadership for the defensive campaign came from several west Texas chambers of commerce, particularly Dalhart's, and from editor John L. McCarty of Dalhart and, later, of Amarillo. McCarty's style was at its shoot-em-up best in his refutation of the *Collier's* article by Walter Davenport: "a vicious libel," "compounded of lies and half-truths," "bunk," "more bunk," "sissy." The outrage lay not only in that outside critics were condemning "a group of courageous Americans for a six-year drouth cycle and national conditions beyond their control"; they were also destroying the property values, bank credit, and business prospects of the region.[8]

A minor but extreme episode in this effort to clear away the dust from the plains' reputation centered on painter Alexandre Hogue. The son of a Missouri minister, Hogue had spent much of his youth on his brother-in-law's ranch near Hartley, Texas, not far from Dalhart, where he had learned to love the country and the cowhand's life. In his mid-thirties when the dusters appeared, he began painting the ravaged panhandle landscape. Dust drifts, starved cattle, broken-down windmills, and rattlesnakes were the principal features of his works, scenes as hopeless and grim as Hogue could manage. The paintings were obviously fictions, exaggerated for dramatic effect—"superrealism" or "psycho-reality" he called his style— but brilliantly conveying the painter's ambivalent mood about the disaster. There was the utter destruction of a rural way of life, which he deeply regretted, but there was also a fascination with the forms of disorder. "They were *not* social comment," Hogue insists; "I did them because to me, aside from the tragedy of the situation, the effects were beautiful, beautiful in a terrifying way." But the Dalhart Chamber of Commerce was not ready for Hogue's aestheticism, and when *Life* magazine published some of his works in 1937 and called him "artist of the dust bowl" (he hated that phrase), the vigilantes went into action. Hogue, they insisted, was "some upstart sent down from New York who knows nothing about the region and so painted isolated cases that are not typical if they even exist." An emissary was sent to Dallas to purchase the painting "Drouth Survivors" from the Pan-American Exposition there; the truth squad planned to burn it on the streets of Dalhart. But when the

Alexandre Hogue, "Drouth Survivors" (1936). Oil on canvas, 30 × 48. The one they wanted to burn.

emissary discovered that he had been given only $50 to buy a $2000 work, he trudged back home—and art triumphed over local pride, or at least cost more.[9]

To admit that the plains had in fact become a disaster area was to give up faith in the future and the productive potential of the land. Many simply could not bring themselves to do it. They were quick to deny, and to repress, the Dust Bowl label. But they were even quicker to announce that the Bowl was shrinking. One month after Black Sunday rain was falling everywhere; Baca County got one inch and a half—it's a "mud bowl" now, they exulted. Floods were rampaging in Hutchinson and Augusta, Kansas, just east of the blow area. It was a short-lived phenomenon, as were other moments of respite in the later part of the decade. But it was enough to renew faith in the future and to vindicate the vigilantes. One year later, in March 1936, Robert Geiger came back to Oklahoma and wrote that, with more rains, "the 'Dust Bowl' is losing its handle." Ida Watkins, a large-scale wheat farmer in southwestern Kansas, was so encouraged that she began planting, explaining to a visitor:

> I guess the good Lord is going to lead us out into the promised Land again.
> . . . For five years we have been living here in the desert of the dust bowl
> and now the abundant rains have taken us up into a high mountain and
> shown us close ahead the bounteous land of Canaan, blossoming with wheat
> and a new prosperity.[10]

Like President Herbert Hoover, who kept reassuring the public that the Depression was almost over, these hopeful souls were false prophets. There were at least five more difficult years ahead, five years when the dust masks came out repeatedly, trains continued to be derailed by dust, and wheat fields often stood empty and dry. Most of those later storms were only "gray zephyrs" compared with those of 1935, but some could be awesomely devastating. One of the biggest ever came three years after Watkins's glimpse of the promised land—on 11 March 1939, when a Stillwater, Oklahoma, agronomist estimated there was enough dirt in the air to cover 5 million acres one foot deep. That storm raged over a 100,000-square-mile spread.[11] A too-ready optimism was no more an effective defense against the winds of ruin than was censorship.

Even as the John McCartys were defending the region's credit rating and the Ida Watkinses were straining their eyes toward Canaan, plains residents were collecting federal aid. The benign arm of Providence could use a little government muscle, apparently. Things were not going to change for the better with time, it was feared— or at least few people were patient enough to wait around for that to happen. The plains were in serious trouble and getting worse, and no amount of faith in the inevitability of progress would save them unless prompt action were taken. What the plains wanted was a speedy restoration of "normal" expectations and the means to satisfy them. The New Deal promised that restoration, just as it offered factory workers the chance to go back to work in the same factory under the old ownership. In the mid-1930s out on the plains, federal money began raining down with the sweet smell of a spring shower, nourishing the seeds of hope that had so persistently been planted. In the absence of the real thing, such outpourings were the best available substitute. And for a while Washington became the new Providence.

It was a long way from the federal government to the Dust Bowl. The region was then, and still is, one of the most remote and rural parts of America. The largest city in the region was Amarillo, with a population of 43,000 in 1930. Denver, with almost 300,000 inhabitants, lay at the extreme northwest corner of the Bowl, out on the fringe, as were all the other state capitals—Topeka, Oklahoma City, Austin, and Albuquerque. Scattered over the SCS's Region VI were 2 million people, most of them living not in cities, but in very small towns or on farms. And they were spiralling downward into desperate poverty as their crops failed year after year. In Hall and Childress counties in Texas, average cotton ginnings fell from 99,000 bales in the late 1920s to 12,500 in 1934. The next year Kansans cut wheat on only half their planted acreage; Stanton County reaped nothing.[12] Those two years were especially bad, to be sure, but with the exception of 1938, a wetter year, not one in the decade saw a significantly improved harvest. As the agricultural base of the region's economy was buried under dust, extreme hardship loomed over the southern plains, and rescue by a distant government was the only hope.

In 1936, to determine which areas were in the most desperate straits, the federal government's Works Progress Administration (WPA) sent out two investigators, Francis Cronin and Howard Beers, to survey the entire Great Plains. Cronin and Beers compiled data in five categories—precipitation, crop production, status of pasturelands, changes in number of cattle, and federal aid per capita—all the way back to 1930. Taken together, the categories gave an index of "intense drought distress." Out of 800 counties they surveyed, from Minnesota and Montana to Texas, two centers of rural poverty emerged: first, an area that covered almost all of North and South Dakota, along with contiguous counties in neighboring states; and second, the Dust Bowl on the southern plains. Altogether, 125 counties from both foci qualified as "very severe" and another 127 as "severe." South Dakota led, with 41 counties in the bottom-most category; North Dakota had 23, as did Texas; Kansas, 20; Oklahoma, 5; Colorado, 2. By 1936, in each of the counties, federal aid for agricultural failure had already totaled at least $175 per person. Other studies revealed that government payments for the fourteen southwestern counties of Kansas came to $100 a year per capita, and Morton received twice that much. One-third to one-half of the farm families in that corner of the state depended upon some kind of government relief in 1935; it was still much less than the 80 per cent found in one North Dakota county, but it was well above the national average. "The prairie," observed a reader of the *Dallas Farm News* in 1939, "once the home of the deer, buffalo and antelope, is now the home of the Dust Bowl and the WPA."[13]

Rural Americans had been more reluctant to ask for outside help than the city poor, even after they too had begun to feel the pinch of hard times. Nowhere was this aversion to "charity" more fierce than on the southern plains. To ask for aid implied personal and providential failure—the very "insult" that the McCarthy brigade had resented. In any case, there was little charity to be had, at least locally: no effective organization to give it out, public or private, in most counties; and nothing to give. State capitals were slow to learn about conditions, and slower to act, excusing themselves by reason of tight budgets. Thus there was only Washington, far away and highly suspect, but the last resort. At the onset of the drought President Hoover turned to the Red Cross, which had performed wonderfully in the Mississippi flood of 1927, to devise another rescue. But the Red Cross leaders, many of them appointed by Hoover, seriously underestimated the Western relief needs, appropriating only a third of what they had spent on the flood. At last, when it became apparent that these private efforts were pathetically inadequate, Congress set up a $45 million seed-and-feed loan fund. Hoover denounced it as "a raid on the public treasury" and a slide toward the degenerate "dole"—but he signed it into

AREAS OF INTENSE DROUGHT DISTRESS

1930-1936

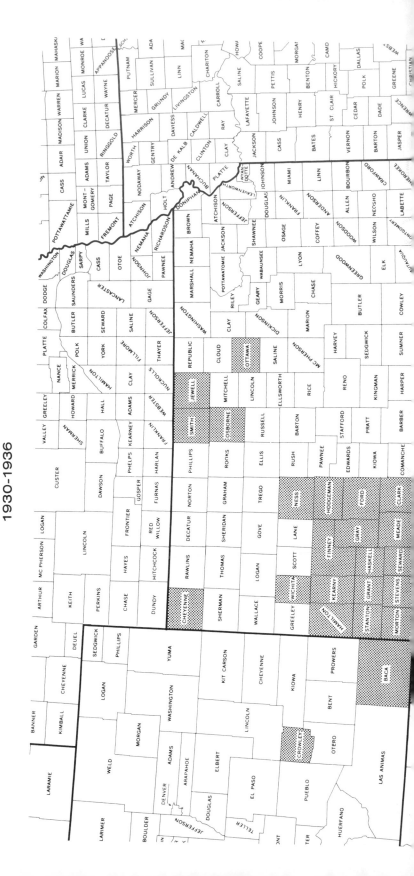

(*Sharon Hagen*)

law.[14] That was the beginning of federal initiatives to save the Great Plains from utter ruin.

The loan fund was not by any token adequate to the relief task, nor by 1932 was Hoover's gloomy mien or budget-consciousness acceptable to most Dust Bowl voters. In the national elections that year, the plains joined with the rest of the nation to elect Franklin Roosevelt, a gentleman farmer from New York, to the presidency. Traditionally Democratic Texas, Oklahoma, and New Mexico gave Roosevelt 88, 73, and 63 per cent of their votes, respectively; while in Kansas and Colorado the victory margin, although below the national level (almost 58 per cent), was a major departure from their loyal Republican past.[15] It was time, the plainsmen agreed, for something beyond rugged individualism, even if they were unsure what and how much the federal government ought to do for them. Perhaps Roosevelt's style, however, was more important to them than any specific program. His easy and buoyant manner appealed to a people who felt their traditional optimism slipping and wanted it shored up.

During his first year in office Roosevelt ignored the Great Plains, as his predecessor had done. It was perhaps understandable: there was a drought going on, but the dust storms had not yet reached continental proportions and he had his hands full with greater emergencies—thousands of bank failures and industrial shutdowns, national income cut in half, one out of every four workers unemployed. He did establish important new programs that would come to play a critical role in the region's recovery, such as the Agricultural Adjustment Administration, the Federal Emergency Relief Administration, and the Farm Credit Administration, all of which were set in motion during the famous first hundred days of the Roosevelt presidency in 1933.[16] But it took the May 1934 dust storm to make the plains visible to Washington. As dust sifted down on the Mall and the White House, Roosevelt was in a press conference promising that the Cabinet was at work on a new Great Plains relief program. Desperate appeals were being heard from farmers, ranchers, politicians, and businessmen out West, some of them demanding money, others, more humble, wanting advice and comfort. "Please do something," one lady wrote, "to help us save our country, where one time we were all so happy."[17] Alf Landon, the governor of Kansas, got letters too, as did other area governors, but in effect they forwarded them to Washington by requesting federal relief money that they could disperse to their voters—the 1930s version of states' rights.

While Roosevelt and his Cabinet worked out a drought relief package, the American public put its own ingenuity to work and sent the results to the President and other public officials. Ideas began coming in during the spring of 1934 and kept coming over the next few years, from citizens in every part of the country and even from observers in China, England, and Czechoslovakia. They came from barnyard inventors and company engineers, from immigrants eager to do something for their adopted Uncle Sam, from former plains farmers retired in Los Angeles, and from the city unemployed who hoped their notions would produce a job or a fat check. The obvious remedy, according to many of these letter writers, was simply to cover the Dust Bowl over. The Sisalkraft Company of Chicago had a tough waterproof paper that could do the job, while the Barber Asphalt Company in New Jersey recommended an "asphalt emulsion" at $5.00 an acre, and a Pittsburgh steel corporation had wire netting for sale. One man urged that the ground be covered with concrete, leaving holes for planting seeds, and another that rocks be hauled in from the mountains. Mrs. M. L. Yearby of Durham, North Carolina, saw a chance to beautify her own state by shipping its junked automobiles out to the plains to anchor the blowing fields, and several others proposed spreading ashes and garbage from Eastern cities or leaves from forests to create a mulch over the plains and restore a binding humus to the soil. Building wind deflectors also appealed to many—cement slabs or board fences, as much as 250 feet high, or shelterbelts of pine trees, alfalfa, greasewood, and even Jerusalem artichokes. An Albuquerque writer blamed the dust storms on "German agents"; a Russian-born chemist in New York City suggested radio waves instead; the Lions Club in Perryton, Texas, pointed to pollution from local gas and oil refineries; and there were some who worried about the carbon-black plant near Amarillo.[18]

But for plains residents the most widely favored panacea was, understandably, water. "You gave us beer," they told Roosevelt, "now give us water." That was all they really needed, they were sure, and the federal government was wasting its time with anything else. "Every draw, arroyo [*sic*], and canyon that could be turned into a lake or lagoon," wrote a clothing store manager, "should be made into one by dams and directed ditches & draws until there are *millions* of them thru these mid western states." A Texas stockman wanted to use natural gas to pump flood waters from the Mississippi River to the plains. Deep-water irrigation wells was another scheme; 5000 of them, it was said, would cost only $17.5 million. And then there were the perennially hopeful rainmakers, long familiar on the southern plains, always popping up with a "scientific" method, new or old, to extract rain out of a cloudless sky. An old soldier from Denver penciled his ideas on ruled tablet paper: stage sham battles with 40,000 Civilian Conservation Corps boys and $20 million worth of ammunition—the noise would be sure to stir up some rain, as it always did in wartime. "Try it," he finished, "if it works send me a check for $5000 for services rendered."[19]

Each of those letters, and dozens more like them, got a patient answer from a federal administrator, but no check. The Roosevelt advisers settled on a more prosaic, if more expensive, program for the Great Plains. On 9 June 1934 the President asked Congress for $525 million in drought relief, and it was promptly given. The biggest chunks, totaling $275 million, were for cattlemen—to provide emergency feed loans, to purchase some of their starving stock, and to slaughter the animals and can their meat for the poor. Destitute farmers would get more public jobs, often building ponds and reservoirs, as well as cash income supplements, costing $125 million. Other features of the program included acquiring submarginal lands, relocating rural people in better environments, creating work camps for young men, and making seed loans for new crops. A few days later Roosevelt squeezed in a shelterbelt program, too.[20] For the remainder of the thirties most of these strategies became familiar fixtures in the federal budget, evolving, along with other farm and relief legislation, into a more specifically directed Dust Bowl rehabilitation effort.

As for the most immediate need to stop the blowing dust, the federal government heeded regional advice and in 1935 adopted a program of emergency "listing."[21] The lister, a standard farm implement on the plains, was a double mold-board that dug deep, broad furrows and threw the dirt up into high ridges. Once used for planting corn, it now served the function of creating a corduroy-like ground surface that would slow erosion, or at least it would if the listing were done crosswise to the prevailing winds. In a stiff blow the ridges would still drift back into the furrows, forcing the farmer to list his fields repeatedly to keep them stabilized. Sometimes a chisel would be employed too, breaking the hard subsurface and bringing up heavy clods to hold down the dust. But when you were broke, with no money for gasoline or tractor repairs, constant lister-plowing or chiseling was impossible. Or if you lived a hundred miles away from your farm, visiting it only twice a year, once at planting and again harvesting time, the work would not get done. The government, therefore, proposed to pay plains farmers for working their own land or having it worked by someone on the scene. And the Texas and Kansas legislatures allowed counties to list the land of irresponsible neighbors, charging the expense to the owner, where all other inducements had failed. As an effort to legalize community control over recalcitrant individuals, these state laws were too hedged about with delays, and too seldom used, to be especially effective.[22] But self-interest, along with government money, was generally adequate to put the bare fields under some control.

Emergency listing continued to get federal funds virtually every year thereafter in the decade. In the 1936 Soil Conservation and Domestic Allotment Act, $2 million was the sum allowed for this work. Kansas and Texas received about half of the money, the other three southern plains states what was left over. In each state the money first passed through the hands of the land-grant colleges and their county extension agents, then through local committees that supervised contracts and made sure the listing was actually done, and done properly. Dust Bowl farmers listed more than 8 million acres in the 12 months prior to July 1937, for which the government paid them 20 cents an acre where they worked their own land, 40 cents where they had to hire others to do it.[23] It was not much money; many thought they should get more. Nor did emergency listing address the deeper issues of man and the land on the southern plains or stop a full-fledged black blizzard. But it gave farmers something to do, and it kept some of the dirt from going too far.

The people of the plains made it clear in the 1936 elections how well they liked this rain of federal money. Despite the fact that the Republican party chose Alf Landon of Kansas for their presidential nominee, Roosevelt was again triumphant in the region, winning 54 per cent of the votes in Kansas, 60 in Colorado, 63 in New Mexico, 67 in Oklahoma, and 87 in Texas. Landon, who conducted a fumbling and waffling campaign, had nothing fresh or appealing to offer the Dust Bowl states and had been regionally upstaged and outmaneuvered by Roosevelt's "fact-finding" swing through the northern Great Plains in September.[24] Two years later Roosevelt and the New Deal were still immensely popular in the Southwest. When the President went to Amarillo on 11 July 1938, in his only venture into the Dust Bowl itself, the city assembled the largest massed marching band in the history of the nation to greet him, thousands lined the streets, and, *mirabile dictu,* rain began to fall shortly before he arrived. As he stood hatless in the downpour, uttering genial platitudes in his clear ringing style, a woman in the audience exclaimed: "I am ready to make him king, anybody who can smile like that."[25] So warm a reception was bound to cool, of course, and by 1940 portions of the dust belt began to defect, reverting to their traditional political views. But throughout the dirty thirties it was all New Deal country.

Some of the most insistent proponents of government intervention were Dust Bowl businessmen. While farmers tended to resist too much interference with their freedom to do as they liked with the land, there were business groups that demanded more authoritarian control by Washington, including a declaration of martial law. The Liberal, Kansas, Chamber of Commerce, for instance, insisted on "a force program, under government supervision," which would see that every field was listed properly. The federal soil erosion agent there noted in 1937 that businessmen, who had been arguing that "the conditions were being over emphasized and this area was getting more than its share of adverse publicity," now were agreed that "the control of wind erosion in the dust bowl is well out of hand and are willing to allow any action that the federal government may take to put into operation." Down in Dalhart the truth squad had to send out a new emissary, this one to a Washington congressional committee, to admit there was some truth in Alexandre Hogue's paintings and to plead for passage of a $10-million water-facilities bill.[26]

But there was one government proposal that never failed to arouse hostility —resettlement or relocation. Leaving the plains meant giving up, admitting defeat, and possibly losing the future altogether; Providence never rewards the quitters. Resettlement was never really a serious idea in Washington either, not at least to the extent of removing all of the people from the Dust Bowl, but plains residents were forever on their guard after the Harold Ickes incident. Secretary of the Interior Ickes, when presented in November 1933 with a proposal to build expensive dams in the Oklahoma panhandle, turned thumbs down; he felt that it would be a waste of money. "We'll have to move them [the people] out of there," he said, "and turn the land back to the public domain." The howls of protest from 40,000 Oklahomans could be heard all the way to Capitol Hill. Ickes is "entirely ignorant of the possibilities this country affords," retorted the *Boise City News*.[27] But the subsequent setting up of a Resettlement Administration in 1935 under Rexford Tugwell, a Columbia University professor, kept the plains wall-eyed. Following Black Sunday, as more rumors of forced evacuation came from the East Coast, John McCarty and his Dalhart boosters organized a Last Man's Club, each member pledging on his sacred honor never to abandon the plains. And farther west, in New Mexico, where the prospects of removal were just as unwelcome, a farmer spoke for many when he warned: "They'll have to take a shotgun to move us out of here. We're going to stay here just as long as we damn please."[28]

That fierce resolve to stay, even as the tawny dust was making their land of opportunity a dreary wasteland, followed in large part from an assumption that the plains people made. It was drought, they were confident, and drought alone, that had made the Dust Bowl: "That drought put the fixins to us." But with a gambler's trust in better luck, they knew the rains would return. "This land will come back," most were sure: "it'll make good agin—it always has." Franklin Roosevelt, although he hardly knew what real drought was, or poverty, for that matter, shared the plainsmen's optimism, and, to a large extent, their analysis of the problem. "Drought relief" was what they most needed, he believed, and when the rains returned the people would be back on their feet, restoring the land to the rich agricultural empire it had been. That confidence was not absolutely misplaced, as later history showed. But it was all too simple and easy, and the farmers too quick to blame nature for the dust storms, too ready to lay all their misfortunes on the lack of rain. Although drought assistance was obviously needed, as flood or earthquake aid was needed elsewhere, a few of Roosevelt's administrators soon began to see that something more was required: a more far-reaching conservation program that would include social and economic changes.

Without the abrupt drop in precipitation the southern plains would never have become so ravaged a country, nor would they perhaps have needed, even during the Depression, much government aid: this much is true. But the drought, though a necessary factor, is not sufficient in itself to explain the black blizzards. Dry spells are an inevitable fact of life on the plains, predictable enough to allow successful settlement, but only if the settlers know how to tread lightly, look ahead, and shape their expectations to fit the qualities of the land. As the federal administrators studied the problem more fully, they came to see that the settlers of the West had never shown those qualities. They had displayed instead a naïve hopefulness that the good times would never run out, that the land would never go back on them. Some officials, therefore, began to call for major revisions in the faulty land system; others emphasized new agronomic techniques, rural rehabilitation, more diversified farming, or extensive grassland restoration. But their common theme was that staying meant changing. The Dust Bowl, in this evolving government view, must be explained as a failure in ecological adaptation—as an absence of environmental realism.

Farmers and ranchers on the plains were not so recalcitrant as to reject that analysis totally, although, understandably, it was hard for them to admit that what they had learned and had always been told was right could now be responsible for their predicament. It was natural for them to be defensive. They felt unfairly singled out for blame and criticism by many outsiders, when it was they who had to face the dust and struggle hard to save the farms that produced much of the nation's food. And they were right to this extent: it was indeed unjust and misdirected to blame everything on the Dust Bowl residents themselves, for they were largely unwitting agents—men and women caught in a larger economic culture, dependent on its demands and rewards, representing its values and patterns of thought. The ultimate meaning of the dust storms in the 1930s was that America as a whole, not just the plains, was badly out of balance with its natural environment. Unbounded optimism about the future, careless disregard of nature's limits and uncertainties, uncritical faith in Providence, devotion to self-aggrandizement—all these were national as well as regional characteristics.

The activism of the federal government was appropriate and essential; a national problem demanded national answers. But the situation also demanded a more than superficial grasp of what was responsible for the disaster and of how it could be prevented from occurring again. What the plainsmen needed was hope, of course—but the mature hope that does not smooth over failure, deny responsibility, or prevent basic change. They needed a disciplined optimism, tempered with restraint and realism toward the land. But all that required a substantial reform of commercial farming, which neither Roosevelt nor most of his New Deal advisers were prepared or able to bring about. Even as it evolved toward a more comprehensive program, the New Deal did not aim to alter fundamentally the American economic culture. Washington became and remained throughout the decade a substitute for a benign Providence, trying to give the plainsmen their "next year."

Okies and

BETWEEN BLACK THURSDAY on Wall Street and the many black days of the Dust Bowl there was no great difference. In each situation die-hard optimists were sure that it could not happen, then were equally sure that it would not last long. And in each there were people who failed to survive. Whether they lost their jobs in Depression cutbacks following the crash or their farms to blowing dirt, the effect could be the same: a shattered morale, an eroded sense of worth, a loss of the future. In the one case a man might walk the city streets for months, trying to find a new position; in the other, he might herd his family into the farm truck and head for California. But there was more to it than a parallel in hardship. Linking the two disasters was a shared cause—a common economic culture, in factories and on farms, based on unregulated private capital seeking its own unlimited increase. In the 1920s that culture had created a high-producing, high-consuming life for Americans. Few people at that time questioned its premises; business was the national faith. But it could also be, as both the bread lines and the dust storms of the following decade revealed, a self-destructive culture, cutting away the ground from under the people's feet.

That was the conclusion reached by a small group of Dust Bowl observers in the thirties—a circle of doubters and critics who saw something besides drought at work on the plains. They included John Steinbeck, Dorothea Lange, and Woody Guthrie, among others. All of them found in the dust storms a potent symbol for the decade, one that could convey in an instant their sense of a wider, national predicament and one that might even move the nation to radical reform. In their view the Dust Bowl stood for an entire continent that had been ravaged by eco-

Chapter Three

Exodusters

nomic ambition. It represented, too, the final destruction of the old Jeffersonian ideal of agrarian harmony with nature: a relationship that would nurture the land while drawing from it an enduring, widely shared security and independence for rural folk. The destruction of that dream was symbolized not only by the desolate Great Plains landscape, but also by the worried faces of its people, especially the outward-bound refugees called "Okies" and "exodusters." In the thirties those refugees became the archetypal victims of hard times; observers read in their eyes the defeat of poor people everywhere. But they were also a warning to the rest of the nation that man's relation with the earth had gone awry.

For a number of writers and artists this collapse was not to be explained by an act of God. The true cause lay in another symbol of the times: the factory farm, built, like the city's assembly lines, on business principles and for exploitative ends. It was most fully developed on the West Coast, where the refugees found themselves serving as a new agricultural proletariat. But as observers traced these workers to their origins, they began to find similar trends at work in Oklahoma, Texas, and Kansas. And they pointed out, albeit more through images than through sociological data, that there was a common thread running through this complex picture, from tractors, banks, and large-scale commercial farming to black blizzards, abandoned farms, and Okies.

One of the most concise and moving expressions of this sense of connection came from the radical poet Archibald MacLeish. In the summer of 1937, on his farm near Conway, Massachusetts, he wrote a poem he entitled *Land of the Free,* which was published, along with 88 photographs, in book form that same year. The title was intentionally ironic: the American land, MacLeish believed, was in fact no longer a means to freedom and dignity for every individual. Its forests, from New England to Wisconsin, were now millions of acres of stumps; its rivers muddied by erosion and polluted with sewage; and, finally, its plains a ruin too. "The land's going out from us, blown by dry wind in the wheat," observed Mac-Leish. As "the dust chokes in our throats we get wondering":

> We wonder whether the dream of American liberty
> Was two hundred years of pine and hardwood
> And three generations of the grass
> And the generations are up: the years over. . . .
> We wonder whether the great American dream
> Was the singing of locusts out of the grass to
>   the West and the
> West is behind us now. . . .
> We wonder if the liberty is done:
> The dreaming is finished.

With the land no longer able to serve as a secure, fruitful base, people were forced to turn elsewhere. "We've got the roads to go by now the land's gone," noted Mac-Leish—but the roads all led to an industrial world owned by a few who had not only property, but the power of law on their side.[1]

Land of the Free began as a poem illustrated by photographs, but "so great was the power and the stubborn inward livingness of these vivid American documents" that it became instead a book of photographs illustrated by a poem. Most of the pictures came from the Farm Security Administration (formerly the Resettlement Administration) and its photographic section under Roy Stryker. From 1935 on Stryker kept at least six of the best photographers of the time busy documenting the rural American scene. The basic concern, according to Stryker, was "with agriculture—dust, migrants, sharecroppers. Our job was to educate the city dweller to needs of the rural population."[2] Among those sent out with a camera were Walker Evans, Ben Shahn, Margaret Bourke-White, John Vachon, and—to the Dust Bowl, in particular—Arthur Rothstein and Dorothea Lange. (Some of their work is reprinted in this book.) It was MacLeish's decision to subordinate his poem to a selection of these FSA photographs, to interpret in words the meaning of those powerful images. Their dominant spirit, he understood, was one of alienation and uncertainty; the faces showed an older, more sober American character; the central truth of the photographs was that a culture was losing its natural heritage, its roots in the land.

There were other literary voices besides MacLeish's expressing the pessimism of the 1930s. In the cotton belt of the South were Richard Wright, James

Agee, and Erskine Caldwell, each of whom collaborated with federal photographers on books.[3] Two of Caldwell's novels, *Tobacco Road* (1932) and *God's Little Acre* (1933), revealed with earthy, sometimes savage humor a depraved and impoverished rural life—the precise opposite of what the idealized American farm family was supposed to be living. Other books of the decade also carried this theme of disillusion: *Land of Plenty* (Robert Cantwell, 1934), *The Day of the Locust* (Nathanael West, 1939), and *The Grapes of Wrath* (John Steinbeck, 1939). A common aim of these writers was to deny one of the most cherished assumptions in the American experience—that a vast open continent of unprecedented natural abundance would make possible a new golden age for mankind. That dream was now seen to be a lie. America was no Garden of Eden after all, MacLeish and others felt, but a wasteland—old, exhausted, sterile. Whatever fruits it did produce belonged to an economic elite, even though those fruits might be harvested by poor laborers. In all those books it was at least hinted that the dream of Paradise had failed not because of an inherent deficiency in the land itself, but because of human greed and violence. Some, like Cantwell, pointed directly to the industrial capitalist system of production; others saw it more as a matter of widely diffused moral values associated with all the forms of capitalism. Since those values were part of almost every American's patrimony, their discrediting in the thirties left people, in MacLeish's words, with a "we don't know" and "we aren't sure" what we must think henceforth.[4]

There was another side to thirties thinking, to be sure, a back-to-the-land movement that seemed to reaffirm the old Jeffersonian dream. Maurice Kains's *Five Acres and Independence* (1935) was a standard guidebook for those who wanted to free themselves from the economic system, raise rabbits and squash, harvest the fruit from their own orchards, and lead a self-sufficient life. The writings of Ralph Borsodi and, in a more philosophical way, of the Nashville Agrarians were other inspirations for those who stubbornly believed that there was salvation in the land.[5] So was *American Magazine,* which observed that "there is still homestead land in this man's country . . . and Americans are still homesteading right here in the good year 1932." How much any of this was accepted may be deduced from a 1937 *Fortune* opinion poll, which revealed that 40 per cent of the public were still sure that this was "a land of opportunity"—although an astonishing 35 percent said no, it was not.[6]

Whether the land offered that vague something called opportunity or whether opportunity was "behind us now," demographers did discover that Americans were in fact moving back to or not leaving rural areas in the Depression years. During the 1920s there had been a net migration of 6 million people, most of them young or black, from farms and small villages to cities. In the next decade that migration was cut to only 2 million, and in 1932 the flow was actually reversed, as urban unemployment peaked. By 1935 there were more people on farms—almost 33 million—than ever before in the nation's history. The increase came mainly from a traditionally high rural birthrate and an unusually low out-migration. But around almost every large city there were also people seeking small homesteads where they could weather economic adversity. The industrial states of southern New England led in that flow to the suburbs and country; Connecticut, for example, registered an 87 per cent gain in rural population from 1930 to 1935. The gains in both Massachusetts and Rhode Island were over 30 per cent, while the national increase was 6.3. One sociologist saw at work here "a great, uncontrolled mass movement to the succoring breast of Mother Earth."[7] Going back to the land was basically a way of coping with hard times, either by a temporary staying-put or by a grim flight from industrial chaos; but in each case the pastoral life had become a more hopeful one, if only by contrast.

Thus, while some of the nation's leading writers were announcing that the agrarian ideal had been shattered, other disillusioned Americans were seeking an escape of sorts from urban factory dependence. It was only superficially a paradox: on analysis these opposing tendencies of thought suggested a fate that MacLeish had found facing city and country alike. In both environments there was a new sense of decay and loss, provoked by an economic system that was destructive of some of the most cherished human ideals: freedom, material sufficiency for all, a life in equilibrium with nature. That was what some Americans were feeling when the dust storms began on the southern plains. For them it was already a dark moment of cultural despair, and the coming of the Dust Bowl confirmed their fears.

"Lord, I'm going down this road feeling bad." The words were Woody Guthrie's, but the mood was that of poor migrants everywhere. National urban-rural population figures said that people began to stay on the farm in the Depression, that fewer men and women were on the move. Compared with the previous decade, or, for that matter, the previous century, Americans were remarkably stationary in the thirties. But there were areas of the nation where the very opposite was true: where there was a tremendous outward flow of bankrupt, deracinated, demoralized folk. Chief among those areas were the Great Plains.

Across the nation the only states that had fewer residents at the end of the decade than at the beginning were all on the plains. South Dakota's drop was the highest rate in the country, at 7.2 percent, followed by North Dakota, Kansas, and Oklahoma. In net loss through migration—outflow minus inflow—Oklahoma was the easy leader: 440,000, or 18.4 per cent of its 1930 population. The net loss in Kansas was 227,000. None of the other southern plains states experienced such adverse imbalances in migration rates; New Mexico and Colorado even showed slight pluses for the ten-year period. But in those states, too, the sight of families on the road—some of them walking, pushing a handcart loaded with their goods—was a familiar one. Texas farmer and painter H. O. Kelly watched his neighbors leave one by one as the years went by; every week a family of movers would stop to trade for some eggs or bacon to carry with them. Almost a million plains people left their farms in the first half of the decade, and 2.5 million left after 1935. Not all were dusted out, but all were uprooted—a generation of human tumbleweeds, cut loose from the soil.[8]

Nowhere in the Great Plains states was the proportion of migrants to residents higher than in the Dust Bowl. Of 32 Texas panhandle counties, 23 lost population and only nine gained—and the latter were all oil and gas counties. Dallam dropped 17 per cent, while the area decline was almost 5 per cent. In southwestern Kansas, Morton County fell 47 per cent; Grant, 37; Stanton, 33; Stevens, 31. During 1938 alone, almost 5000 exodusters left the 19 counties in this corner of the state. Across the line, in Baca County, Colorado, the 1931-36 decrease was 33 per cent. The Resettlement Administration, surveying forty Dust Bowl counties, discovered that from 1930 to 1935 their farm population had decreased less than 3 per cent; from 1935 to 1937, after the dust storms began, over 34 per cent left. There once had been a farmhouse on every quarter section in the region, and now there were often as many houses abandoned as occupied. The people did not stop to shut the door—they just walked out, leaving behind them the wreckage of their labors: an ugly little shack with broken windows covered by cardboard, a sagging ridgepole, a barren, dusty yard, the windmill creaking in the wind. Ten thousand abandoned houses on the high plains; 9 million acres of farmland turned back to nature.[9]

In the words of Guthrie again: "We loaded our jalopies and piled our families in, / We rattled down the highway to never come back again." Where did they all go? The majority of those 2.5 million moving from their farms did not travel far—into town or to the next county, in most cases. Nor were those who moved to another state always long-distance migrants; leaving Oklahoma from 1935 to 1940 were a total of 309,000 residents: 142,000 went to a contiguous state such as Texas, 167,000 to noncontiguous states. In the early 1930s one group of west Texans migrated as a colony to the pueblo plateau country of western New Mexico. Over 500 families moved into Mesa County, Colorado, in a five-year period, most of them from dust-belt farms around Springfield, Lamar, La Junta, and Cheyenne Wells. The impact on Mesa County was phenomenal: the school population skyrocketed, only one in five migrant families arrived with some money, only one in twenty had enough cash to rent a farm, there were few jobs for the rest. One-half applied for relief, virtually all were in debt. The Resettlement Administration established a project in near-by Delta County, where sixty farm families were placed on farms of 45 to 60 acres each, with electricity and adobe block houses.[10] But that was like trying to contain a flood with a mop.

Most of the long-distance migrants—"tin-can tourists" they were called—went farther west, as Americans have always done. The Pacific Northwest gained 460,000 migrants during the thirties; 25 per cent came from the northern plains along the "Lincoln Highway," 14 per cent from the southern plains. There was, as in Mesa County, very little good farming land for those who wanted it, and almost all were forced to settle on abandoned or cutover property, become seasonal agricultural laborers, or seek relief in the cities. The building of Bonneville Dam on the Columbia River opened up new irrigation possibilities for a small number of these plainsmen; others went farther north to the Matanuska colony, organized in Alaska by the federal government. But the vast majority did not share in those opportunities, nor did they find their life easier in their new homeland.[11]

It was California, however, that had long been the American ideal of Paradise, and now all it cost to get there, if you had a car, was $10 for gas and a bit of food. In a single fifteen-month period, 86,546 destitute migrants went to the Golden State, slightly more than had migrated there in the two years following the discovery of gold in 1849. Exact numbers are not wholly reliable here, for the border patrol at places like Needles or Yuma counted only those whom they guessed were "in need of manual employment." But taking these figures as the best available, it was unmistakenly one of the most spectacular migrations in American history: almost 300,000 poor people entering the state by automobile alone in the second half of the decade. California was the destination for two out of every five migrants across state lines in the nation over this period, and its population consequently showed the greatest gain of any state—a 1.1 million net increase from migration, rich and poor, adding almost 20 per cent to the 1930 population.[12] Obviously, the utterly destitute were a minority in this influx, and the Dust Bowlers a still smaller portion. But it was the exoduster who gave the movement its image and mythology.

Federal statisticians were on hand to compile records as to where the impoverished migrants came from, and why. In two samples taken during 1935 and 1936, using the California border patrol's "guestimates," they found that Oklahoma furnished by far the most numerous group of destitute entrants; Texas was third, behind either Oregon or Arizona (many of the migrants from these last two states were originally from the plains, too). Some 75,000, or one-fourth of all the poor migrants arriving in 1935 and after, came from Oklahoma. Texas, Arkansas, and Missouri together sent another 75,000; Kansas and Colorado, roughly 10,000 each. If you had been among this class of migrants, chances are high you would not have been a farmer. Interviews with those who registered at Federal Emergency

Drought refugees near Tracy, California, 1937. (*Lange, Library of Congress*)

Relief offices around the nation showed that the typical migrant family of the 1930s was a young married couple with a single child; they were white, native-born, leaving some town or city on the plains or in the South and going to another town farther west. Only 12 per cent of the Oklahoma families interviewed blamed their migration on farm failure; in Kansas it was 17 per cent, in Colorado, 16. Unemployment or layoffs accounted for 38 per cent of the relief-seeking Oklahomans, ill health, another 12, inadequate earnings, 11.[13] But no matter what your reason for being poor, or your place of origin in the southern plains states, once across the Colorado River you became an "Okie."

All along U.S. Route 66 in New Mexico and Arizona down-and-out migrants could be seen chugging west: "Beating a hot old dusty trail to the California line," the song went. Their wheezy cars, coated with red or brown dirt, were loaded high with whatever they thought was worth salvaging from their past: bedsprings and mattresses, a cookstove, a box of old dishes, buckets and odd pieces of lumber, the kitchen table, a bewildered goat caged and tied to the running board. In the

Migrants camped by a pea field, Calipatria, California, 1937. (*Lange, Library of Congress*)

desert noon they camped beside billboards, discussing what it would be like when they bought a little white house in an orange grove. In the late afternoon they gathered at filling stations, spending what little cash they had on gasoline and oil while they compared notes on where they could sleep free that night. At the port of entry the Los Angeles police met them with a "bum blockade"—no more Okies wanted. Woody Guthrie warned them too: "If you ain't got the Do Re Mi, boys, better go back to beautiful Texas, Oklahoma, Kansas, Georgia, Tennessee."

The popular reception these travelers received in California, when they were not discouraged from entering, was unlike anything native whites had faced there before. It was most tersely summed up in a San Joaquin Valley theater sign: "Negroes and Okies upstairs." The large growers, however, were glad to see this new labor pool arrive. They had over 200 commercial crops on their farms, most of them needing hand labor for brief periods: peaches and prunes, lemons and oranges, lettuce and asparagus, cotton and flax, all to be picked and boxed or baled. Their former supply of cheap Mexican workers had been cut off in 1929 by immigration restriction. Oklahomans and Texans now came to fill the jobs the Mexicans had held. The laborers started down near Brawley in the Imperial Valley, worked their way up the coast to Santa Barbara, then over to the Central Valley, and on north to Washington State. Most of the farms provided temporary lodging—tents or rude cabins—but with only three state inspectors and 8000 camps to inspect, the quarters were bound to be generally poor. Any family entering this stoop-and-pick life could expect to work about half the year and earn $350 to $450, only 50 per cent of what the California Relief Administration estimated to be a subsistence level. It was take it or leave it; strikes for higher wages were squelched and radical organizers beaten, shot, and jailed. With only 175,000 workers needed at peak season and at least two or three desperate migrants for every job, the growers could name the terms.[14]

But those who did get jobs were the fortunate ones; much worse off were the thousands forced to squat by the side of the road, having no prospects of work at all and denied public relief funds for an entire year. They formed wretched squatter camps called "little Oklahomas." Those down in the Imperial Valley were rated by *Fortune* as "the absolute low for the entire state." Relief officials found a family in one of them that had only a 1921 Ford to shelter ten people. The mother, suffering from tuberculosis and pellagra, was trying to carry on a homelife as best she could, using cupboards and tables made of old boxes, a rusty tin can as her stewpot, wash water taken out of an irrigation ditch, the sides of which served as their toilet. Told that they would have to leave, she responded vacantly, "I wonder where we can go."[15] They had reached the end of their road.

H. L. Mencken, the barbed wit of the iconoclastic twenties, had once attracted a large following by ridiculing rural people. In the thirties he was outraged by pleas for help from sharecroppers and exodusters. "They are simply, by God's inscrutable will, inferior men," he wrote, "and inferior they will remain until, by a stupendous miracle, He gives them equality among His angels." The best solution, Mencken supposed, was to move the Dust Bowlers away from the plains, out of farming and even out of childbearing—bribe them to be sterilized, he urged.[16] Many Californians shared Mencken's view that failure on the Great Plains was a sign of biological inferiority—that that was what "Okie" meant—although they were much less ready to have them resettled in Kern or Kings County. The Californians' popular analysis was also more ambivalent than Mencken's, to a point: the Okie was widely presumed to be a "Dust Bowl refugee," suggesting that a natural calamity rather than personal biology was responsible for his leaving home. Prejudice, of course, never waits for the facts, especially when they are complex; to get to the truth of the difficult situation required an empathy with the Okies that neither Mencken nor many Californians had. It was easier, and perhaps more human, to feel hostility toward them than attempt to resolve the contradictions.

There were a few Californians, however, who did not share that hostility. They recognized in the Okies the need of all men and women for acceptance and for a secure, decent life. It was they, therefore, who assumed responsibility for bringing the plight of these migrants before the nation in the late 1930s. They explored the Okie background, trying thereby to unravel the complicated story behind their West Coast presence. Unlike Mencken, this group was convinced that external factors, not genetics, explained the influx from Oklahoma and Kansas. But they did not find that dust storms were the most important of those factors. More fundamental, they realized, was the kind of agriculture evolving in America. What later generations would call "agribusiness," or business farming, was everywhere on the rise—it had been for some time—and it was severing an historical and valuable connection between a rural culture and the land. It was here that one had to seek an understanding of the refugee squatting by an irrigation ditch. He was there not because of the dust, but for the same reason that the dust was blowing so violently: both calamities were consequences of commercial agriculture's aggressive energies.

Easily the most influential spokesman for this more radical argument was John Steinbeck. He was, of course, primarily a novelist, not a social critic, but *The Grapes of Wrath* was one of the most socially committed works of art the decade produced. No other novel of the thirties had anything like its national impact; it taught an entire reading public what to think about the Okies and exodusters, and it would endure, for all its aesthetic and analytical faults, as one of the great American works of literature. When director John Ford made a movie out of the book one year after its publication in 1939—featuring Jane Darwell and Henry Fonda as Ma and Tom Joad, the most powerful mother-son match ever put on the screen—it became an instant film classic. The story of the heroic, embattled, tenacious Joads, encountered in either the novel or the movie version, was that of every ordinary family that had experienced defeat during the Depression and the Dust Bowl years. But the Joad story was also a way of explaining why it had happened and where the nation was heading; it was a glimpse into the American future as much as a glance back at a passing decade.

Not everyone was ready to appreciate Steinbeck's choice of subject, to accept his radical opinions, or to like his colloquial style. Some literary critics complained that mawkish sentimentality spoiled parts of the book. Edmund Wilson disliked the way the novel reduced humans to an animal level and made them too much a part of nature, too coarse and debased. Less highbrow critics said much the same thing in their own way: the book was banned in Kansas City, Missouri, East St. Louis, Illinois, and Kern County, California, for its sexual frankness as well as for its political views. Oklahoma boosters described the Joads's language as "morbid"

'Now Eat Every Gol-Durn Word of It!'

Daily Oklahoman (Oklahoma City), 25 September 1941.

and "filthy" and complained that the novel gave their state's fine, progressive people a degenerate reputation; "it pictures Oklahoma with complete and absurd untruthfulness," wrote one newspaper. An English professor at the University of Oklahoma defended his state's honor by arguing that "the folks in the Dust Bowl are not proletarian in thought or speech. They were never ashamed of poverty nor so weak as to think it an excuse for laxity in living up to their traditional code." Despite these censures, *The Grapes of Wrath* was as widely read in Oklahoma as elsewhere; it sold sensationally, and the Tulsa library had to buy twenty-eight copies to meet the demand. Nationally, it outdid everything on the bestseller list, except *Gone with the Wind,* and it won both a Pulitzer Prize and a Nobel Prize for its author.[17]

Steinbeck, long a resident of California's Salinas Valley, was already a recognized writer when he came upon the Okie story, lying, as it were, on his doorstep. In October 1936 the *San Francisco News* published seven articles he wrote on the agricultural migrant, along with several FSA photographs taken by Dorothea Lange. Two years later those articles and pictures appeared again as a pamphlet entitled *Their Blood Is Strong,* which served as Steinbeck's journalistic base for the great novel to follow. "Our agriculture," he wrote then, in what would also be his later theme, "for all its great produce is a failure." It reduced the very people who harvested its crops to hunger and nakedness, and it kept them there by legalized violence. At this point Steinbeck assumed that he was talking only about California farms. The migrants had come from "the prairies where industrialization never penetrated," he believed; they had jumped with no transition

> from the old agrarian, self-containing farm where nearly everything used was raised or manufactured, to a system of agriculture so industrialized that the man who plants a crop does not often see, let alone harvest, the fruit of his planting, where the migrant has no contact with the growing cycle.

In their old homes, he went on, these people had lived in a small-scale, classless world of Jeffersonian democracy, where every man and woman had a say. All of that had been destroyed by drought; they were now refugees from dust. Out in California, through no fault of their own, they had become a disfranchised, exploited class of workers, supporting with hard labor their rich, absentee masters. "Must the hunger become anger," Steinbeck demanded to know, "and the anger fury before anything will be done?"[18]

There was confirmation of Steinbeck's outraged views in no less a source than *Fortune* magazine. Just a few months before *The Grapes of Wrath* appeared, *Fortune* had described not only the squatter camps, but also the kind of agriculture found in California. One in ten farms in the state grew more than one-half the crops; these were gigantic "factories in the field," which were more highly developed here than anywhere else in the world. One-third of all American farms that produced at least a $30,000 annual crop value were in the state. Yet for all its giantism, it was a most unstable business, with expensive irrigation costs, high taxes, and cutthroat competition. "Speculative feverishness"—the desire to beat out rivals and maximize profits in order to grow even bigger—led to "periodic overproduction in one crop after another." Then, as in the rest of industrial America, the strategy was to cut costs by cutting wages to the barest subsistence level. The migrants' desperate status, *Fortune* decided, was properly seen as the culmination of "the whole tragic history of American agriculture, dating from the earliest misuse of the soil."[19] Exploitation of the land through profit-seeking factory farming, directly connected to the exploitation of farm workers, was where the nation's farms long had been going, and now, at least in one state, where they had arrived.

Other Californians echoed *Fortune* and Steinbeck: notably, Dorothea Lange's husband, Paul Taylor, University of California economist; and Carey McWilliams, director of the state's Immigration and Housing Office under Governor Culbert Olson. The agricultural structure, they too maintained, was unlike anything Americans had supposed was true of farming, based as it was on a caste system similar to that found in any factory. "We are not husbandmen," Taylor quoted an agricultural spokesman as saying, "we are not farmers. We are producing a product to sell." And the profitability of that product always depended upon pushing the land as far as it could go, and the farm laborer too. The lords of this self-aggrandizing economic order were those who owned the land *in absentia:* "such earth-stained toilers," wrote Steinbeck, "as chain banks, public utilities, railroad companies and those huge corporations called land companies."[20] Taylor and McWilliams were agreed: there was no longer an immediate working bond between the land and its owners, nor was there any identity between those who labored in the earth and those who enjoyed its fruits.

After studying their own state's corporate farms, all of these Californians went to the Great Plains, traveling east on Highway 66, wanting to know more about the abused Okies and to learn for themselves what conditions were like back there. Steinbeck passed through Oklahoma in 1938, before he wrote *The Grapes of Wrath*. Lange and Taylor went to Texas to take photographs of the Dust Bowl and cotton belt people and to hear their stories, both of which made up their book, *An American Exodus* (1939). Carey McWilliams followed after them, as did Congressman John Toland of Oakland and his House Committee on Interstate Migration of Destitute Citizens, which held exhaustive hearings during 1940.[21] What all of these people discovered, much to their surprise, was that industrial farming was advancing across the flat midsections of the country too, and that the migrants were fleeing not only drought, but the machine as well. In the plains states it was often the owner of a tractor who was putting the Okies off the land, just as in the San Joaquin Valley it was the machine-like economic system that was ensnaring them in a new bondage.

This was precisely what had happened to the fictional Joads. Tractors belonging to the land's owners came and Joads had to go. Their house was bulldozed away, and there were no choices left to them. Steinbeck, however, could not avoid beginning his book by reaffirming the popular image of the Okie refugees as dust-storm victims. The very first chapter of *The Grapes of Wrath* told again of blowing dirt, darkness at midday, and crops destroyed. The Joads were then placed in Sallisaw, Oklahoma, almost on the Arkansas border and 400 miles east of Guymon and the panhandle dust center. Corn, not wheat, was the crop they raised; hills and oaks, not shortgrass, filled their native landscape. Steinbeck's geography, like that of most Americans, was a bit hazy; any place in Oklahoma, even on the Ozark plateau, must be Dust Bowl country, he assumed. But confirm though he did this misapprehension and thereby, for the hasty reader, the widely confused explanation of the Okie/exoduster migration, Steinbeck did go on to show that it was not nature that "broke" people like the Joads—they could handle the drought. It was business farming, seeking a better return on land investments and buying tractors to pursue it, that had broken these people, smashing their identity as natural beings wedded to the land. Against this economic force there was no defense; "there wasn't nobody you could lay for," neighbor Muley complained.[22]

Steinbeck was never able to put his finger firmly and accurately on the economic institutions responsible for the Joads's·exodus. Just as he moved dust storms in from the plains, so he turned eastern Oklahoma farming into a near replica of the Salinas orchards. Great invisible corporations interlocked with banks supposedly controlled the land around Sallisaw. It made a good story and a familiar one, not only for readers on the West Coast, but for those in the Northeastern urban centers. In fact, however, there were few farming corporations anywhere in Oklahoma. Agriculture there was more primitively organized than that; independent operators were the rule, some of them large landowners, others not so large but caught up just as firmly in the web of commercialism. The businessman as farmer wore many guises, and it did the cause of reform no good to focus, as Steinbeck did, on distant conspiratorial shareholders or boards of directors. More important than the precise pattern of private ownership was the widespread drive in American farming to maximize profits from the land and the increasing use of machinery to do just that. Those were among the major factors accounting for people like the Joads going west.

On the Ozark plateau, down along the Mississippi, up in the Illinois corn belt, out on the west Texas plain, Paul Taylor likewise observed·this industrial invasion under way. Great phalanxes of clanking, smoking machines were remaking the face of the earth and grinding under its rural culture. One panhandle family, with seven sturdy young sons, was living on relief checks, he discovered. They could find no land to farm, for it was all being consolidated with the aid of tractors, and the tenants were being told—sometimes gruffly, sometimes in anguish— that there was no alternative but to start packing. Federal agriculture programs designed to control surplus crops put money into the hands of landlords, almost never into the hands of their tenants. "I let 'em all go," explained one owner:

> In '34 I had I reckon four renters and I didn't make anything. I bought tractors on the money the government give me and get shet o' my renters. You'll find it everywhere all over the country thataway. I did everything the government said—except keep my renters. The renters have been having it this way ever since the government come in. They've got their choice— California or WPA.

According to Taylor, the number of tractors on Oklahoma farms increased, despite the drought and Depression, by 25 per cent between 1929 and 1936. The effect of such mechanization was to create a contemporary equivalent to the English enclosures of the sixteenth to nineteenth centuries, when early commercial farmers "modernized" the social and ecological order of their nation. Where would it stop this time? Taylor wondered. Where would the common people turn? Was it all an inevitable price of progress?[23]

The machines were a tangible threat in American agriculture, easy to isolate, as Taylor did to account for Okie migration. But behind the tractors were economic values, and they were old and familiar, especially in the cotton belt. Since the founding of the cotton and tobacco plantation systems, long before lettuce growers appeared in Imperial Valley, the South had been leading America along the route toward large-scale business farming, first with slave labor and then with tenants and sharecroppers. Southerners might have known little about the capitalism of huge factories and Wall Street investors, but they understood very well the idea of using the land without restraint. They were, in fact, pioneers in commercial, specialized monoculture and in international marketing and trade of farm products. From the Carolina piedmont to the Oklahoma red hills and the Texas black wax prairie, their one-crop agriculture had left a trail of exploitation: a permanently submerged class of transient farmers who had become shiftless and uncaring, without the power to change their lives for the better; and a barren earth, marked by deep gullies, slashed timber, and thinning soils.[24] Steinbeck and Taylor, sensitized as others in their generation were to the American economy's failures, now began to see, though sometimes confusedly, a larger pattern that included on one side of the ledger the Wall Street broker who bought and sold on margin, the small-town banker who frittered away other people's savings, the factory owner who laid off workers to shave costs, and the commercial farmer who saw a new way to make a profit on cotton or some other cash crop. And on the other side of the ledger was entered the simple word "erosion"—personal, cultural, geological.

No one understood this pattern better than Carey McWilliams. In *Ill Fares the Land* (1942) he told Americans that the Joads of the nation were "the victims of grab and greed as much as dust and tractors."

> Their distress is the end product of a process of social disintegration set in motion as early as 1900. Their problem is distinctly a man-made problem. Their tragedy is part of a greater tragedy,—the wasteful and senseless exploitation of a rich domain,—the insane scramble of conflicting group interests which frustrated the promise of the frontier and (within a decade) converted a pioneer territory into a sink of poverty.

Most of the Oklahoma refugees came from a broad zone stretching northeast to southwest across the state. Within that area tuberculosis and other diseases were rife, as was illiteracy. Farms often amounted to no more than forty or fifty acres

Typical Okie homestead, well-removed from the plains and dust storms. This one was in Atoka County, Oklahoma, and rented for $6.00 a year. (*Dorothea Lange, Library of Congress*)

apiece, 61.2 per cent of them were operated in 1935 by tenants, and each year 28 per cent of the farm population—275,000 people—moved to a new farm. Out of this rootless countryside came the westward-moving migrants, still eager to find what they had never had, "a place to stay still," as one of them put it. McWilliams was shocked to see here, in an American state only thirty years old, "humanity at its lowest possible level of degradation and decay."[25]

Even without tractors Oklahoma could not have provided a permanent home for people like the Joads: too much of its soil had been destroyed. A scientist declared in 1938 that since agricultural occupation, Oklahoma had suffered as much erosion as some of the oldest farming districts of the United States. Hugh Hammond Bennett, head of the Soil Conservation Service, had said the same thing ten years earlier. On a representative red-plains farm where 74 acres had been broken out and cultivated, 92 per cent of the land showed heavy losses to sheet erosion, he noted; 25 acres had lost an average of eight inches of topsoil; 23 acres had lost thirteen inches, and on one acre *five feet* of earth had been washed away. Over all of Oklahoma, the state agricultural college at Stillwater calculated, 13 million out of 16 million cultivated acres suffered from erosion, nearly half of them being gullied; consequently, the state's average cotton yield had skidded down 100 pounds per acre in only twenty years.[26] In China or Japan a large family could support itself in at least limited comfort on a mere two acres, but that required intensive husbandry, well-developed skills, and a stabilized social framework. In Oklahoma even a 160-acre spread, owned in fee simple, could not prevent a family's joining the relief rolls. How much worse off then was the tenant farmer, aware as he was that next year would be moving time again, knowing as he did that the land was someone else's and might be claimed any day? The result could only be, according to Carey McWilliams, a "sumphole" of human misery and a land covered with red, running sores.

The Joads and their fellow migrants thus had not come to California out of a sturdy yeoman farmer tradition, nor out of a pastoral landscape. They had been victims at home too of an exploitative agricultural system: of tractors, one-crop specialization, tenant insecurity, disease, and soil abuse. Apparently, their predicament had little to do with dust storms after all, and they were not really, for the most part, exodusters. Of Oklahoma's total net migration loss of 500,000, perhaps only 2 or 3 per cent were from the westernmost part of the state, where the black blizzards were.[27] This was the conclusion toward which McWilliams in particular moved after his fact-finding tour; a "Dust Bowl refugee" was for him a stereotype built on a myth, on geographical confusion, and on shallow causative thinking—as false as Mencken's "bad genes" argument.

The upshot of Carey McWilliams's analysis was to shift attention away from dust storms to economic conditions in explaining the migrant labor problem. But in that process the danger was that the plains would be forgotten and the black clouds set aside as another issue altogether, unrelated to the progress of commercial farming. The truth was more complex than either McWilliams or the "refugee" stereotype allowed. Although few of the Okies were in fact from the Dust Bowl, the exodusters were rightly lumped together with the despised Okies; they had many things in common. First of all, throughout the panhandle area, but especially from Lubbock to Amarillo, the cultural patterns were almost identical to those farther east, which was not surprising, since both sections were part of the cotton kingdom. There were sharecroppers and tenants, mules and gins, in Childress, Floyd, Hale, and Bailey counties of the Texas plains. Up north, in the wheat and cattle country, many of the residents had also come out of eastern Oklahoma or Arkansas, and their background was largely Southern poor white. Woody Guthrie is a case in point: born in 1912 in Okemah, Oklahoma, he moved to Pampa, over in the Texas panhandle, in 1929 and remained there through the dust storms until he hitched a ride to California in 1937. He had rambled around until cotton, oil, wheat, corn, and white faced steers were all mixed into his songs, as they were mixed into the lives of his people.[28] The Okie type, it is true, was not common farther north in the Kansas or Colorado part of the Dust Bowl. As a rule, the Dust Bowlers were healthier than the typical Okie, and more often knew how to read and write. But otherwise, in speech, religion, diet, and kinship, the southern plains families were often hard to distinguish from the Joads.

Furthermore, similar economic forces were at work on the High Plains, creating an impoverished economic class and putting people off the land in wholesale quantities there, as in Sallisaw. Mechanization of farming was more advanced in this region than anywhere else in America, including California, leading to the familiar process of, in Paul Taylor's phrase, "bigger farms and fewer men." Tenants were a growing class on the plains, just as they were in the red hills, growing first in numbers and then, with more tractors at work, growing in insecurity. In most Dust Bowl counties less than half the land was owned by residents, and at least 40 per cent of all operators were tenants—a lower figure than the Oklahoma average, but far higher than was suggested by the outmoded American image of the self-reliant farmer. In Baca County, Colorado, the tenant rate had increased from 3 per cent in 1910 to 44 per cent in 1935. Most of the newcomers after 1927 had been renters, and they were the first to leave in the thirties, possessing insufficient capital either to compete against their neighbors or to survive drought and dust.[29] Technological and economic developments on the Great Plains made it most misleading to distinguish the Dust Bowler from the Okie completely. There were important differences between the two rural types, but the similarities in agricultural structure, and, for many, in cultural origins, were more compelling.

But behind twangy voices and salt-pork diet, behind the statistics on machines and tenantry, lay a further characteristic that all these people shared: a condition of profound ecological disequilibrium. The people-land symbiosis, never perfectly achieved nor perhaps widely desired, was in utter disintegration. Thousands of cars on the road west were one kind of evidence, whether they came from Ulysses, Kansas, or Muskogee, Oklahoma. Rivers stained red with precious topsoil were another proof. And then there were the dusters, piling great dunes up against the houses and barns, leaving the plains a Sahara. More than anything else, the destruction of the land was a shared phenomenon, caused by a fundamentally similar economic order. California-bound migrants were to a substantial extent "ecological refugees," regardless of where they came from. It was important to collect precise data and make careful distinctions so that "Dust Bowl refugee" did not become a way of dismissing a complex social problem. But it was also necessary to see, and to feel, the underlying connections. Dorothea Lange understood that she was photographing a common ecological story when she took pictures of hungry families rocking on the porches of their sharecropper cabins, of panhandle farms blowing down to hardpan, or of migrant mothers camping along the highway to Bakersfield. Woody Guthrie, who knew the landscape and people better than any of the Californians, made the same linkage in his Dust Bowl ballads. And John Steinbeck, though technically wrong in putting his dust storm in Sallisaw, also knew that his fiction spoke a deep truth about man and the earth in thirties America.

"The land bore under iron, and under iron gradually died." This was the truth Steinbeck wanted Americans to realize about industrializing, commercial agriculture. It had, he feared, no respect for or sympathetic understanding of the natural world that produced its profits, any more than it cared about the fate of a rural way of life.

> The man who is more than his chemistry, walking on the earth, turning his plow point for a stone, dropping his handles to slide over an outcropping, kneeling in the earth to eat his lunch; that man who is more than his element knows the land that is more than its analysis. But the machine man, driving a dead tractor on land he does not know and love, understands only chemistry; and he is contemptuous of the land and of himself. When the corrugated iron doors are shut, he goes home, and his home is not the land.

Uprooting the Joads from their place, giving them nowhere to stand and to "stay still," was the result of this business mentality. Herein also lay, as Steinbeck strongly implied, the ultimate explanation of the Dust Bowl: the alienation of man from the land, its commercialization, and its consequent abuse. The tractor was not the true problem, nor was the corporate phase of farming. There was something more basic and general than these—an economic culture that now dominated the rural landscape of America. Its approach to the land had never recognized any limits nor restrained the appetite for gain. "When the monster stops growing, it dies," Steinbeck wrote; "It can't stay one size."[30] But as it grew and as it gained new technological power, it destroyed more thoroughly than ever—until one day there would be nothing remaining to the nation but a man-made desert.

Too pessimistic, a later generation might respond. Steinbeck, MacLeish, and the rest were too impressed by a few dust storms and marginal farmers on the road; too quick to blame it all on capitalism; too easily convinced that the world would never get better, even for the Okies—so one could argue. But if the photographs of the period can be taken as accurate to any degree whatsoever, there was much to be pessimistic and critical about, whether in California or in Oklahoma. Those photographs make a convincing argument that the dust storms were neither a trivial matter nor an isolated phenomenon, that everywhere in America the land was in a bankrupt state, just as the people on it were. The Dust Bowl rightly became the dominant national symbol of this bankruptcy and ecological decay, fusing into itself all the environmental complexities of the time. Neither photographs nor literary symbols could illustrate precisely how this massive disorder had come about. That required a more complete examination of the ecology of the southern plains and the history of their settlement. But the chapters to come will justify the radical sensibility of John Steinbeck and others. If their pessimism was deeply felt, it was because the causes of the Dust Bowl were deeply entrenched in the American economic ethos.

Part II

PRELUDE TO DUST

There was always the grass ahead
of us on and on
Father to father's son.

Archibald MacLeish,
Land of the Free

What Holds

"THE MEANING OF THE DUST STORMS," wrote Archibald MacLeish, "was that grass was dead."[1] An old and unique ecological complex had been destroyed by man, leaving him with no buffer against the elements, leaving the land free to blow away. It was not the first time some large part of the natural vegetation had died, but it was the only time that it had happened because of a deliberate strategy carried out by human beings. Before the coming of Europeans to the plains there had long been cycles of drought and rainfall, following, like summer after winter, a continual building up and tearing down by the inanimate forces that control life on this planet. Against these powerful forces organic nature had struggled over millions of years, determining by trial and error what would flourish best in this dry corner of the good earth—now losing ground, now gaining it back. Nothing was fixed or permanent; man did not come into a perfectly stable or finished world on the plains. But he did encounter there an ancient set of alliances that might have helped him survive. All the living things needed each other, depended on each other, to withstand the harsher side of climate. The earliest humans to settle in the region understood that interdependency well, and respected it, but the white man did neither.

The white man, however, was not the first agency to effect a total reorganization of plains ecology. Nature herself had created here, as elsewhere, a succession of regimes and revolutions before the days of grass. In the mid-thirties WPA workers began excavating a dinosaur graveyard in northwestern Cimarron County, Oklahoma, unearthing, among other bony treasures, a 65-foot-long Brontosaurus skeleton. A few miles away, on Elzy Tanner's farm, they also found gigantic petrified

the Earth Together

logs that had once been living redwood-like trees as much as six feet in diameter.[2] Those fossil remains told of an eerily different Mesozoic past, when vast inland seas had ebbed and flowed across what was now the Dust Bowl. In those seas had swum ancient turtles and plesiosaurs, and along the warm swampy edges had grown tropical forests of trees and ferns where enormous reptiles, vegetarian and carnivorous, had lumbered about for more than 100 million years. Then it all had abruptly disappeared: the climate of the earth had become colder and drier; violent crunching of the continental plates against each other had thrust up new mountain ranges, producing a far more diversified set of habitats; and the largest reptiles, unable to adapt to the new order, had died out. Nothing man would ever do could be compared to that tumult wrought by nature.

For the Great Plains the most dramatic of those upheavals had come with the Laramide Revolution of 60 million years ago, which had created the Rocky Mountains. In a geological instant the immense trough through which Pacific and Arctic waters had once invaded the North American interior was plugged. The Rockies had also fundamentally altered the climates east of them, distilling out the moisture that air currents brought from the ocean and leaving the plains lying in a wide rain-shadow. The heavy rains and snows that had fallen on the mountaintops now washed away the softer, sedimentary layers and redeposited them in a broad apron, or alluvial fan, at the base. Year by year in the Tertiary period, that apron spread eastward from the mountains, covering the old seabed of shale and sandstone with loose, unconsolidated silt and smaller quantities of sand and gravel, as much as 500 feet thick. Irregularities in the old surface were smoothed away to

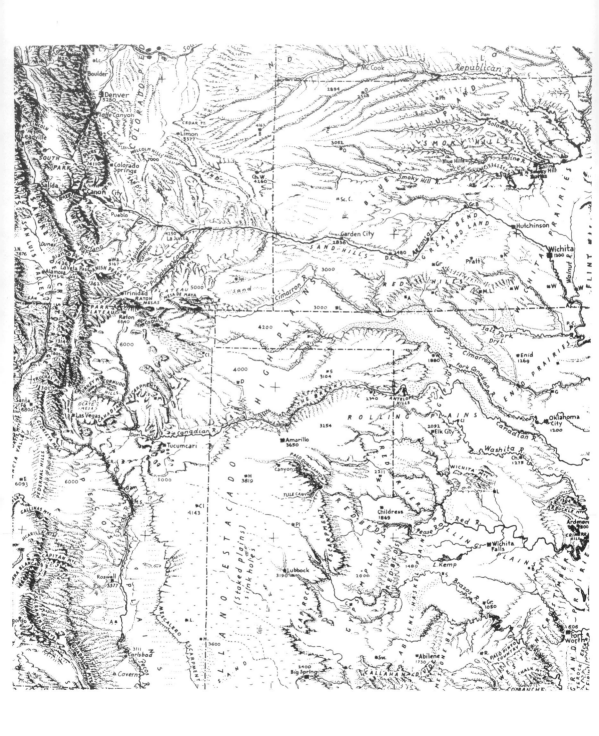

Landforms of the Southern Plains. (*From Erwin Raisz, "Landforms of the U.S."*)

produce one of the most monotonously level landforms on the face of the earth: the soft tableland of the High Plains, ranging from 3000 to 4000 feet in elevation. There was not enough rain on the plains to erode the smoothness; the rivers that flowed through eventually carried less new sediment and stayed roughly in their courses, having little more regional effect.[3]

During the past million years, the so-called Pleistocene epoch, massive ice-sheets formed, and they crept down from the mountain valleys and south from Hudson's Bay. On four occasions the glaciers spread into the plains, but they never reached the southern latitudes of the continent. Then, with the retreat of the ice, large sections of the land lay bare and dry. Winds began to pick up the soil, and interglacial dust storms occurred—far greater and more protracted than those of the 1930s—leaving behind them deposits we call loess. In Nebraska some 42,000 square miles of loess were laid down, sometimes twenty or more feet thick; much of the fertile farmland of Iowa, Illinois, Wisconsin, and Indiana also originated in the days of prehistoric wind erosion, gaining a gift of rich soil from the plains to the west. There was potential good in blowing dust then, but at the immediate and severe cost of transforming parts of the Great Plains into areas of Martian sterility, swept by tyrannic tidal winds. Fortunately for man, that ancient "dust bowl" ended long ago; according to an Illinois geologist writing in 1938, "no appreciable amount of material has been added to the loess of the Mississippi Valley since the last glacial epoch."[4]

From those chaotic, erosive forces soil patterns emerged. Curtis F. Marbut, the most authoritative student of the subject, isolated two universal characteristics in matured soils of the Great Plains, including eolian, or wind-deposited, loess. The first was a dark surface layer containing organic matter, ranging in color from black in the east—similar to the chernozem of the Eurasian steppe—to shades of brown as one approached the Rocky Mountains. The second was a zone of alkaline salt accumulation, usually lime carbonate, created by the leaching effect of limited rain. On the extreme eastern edge of the Great Plains there was no alkaline zone because the rain was heavy enough to wash the salts down to the groundwater level. But farther west it appeared, first at a depth of 16 to 20 inches, then only 13 or 14 inches down. This calcereous material under the loose surface formed a hardpan, or, more technically, a caliche deposit, beneath which the earth stayed dry. Soils with this layer were called "pedocals," indicating that they had lost less mineral matter than had those of humid climates. Give them rain and they would support a rich vegetation—but then the same rain would eventually leach away their soluble nutrients.[5]

So little moisture falls on the southern plains today that they are classed as semiarid: not quite a desert, but very dry, receiving an average of twenty inches or less of precipitation a year.

The virgin land—shortgrass plains and an old buffalo wallow. (*Kansas State Historical Society*)

But the most important fact about the climate, after the dryness, is its unpredictability. There are years when the Oklahoma panhandle enjoys Iowa weather; then it will get a year or two of Utah skies—of dry crackling air that can turn the bare earth to powder. Most of the moisture falls during the spring and summer growing season, but high temperatures can quickly evaporate it before there is much penetration to plant roots. The land is not one of steady deficiency that men can count on, as is the true desert, but one of sharp extremes—heat and cold, floods and droughts, cyclones and blizzards. It is an unreliable, intractable place, wildly oscillating around an almost meaningless mean. The only certainty is that droughts will come, and come often, and that in "normal" years the region lies at or below the rainfall margin for most farming.

Why the climate should be so volatile is clear enough when one understands the peculiar meteorological situation. The high-level winds of three powerful weather empires meet and clash here. Mild, dry air moves across the cordillera; cold, dry fronts roll heavily down from the Arctic; and warm, moist currents flow up from the Gulf of Mexico. Where and how they meet determines what the plains will be like from week to week as well as from century to century. The sudden encounter of polar cold and tropical warmth, sometimes with hail and thunderous *éclat,* can produce in a single day a torrential downpour of one-third the average annual precipitation. Over the years a rough balance of power emerges in this warfare: a series of rainfall zones shades from north to south and from east to west. The Dust Bowl lies most fully under the power of the dessicated westerlies that flow over the mountains: rain makes its way from the Gulf on only a few unguarded occasions. All of this takes place as a grand, upper atmospheric drama. Down at ground level, however, the winds usually blow out of the southwest; their average velocity in midafternoon is 15 miles per hour. They are the one steady ingredient in plains weather—always ready to tear away whatever is not firmly rooted or nailed down.[6] The climate of the plains then, like its geological history, confronts man with nature's capacity for violence.

There were not many kinds of plants that had sufficient resilience for such conditions. In particular, almost all trees needed more soil moisture than the plains could offer, except along river bottoms, where cottonwood, hackberry, willow, and wild plum found a wetter, less windblown refuge. For the most part the plains had to be given over to the grasses. In the post-Mesozoic era the grasses began to appear on the earth, some of them destined to furnish man with his important cereal foods, such as wheat, rice, and corn. Eventually the grasses covered one-quarter of the earth's total land mass. Out of some 4500 species of grasses that evolved, the Great Plains became the home of several hundred. As many as 50 to 75 species could be found in a single area.[7] Together they created a series of ecological communities, or ecosystems, that were nowhere duplicated in the world. Those communities could be disrupted by drought, silting, or Ice Age climate shifts; and their boundaries were never rigidly fixed, but expanded or contracted with yearly weather patterns. Even so, the grasses endured those trials. They created a new, living, inland sea that lasted for millions of years. They helped preserve the soft plateau from further erosion by wind and water. "There is no run-off," noted the geologist Willard Johnson. "Even heavy downpours . . . are here rendered practically inert by the grass mat until disposed of through ground absorption and evaporation. The High Plains . . . are held by their sod." The grasses were described less prosaically by an early Kansas Senator as "the forgiveness of nature—her constant benediction."[8] They came as a pacifying force, unable to tame the elements, but moderating their effect and creating a more benign world for other forms of life.

Before the white man appeared, the North American grassland extended from the oak openings of Ohio all the way to the Rockies, and beyond in isolated pockets. Its most impressive domain, however, was what became the Great Plains states. On the eastern edge of that country, where the rainfall was 25 to 30 inches annually, grew the tall grasses—big bluestem, switch grass, and Indian grass, some of these eight feet high with roots going six feet into the ground. That was the true prairie of black chernozem soil. But the Dust Bowl, lying hundreds of miles southwest of the prairie and beyond the 20-inch isohyet, was a world of brown soils and short grasses. Not one, however, but four major plant associations were widely established on these southern plains: grama–buffalo grass, wire grass, bluestem–bunch grass, and sand grass–sand sage. Of all these the first was the most common, forming a tough fibrous mat that looked precisely like a well-grazed meadow. Flowerstalks of the blue grama, each bearing two or three right-angled seed spikes, were no more than a foot high. The buffalo grass was even shorter—four or five inches above the ground—with its seed heads hidden in its curling foliage. The wire grass association, which was the same shortgrass sod overtopped by a taller species, could be found where there was slightly more rainfall, 18 to 22 inches. Both of these vegetative types required tight soils that held the water close to the surface, within reach of their roots. On the looser, sandier areas grew the remaining associations. Water penetrated those lighter soils more quickly and went to a greater depth, where only bunch grasses with long roots, such as the bluestem, could tap it. Thus, in the western sandhills, the tallgrass prairie had an outlying toehold of sorts, and the plains offered a wider array of habitats than its over-all visual monotony suggested.[9]

These were only the ecological dominants of the shortgrass country. A miscellany of other grasses sprouted, too: galleta, western wheat grass, salt grass, sand dropseed, needle grass, sideoats grama, six-weeks fescue, prairie three-awn. Soapweed, or yucca, bristled its way in here and there, raising its creamy white stalks above the rest, and the pungent sagebrush and the delicately green mesquite tree were scattered along the plains border. Other conjoiners were the brown snakeweed, found in thin, frail clumps; yellow broomweed; and curlycup gumweed. There were bright-colored plants such as the yellow sunflower, butterweed, tetraneuris, and sundrop; the pinkish-purple dotted gayfeather; the deep red cups of low poppymallow; and the red-orange of Indian blanket. Where the grasses' hold was temporarily broken, buffalo bur, sneezeweed, bee balm, or woolly plantain seized the ground. Some of these plants were annuals, others perennials. But long before man came to give them names, long before man even existed, these plants yearly shared their variegated beauty with the sky.

Complexity, adaptation, and loveliness were all parts of organic nature's way of meeting the challenge of the plains. One effect of the grasses and other plants was to keep the dirt in one place; another was to transform the sun's energy into foodstuffs on which other organisms could subsist. As the grasses evolved, so did animals equipped to eat them, the most important of those animals being the hoofed herbivores. Horses and camels began their existence 45 million years ago in the North American grassland, migrating later across the Bering land-bridge to Asia. Bison followed the same route in reverse during the Ice Age and discovered a domain in which they could thrive. Ernest Thompson Seton made the most elaborate calculation of how many buffalo eventually roamed over the continent. On the shortgrass plains, he figured, it takes 30 acres of vegetation to support one large grazing animal; allow one-third off for other creatures, and the bison could have numbered 20 million on the plains. Add another 45 million living in the prairies, woods, and

Native sandhill vegetation, including bluestem bunch grass and yucca. (*Author*)

mountains, and one reaches a maximum potential of 65 million head. There also were 20 million pronghorn antelopes here, Seton believed, concentrated on the plains margin, where the sagebrush grows: a wildlife species unique to America.[10] Both the buffalo and the antelope had sharp, broad incisors, beautifully equipping them for eating grasses and shrubs and for keeping out invading weeds. They could run, too, and herded together for protection. Even their stomachs were especially adapted, with four separate compartments that enabled them, like other ruminants, to digest the plains diet efficiently. They were preeminently creatures of the grassland.

In the plains ecosystem there were many other animals that depended directly on the plant life. The blacktailed jackrabbit, able to bound away from danger in 20-foot leaps, was a constant nibbler on the broadleaved herbs. So were the hundreds of grasshopper and locust species, some of which lived mainly on grasses, others on flowering plants; a two-acre population of them could eat as much as a buffalo could. Mice, pocket gophers, kangaroo rats, and prairie dogs were also primary consumers, sometimes with major impact: one unusually large prairie-dog

"town" in Texas covered 25,000 square miles and housed 400 million of the rodents.[11] These plant eaters, in turn, were eaten by the predators of the grassland
food chain. There were insectivorous moles, rattlesnakes, burrowing badgers, black-
footed ferrets and skunks, soaring hawks and eagles, coyotes and wolves yapping
and howling in the moonlight. And there were birds everywhere, making their
nests in the grasses or prairie swales. The lesser prairie chicken could be heard
booming in the sandhills, the horned lark jingling from its perch on a swaying
rosinweed; the great white crane whooping its way toward the northern wetlands.
As long as the grasses flourished, the plain was no silent, empty wasteland. It could
still be a hard, demanding world, but in most years for these creatures it provided
abundantly all the conditions that make for success in nature's economy.

The first men to come into this shortgrass ecological community had neither the
means nor the intention to change it significantly. They followed the same path
taken by the bison across the Bering-Chukchi Platform around 40,000 years ago,
and with their rude stone weapons perhaps helped a few of the more endangered
Pleistocene species—ground sloths, mastodons—along the way to extinction. Subsequently, ancient man devoted himself for the most part to collecting berries, seeds,
and roots, and to hunting small game. But he continued to go out for bigger animals, too. In 1926, at Folsom, New Mexico, just a short drive from the Oklahoma
dinosaur quarry, Denver naturalist J. D. Figgins found beautifully fluted flint points
buried along with the bones of a now extinct giant bison; the points belonged, he
decided, to a paleolithic wanderer who lived 10,000 or 12,000 years ago.[12] All
along the Rocky Mountain piedmont Folsom man camped and hunted; it is clear,
however, that his environmental impact was far less than that of the bison or the
prairie dog. The same could be said for every other group of humans who came to
the sea of grass before the nineteenth century.

As the dust storms blanketed houses and crops in the 1930s, scholars began
to look more intensely at the experience of prehistoric man on the plains, and
especially at his agricultural settlements. For several thousand years after Folsom
man there was hardly any evidence of human activity of any kind, aside from a few
sites where bison had been stampeded over cliffs. It is possible that hunters continued
to roam here, leaving, as usual, no traces of their lives; if so, they were far out on
the cultural margins of North American Indian development. But sometime before
A.D. 500 a new group appeared on the plains: the Signal Butte people, who settled
on a windswept plateau near the present Wyoming-Nebraska line. They were
hunters, living in skin tents, with no pottery or bow and arrow, a spear serving as
their only weapon. The Signal Butte site, excavated in 1932 by W. D. Strong,
showed three distinct occupation periods, separated by layers of wind-deposited dirt

up to two feet thick. Evidently man had been repeatedly driven away from Signal Butte by drought and local dust-blowing. Later a handful of more economically advanced settlements were made along several rivers by agricultural Indians migrating from the east; these sites showed a similar pattern of defeat and abandonment, although in none of these were the dust deposits as important as they had been at Signal Butte. Most prominent of these late prehistoric villages, which appeared between 500 and 1600, were those on the Upper Republican River in Nebraska and on Antelope Creek in the Texas panhandle; both were occupied by sedentary peoples who built stone and wood structures, scratched the alluvial plain with their bone hoes, raised corn and beans, and even dug small irrigation ditches. These early farmers, wrote Waldo Wedel of the Smithsonian, apparently "ventured far out into the Great Plains during favorable times only to withdraw when droughts set in."[13]

In the thirties a number of archaeologists also began to take up the analysis of tree rings, hoping that these might furnish a calendar of droughts for at least the last few centuries. Such a calendar could tell how often those droughts had come, and how long they had lasted. The tree-ring technique was the invention of Andrew Douglass, director of the University of Arizona's Steward Observatory. Back in 1901 he began measuring the thickness of rings on stumps as a clue to rainfall cycles. With the added help of old pueblo beams he discovered that there had been a major drought in the Southwest from 1276 to 1299, forcing the Anasazis to abandon their Mesa Verde cliff dwellings.[14] Could the Great Plains have been affected by this disaster too? It was impossible to say; there were few trees to analyze here, especially trees of any real antiquity. But one student, Harry Weakly, did manage to find enough plains trees to construct a drought calendar for Nebraska: the narrowest rings (indicating, of course, low precipitation) were those of 1439-54, 1459-68, 1539-64, and 1587-1605, all well after Douglass's great Southwestern drought. Undoubtedly, dry spells of such duration—one of them lasting 26 years— must have killed not only crops but sometimes the grasses too, so that dirt was laid bare and began to blow, though nowhere so seriously as in modern times.[15] The conclusion of these researchers was that agricultural man had long faced severe tests on the Great Plains, and that there were a few exodusters even before the Europeans came. Wherever farming had been tried, in fact, it eventually had failed. A settled village life, depending on its own introduced crops, could not survive the ancient cycle of aridity.

In the light of this record of human failure, it was ironic that European man's first venture into the Dust Bowl was a quest for Gran Quivira, a great city supposedly built on the plains and paved with gold. Just fifty years after Columbus arrived in the New World the Spanish conquistador Francisco Vásquez de Coronado made that futile search, crossing in 1540-42 from Santa Fe into the panhandle area and northwest to present-day Great Bend, Kansas, where at least he located about twenty-five wretched villages of the Wichita Indians. On his way home to the Rio Grande Valley, he and his troops encountered the nomadic "Querecho" (Apaches), who "lived like Arabs" in tents, hunting the "hump-backed cows."[16] And that was all he had to report: no wealth, no cities, a tiny handful of humans lost in the immensity of grass. To make the impression even worse, Coronado arrived during one of Harry Weakly's worst droughts. Thus, 400 years before the dirty thirties, civilization came to the southern plains and left in disappointment along essentially the same route the Okies took west.

The Indians Coronado visited were among the most backward on the continent. But two centuries after his expedition, and a full century after the founding of Jamestown, the grasslands were the scene of an incredible explosion: the birth of the Plains Indian culture, which eventually came to symbolize for the entire world the aboriginal man of North America. It was the last Indian culture to evolve, and in many ways it was the most impressive. Around 1700 the Comanches appeared on the southernmost plains, emigrating, for some unknown reason, from their former home in Wyoming. Stealing horses from the Apaches, who in turn had obtained them from the Spanish in the 1630s, the Comanches took over the buffalo-hunting grounds. Then came the Kiowas out of the Yellowstone area, driven by the northern Sioux into the Dust Bowl heartland; they too became skilled horsemen, and from their panhandle base they raided all the way to Arizona. Cheyennes and Arapahoes emigrated from the upper Mississippi River to complete the circle of southern plains Indian tribes. In none of these cases had the way been easy, and the Indians were consequently not pacific peoples; to them warrior heroism and implacable hostility toward their enemies became cardinal virtues.[17]

Because it was so vivid, straightforward, and heartfelt in its violence, this Plains culture became the most familiar of all primitive cultures in the world. The major material elements were taken over from the Apaches, who had inherited many of them from the paleo-hunters of the plains. Hunting the buffalo, for example, was once again made the basis of human economics; agriculture had never been dependable enough. The horse, however, gave unprecedented locomotion to the hunt; its revolutionary influence has undoubtedly been exaggerated, but it became an essential part of the emerging way of life. As anthropologist Mildred Mayhill points out, "The real area of the plains was not habitable and serviceable in its length and breadth until the use of the horse opened it up and characterized it, and became its *modus vivendi*."[18] By 1775 this culture was in full maturity, with tepees spotted over the landscape, horses tethered and hobbled, haunches of buffalo meat roasting on sticks, and a rich, imaginative mythos sung around the campfires. For the first time in its history the grassland began to experience the presence of man.

But for all their creative, exuberant force, these Indians did not drastically alter the ecological order. Wild claims have been made about their burning the entire Great Plains vegetative cover to provide better forage for game (which supposedly was what kept the grassland free of trees) or about their depleting the bison, or about their overbreeding to the point of Malthusian disaster.[19] The truth, however, is that the Plains Indians completely merged into the natural economy; they simply became another predator—successful, highly intelligent, making themselves felt as other creatures did, but accepting in every way the primacy of the grass. They did so not because they were especially noble or righteous, although they had those qualities too, at times. More important to their adaptiveness was their assumption of complete dependence: their unwillingness to consider that any other relationship with the grassland might be possible. From the beginning of their occupancy there was a limit on these Plains people's potential due to their full acceptance of the natural order, but at the same time that acceptance enforced a pattern of ecological restraint in their behavior. They carefully kept their numbers down to what the ecological community could support.[20] They wasted little of the resources they could tap. They thrived, if not in great affluence, at least with enough security to develop a unique and in many ways an appealing and satisfying culture.

A modern Kiowan, N. Scott Momaday, argues that, wherever they lived, his people followed a conservation ethic, practical in its effects, perhaps, but spiritual in its origins. They realized that they were part and parcel of nature and yet that there was something in the land beyond man's understanding—something to be revered. "Inasmuch as I am in the land, it is appropriate that I should affirm myself in the spirit of my land," writes Momaday; "I shall celebrate my life in the world and the world in my life."[21] For the Plains Indian, use was definitely implied in man's relation with the ecological community, but reverence, it was always insisted, was where use must begin. There is nothing unusual in this ethical-religious stance. It seems to be the way of thinking everywhere among peoples who have lived for a very long time in intimacy with the land, who have never thought about devising elaborate technologies, who have scaled their wants to a limited world, and, above all, who have a lively sense of their dependence upon nature. The Kiowans undoubtedly brought such thinking with them to the southern plains, as did the other tribes, and it served them well in their new homeland.

By 1876, Walter Prescott Webb tells us, the Plains Indians were a broken, defeated people, pushed onto reservations.[22] The buffalo, 20 million of them, were virtually all gone. It was not drought that had ended this last and most successful aboriginal occupation; it was the United States Army. By the mid-nineteenth century the white man had come to the plains, clanking along with military hardware and seeking new forms of gold. But this time settlers came too: people wanting

Cimarron River meandering through southwestern Kansas. The Santa Fe Trail ran along the near side of the river. This area is now part of the Cimarron National Grassland. (*Author*)

farms, wanting railroads, wanting fences and deeds. Against this land hunger the plains had little defense. In the war over possession between whites and Indians, the bison became innocent victims; they were viewed as "the Indian's commissary" and therefore required extermination.[23] As they disappeared, so did the predators they supported, including the red man. In a very few years the plains went through more profound changes than it had known in 40 millennia, and more sudden ones than it had ever passed through before, even during the geological revolutions of the past. Changes now were to be measured in decades, not epochs.

For another ten years after 1876, the grass still rippled under the wind. All the recent tumults had disturbed it no more than a ship's passing changes the ocean. Where the bison had wallowed and laid bare the soil, or where the Indians had trodden out the grass with their moccasins, the land was soon revegetated. The white men and women who came now into the grassland sometimes marveled at its beauty, and a few understood its ecological value. Among those few was a Texas sheepherder, who observed, "Grass is what counts. It's what saves us all—far as we get saved. . . . Grass is what holds the earth together."[24] Not many newcomers shared that appreciation, however; the grass was destined to disappear too—to be turned under by the plow, not in isolated patches here and there, but across millions and millions of acres. When the plowing was done, the land would fall apart, and the outcome would be the most desolate event that humans had ever experienced on the plains.

Sodbusting

MUCH OF WHAT WAS TO BECOME the Dust Bowl first came into American hands with the Louisiana Purchase of 1803. President Thomas Jefferson, who promoted that real-estate deal, wanted the land as an insurance plan for his democracy of small farmers. As the population mounted, he argued, opportunity to own rural property would diminish unless more land could be acquired and reserved for settlement. No single idea has been more deeply embedded in the American mind than this notion of a democratic society that must always have more of something to be secure and at peace with itself. Justice and equality, Jefferson's theory suggested, require continual economic expansion, which to his mind meant simply more farmland for the nation. The Plains Indian, though he lived in a far more egalitarian culture than Jefferson's, would not have understood that thinking. First control your numbers, he would have said; then simplify your wants and see the earth as everybody's mother rather than as a piece of property to be divided by competing individuals. But the white man did not view land and society in that way. He based his democratic ideals at first on geographical expansion: as long as there is more of nature somewhere else, there is no need to share here—every person may build his own Monticello over yonder hill. Later that view would take on extravagant proportions.

Those Americans who did not take up the expansionary attitude were frequently accused of being elitists. In some cases the charge was accurate; in others it was most erroneous, for there were in fact other ways to get to democracy besides physical growth. One of Jefferson's own army officers, Lieutenant Zebulon Pike, was an anti-expansionist, and apparently no elitist—not a man, that is, of high social or economic rank who might be threatened by new sources of wealth. His 1806 report on the southern plains (he was the first American ever to visit the area) began a century-long dispute over that region and its value for the new nation. Pike followed the Arkansas River west up into the mountains. What he saw on that part of his explorations were for the most part the extensive riparian dunes that had blown out of the riverbed in dry seasons; if that was what all the plains were like, he concluded, then the nation had purchased a veritable desert. Yet Pike could still find a blessing in that sandy waste: "the restriction of our population to some certain limits, and thereby a continuation of the union."[1] Having a wide desert on the western side and an ocean on the eastern, the United States would be more politically cohesive and safe. It was an appealing prospect for others who came after Pike, too. "Great American Desert," they began to write on maps of the interior plains, and what they usually meant was that Americans had better stay put and tend their gardens rather than go adventuring westward. Of course, they exaggerated the aridity of the plains—not, however, the anarchic tendencies of their society.

Neither Pike nor other "desert" proponents had the slightest effect on the pace of plains settlement.[2] They were seen as enemies by all who identified freedom and democracy with national increase. Charles Dana Wilber, a town builder in Nebraska, felt compelled to answer them by an appeal to the Creator: it has never been God's intention, he announced, that any part of the earth be "perpetual desert." Wherever man "has been aggressive," he has made the land suitable for farming—"so that in reality there is no desert anywhere except by man's permission or neglect." If the plains were not all that Jefferson had hoped they would be, the farmer

Early cattle ranching in Kiowa County, Kansas. (*Kansas State Historical Society*)

could remedy their deficiencies. Rain would follow the plow, Wilber predicted; that was the way the Creator expected men to think. Turn the grasses under and the skies would fill with clouds. There were thus no restrictions in nature that man must observe; on the contrary, all ecological limits were simply challenges to be overcome by human energy. Neither was there any ceiling on the number of people who could come to the plains to be free, prosperous, and self-respecting. So went the expansionist argument against anyone who thought America was already large enough.[3]

Under the Homestead Act of 1862, any person who settled on 160 acres of shortgrass, stayed there for five years, made "improvements," and paid a filing fee became part of the landed gentry. But farmers were slow to go that far west, having rich black prairies to take up first, and when they did arrive they found the country in the hands of cattle barons. Even before the Indians and bison were out of the way, the cattlemen had come in, seeking to exploit the grass—without, in many cases, bearing the burden of ownership. Charles Goodnight was among the earliest ranchers in the Dust Bowl vicinity, trailing steers down from the Colorado gold camps in 1877 to the Palo Duro Canyon on the edge of the Texas High Plains. To the southeast of him the "beef bonanza," as it was called, was already organized; there were close to 5 million head in Texas alone, and more than 650,000 were driven north to Abilene, Kansas, and to other railheads that year. By 1880 the prospects were glittering as slaughterhouse prices soared from $3.00 to $60 per animal.

Two members of the British Parliament toured the plains and found annual profits of 33.3 per cent on investment, a fact they quickly reported to investors back home. English, Irish, and Scottish capital subsequently poured into the plains, along with money from Eastern lawyers and bankers. Among the largest of the enterprises formed was the XIT ranch in the panhandle (the brand stood for "ten counties in Texas"), which sprawled over 3 million acres and ran 150,000 head. The cattle kingdom, the first major use to which Americans put the plains, was in its glory.[4]

The world of cowboys, roundups, and cattle drives has been recalled many times, but not the ecological story. Whether they held title or not, the cattlemen pushed the land as far as it would go, and then pushed some more. They generally viewed the southern plains as another Comstock Lode, to be mined as thoroughly as possible by overstocking the range. In some areas they ran four times as many cattle as the grass could carry, resulting in depletion and long-lasting damage. By 1880 a steer on one range needed 50 acres to fatten up, where a decade earlier 5 acres had been sufficient. The winter of 1885-86 proved to be the harshest in the recorded history of the region, and with severely diminished buffalo grass for forage, it was a fatal blow. Eighty-five per cent of the cattle perished on some ranches, and their carcasses lay black and stinking across the spring landscape.[5] The longhorns had never really counted for very much in their own right; they were merely the impersonal, massed mechanism for turning grass into money. Now, in the face of this collapse, the beef entrepreneurs retreated right and left, their "industry" bankrupted by weather and, more, by overexpansion. Altogether, their hegemony had lasted a scant two decades before it self-destructed. Had anyone cared to notice then, it was a foretaste of later developments on the plains. But for most Americans at the time, the more important issue was that the cattle kings had monopolized a resource that others now wanted.

Into the post-1886 vacuum poured the waiting farmers, armed with iron plows to "break the land" and establish a more democratic tenure. Unlike the cattlemen, they came without much capital—as little as a team of oxen and a dollar gold piece. One family arrived in western Kansas with "nine children and eleven cents."[6] Out of the sod itself they made their houses, with walls two feet thick, dirt roofs that leaked muddy water, and straw-filled mattresses that swarmed with bedbugs and fleas. Their diet was cornmeal and molasses, baking-soda biscuits, coffee made from roasted rye. It was as hard a life as any that Americans have made for themselves, yet they liked it well enough. "The choice," writes Edward Higbee, "was between the dry plains or no land at all worth having." By 1890 there were 6

Sod house, location unknown. The menfolk may be off farming or looking for work. (*Western History Collection, University of Oklahoma Library*)

million people on the Great Plains; Colorado had 413,000, and Texas and Kansas over a million each. Like California a half-century earlier, the Dust Bowl was boom country, doubling its numbers in less than a decade, and in some panhandle counties the increase was 600 per cent. In the majority of cases they came wanting not a place to stay forever, but simply cash—a stake to take with them someplace else. "Few of them thought of the farm in terms of a permanent home," notes historian James Malin, ". . . but rather as a speculation which would be improved and developed with a hope of a sale sooner or later at a profit." Consequently, the mobility of the soddy entrepreneur was phenomenally high.[7]

The sod-house era did not even last as long as the cattle bonanza had. Beginning in 1889, drought scorched the plains for most of the next six years; at times it was as severe as in the 1930s. Luckily, there was little dust blowing, for most of the grassland still remained in sod. But in some cases the economic hardships were worse than those in the Dust Bowl years. In Kit Carson County, Colorado, a farm family had to get along for six weeks on nothing but squash; there was no money to buy fuel or shoes, either, so they wrapped themselves in rags. Some relief came from the Colorado Springs Board of Trade, but it was not enough to stop a massive exodus. By 1900 the population of Kit Carson had dropped 36 per cent from what it had been a decade earlier. In other counties of the region the decline was as much as 60 and even 90 per cent. God supposedly had assigned the plains to the farmer, urging him to plow and bring rain; now it was clear, as some declared, that "there is no god west of Salina."[8] The cattlemen, chastened by their

An old couple standing by their sod house, which is built into a bank. Decatur County, Kansas, 1890. (*Western History Collection, University of Oklahoma Library*)

failure, began to reacquire the land, buying up relinquishments from one failed farmer after another. And "the little sod shanty on the claim" crumbled back into the soil.

There was one man in Washington who found vindication in these unhappy events—John Wesley Powell. Now director of the U.S. Geological Survey, Powell had recommended in his *Report on the Lands of the Arid Region of the United States* (1878) a very different blueprint for plains settlement than had been followed. Beyond the 100th meridian, he believed, there was not enough rainfall for traditional farming; a 160-acre homestead there would not produce enough to maintain an American family. Powell's own proposal was to cut up the plains into much larger "pasturage farms," each covering four square miles, or 2560 acres, which would be sufficient to raise livestock profitably. The use of the word "farms" here was an obvious strategy to avoid the more aristocratic "ranches." But neither Congress nor most sodbusters were fooled; Powell's scheme would have made rural homes for only *one-sixteenth* as many families as the Homestead Act had. It was, they retorted, flagrantly restrictive, undemocratic, and too pessimistic about the carrying capacity of the region.[9] But then, in the 1890s, with thousands unable to make a living on their quarter sections, Powell began to look like a prophet at last. And in the 1930s, when the same sequence of disasters occurred, his book was dusted off again and read by one bureaucrat after another. The key to successful plains occupancy, many began to argue, lay in bigger units and more cattle ranching. Instead of trying to accommodate everyone, the goal ought to be to remove as many farmers as possible to some other—usually undefined—spot, or take them out of agriculture altogether, allowing those who stayed to establish viable economic units.

Powell's "pasturage farms" would not have prevented the dirty thirties, if the beef bonanza could be taken as a precedent. But at least the idea was founded on a more informed, more realistic view of the plains environment. It came, as Wallace Stegner writes, from a "willingness to look at what was, rather than at what fantasy, hope, or private interest said there should be."[10] Powell, moreover, was not an elitist; on the contrary, he was an unusually far-sighted social democrat in an age of grab, one who was willing to use the power of government to save as much of the region for the common people as possible. Admittedly, his land policy would have given far fewer citizens a chance to achieve their own farm, but for those few it might have made opportunity more secure and genuine. Like Thomas Jefferson, Powell was a geographical expansionist, seeking to redeem the West from its worthless state and make it over into a garden for the dispossessed. But he realized, as had Zebulon Pike, that the natural world places "certain limits" on what man can do. A more ecologically adaptive democracy was what he had in mind. The unasked question, however, is whether that was enough. Did Powell's land proposals, good as they were, go far enough toward adaptation? The answer is no.

"The environment demanded relatively large acreages," writes Gilbert Fite— just as Powell had said.[11] That is at best a half-truth, and like all half-truths what is missing is the more telling part. Nature did not "demand" 2560 acres per family. To Powell, as to everyone else, the size of individual holdings was controlled primarily by economics: he simply took the American standard of living for granted, and then wondered how much land was needed to support it in the West. In his "pasturage farm" ideal he also naïvely assumed that the standard would forever remain the same. Down on the XIT ranch that acreage was already laughably below their expectations of wealth. On the other hand, there were some farmers on the plains—the Amish, and some of the Mennonites, especially—for whom 160 acres was sufficient in 1878 and still was in 1935. With the coming of mechanization, those small-scale operations increasingly became "Old World" anomalies in progressive America, but they showed that it was possible to endure on the plains, and eat something besides hardtack, without constantly needing more land. However, for most plainsmen who survived the nineties, the unending escalation of wants brought a cutthroat competition for scarcer and scarcer resources that has lasted through the twentieth century. If there was one factor that would defeat broadly diffused, democratic tenure in the region, it was precisely the demand for ever higher living standards. The quarter-section farm eventually disappeared, the big farmers bought out the small ones, and the land moved toward oligarchy. Nothing in Powell's proposals would have stopped that process, for he had not begun to question the underlying economic values of the culture. From the beginning, Americans were on a hopeless ecological course: there would never be enough land to satisfy everyone's demands, especially if those demands were constantly growing.

John Wesley Powell, for all his common sense, did not come to grips with the expansionary drive of American culture, nor did he anticipate the tenacity of row-crop agriculture on the plains. In the wake of the 1890s débacle a new technique called "dry farming" began to appear. With changes in method, it was argued in dry-farming congresses and manuals, the land could be kept from reverting to useless grass and imperial cattlemen. The most famous spokesman for this movement was Hardy Campbell, who had worked out what he thought was a climate-free system of land use: deep plowing in the fall, packing the subsoil, frequently stirring up a dust mulch, and summer fallowing—leaving part of the ground unplanted each year to restore moisture.[12] Corn had been the chief crop on the plains before 1890; now farmers put their fields into more drought-resistant grains, especially Turkey Red, a hard winter wheat, and the sorghums. In 1909, to satisfy dry-farming agitation, Congress passed an Enlarged Homestead Act, which gave each settler 320 acres. Once again the plains became a feverish scene, as thousands rushed to get their share of the last agricultural frontier. It was in this latest surge of settlement, from 1910 to 1930, that a dust bowl was prepared.

The most important new wrinkle was the machine. Neither the cowboy nor the sod-house farmer knew much about technology; their methods were almost as old as agriculture itself—herding animals by horseback, walking behind a plow and team. But America had changed rapidly since these earlier waves of settlement; there were now long assembly lines turning out automobiles, trucks, and tractors. Henry Ford, who had been a farm boy in Michigan, represented those new economic developments, and it was his spirit, his machines, and his techniques that came to the southern plains in the early twentieth century. The grassland was to be torn up to make a vast wheat factory: a landscape tailored to the industrial age. Specialized, one-crop farming became the common practice, and business economics the standard of success or failure. Above all, the new-style sodbuster was an expansionist, feeling all the old land hunger of an opportunity-seeking democrat, but adding an intense desire to make his new machines profitable that would have shocked Thomas Jefferson's agrarian idealism.

Cutting prairie hay on the High Plains. (*Kansas State Historical Society*)

Under the new homestead policy, land entries skyrocketed nationally, especially after 1912, when Congress reduced the proving-up time from five to three years. In 1912, there were 24,000 entries in the West; in the next year, 53,000—and they remained at over 30,000 annually until the early twenties. Less than one-fifth of the filings in Colorado during this period resulted in permanent farms, again the movement out being almost as heavy as the migration in. In addition to the public domain, there was much private land put on the market at cheap prices. Finding that they could not make a profit on cattle, the owners of the XIT ranch, with their 3-million-acre land grant from the Texas legislature, went into the real-estate business. They sold farms for less than $13 an acre, at a time when land was being sold for $150 an acre in the midwest. Iowa and Illinois farmers needed no better inducement; they packed into railroad cars by the thousands for promotion tours of the Texas panhandle and plunked down cash for as much land as they could afford, commonly getting more than they could at the moment farm efficiently. A study of 22 High Plains counties in Kansas, Colorado, and Texas suggests the magnitude of population ebb and flow and the emerging scale of modern agriculture. In 1890 there were 5762 farms in those counties, and the average size of a unit, including a few ranches, was 256 acres. By 1900, with the swing back to cattle, there were only 4087 farms, and the average holding was up to 1730 acres. The year 1910 found 11,422 farms, averaging 520 acres each, as crops once more replaced pastures. The enlarging size of these wheat-belt farms was clear evidence that, despite what the public land laws indicated as best, Americans on the frontier always wanted—and got—more. In 1920 the average unit in these counties was 771 acres, and in 1930, 813.[13]

These were halcyon days for all the nation's farmers, setting a standard of prosperity against which subsequent experience would always be measured. A growing urban population at home and bigger markets abroad meant high prices, substantial profits, and more money to expand. Wheat fetched from $1.04 a bushel in 1909 to 93 cents in 1914 on the southern plains; these were the so-called "parity years," when agriculturists stood on a roughly equal footing in purchasing power with manufacturers. But it was World War I that put the American farmer into a happy dither. As the Turks cut off wheat shipments from Russia, the largest producer and exporter in the world, Europeans turned to the Great Plains. The effect of this new and heavy demand was that in 1919 the price of American wheat reached 2.5 times its 1914 level. From Washington, as the Wilson administration led the United States into the war, there began to come a patriotic appeal to augment that of high prices: "Plant more wheat! Wheat will win the war!" These pressures, according to a later government official, lifted agricultural development "from its rational course of progress and forced it to an unnatural exertion in response to an abnormal demand."[14] Never mind for the moment what was meant here by "rational," "normal," or "natural." The fact is that the bloody conflict in Europe had a profound impact on the southern plains of America—not by sending it in a radically different direction, but by hastening trends already under way.

Under the wartime Food Control Act of 1917, the government guaranteed wheat prices of over $2.00 a bushel. Americans that year harvested 45 million acres of wheat, down (due to droughty weather) from 60 million in 1915, and providing only 133 million bushels for export. When the war ended Europe still needed food imports, and by 1919 the nation, under government-set goals, harvested 74 million acres—yielding 952 million bushels in all, a 38 per cent increase over the 1909-13 period, and providing 330 million bushels for shipment abroad. Most of this gain came in winter wheat, which was the standard variety grown on the southern plains: planted in the fall, cut in the following mid-summer. Kansas, Colorado, Nebraska, Oklahoma, and Texas had expanded their wheatlands by 13.5 million acres by 1919, mainly by plowing up 11 million acres of native grass. In Finney County, Kansas, there were 76,000 acres of field crops in 1914; there were 122,000 in 1919.[15] By that time the Western wheat farmer was no longer interested in merely raising food for himself and his family. More than any other part of the nation's agriculture, he was a cog in an international wheel. As long as it kept turning, he would roll along with it. But if it suddenly stopped, he would be crushed.

One of the most important facts of the period was that more acres in wheat did not mean more work in man-hours. In the 20 years after 1910 the labor needed

Busting sod with a Reeves steam tractor and plow. (*Kansas State Historical Society*)

to plant and harvest the nation's wheat fell by one-third, while the acreage jumped by almost the same amount. The reason for this disparity lay, of course, in mechanization: an industrial revolution, supplanting men and animals with fossil-fuel power, had come to American agriculture. Back in 1830 it had taken 58 hours of work to bring an acre of wheat to the granaries. A hundred years later it required 18 hours in Lancaster, Pennsylvania, one of the nation's first breadbaskets, 6 hours nationally, and less than 3 hours in the most advanced sections of the Great Plains. The wide flatlands of the Dust Bowl were especially suitable for mechanized farming. With surplus money in their pockets from the war, the region's wheat farmers rushed to county fairs to examine tractors, plows, and threshers. Some were observed dropping to one knee in the dirt to write their checks. As a businessman told Henry Ford, "You never saw the farmer so ripe for anything and plucking should not long be delayed."[16]

Ford, however, did delay and so lost his chance to duplicate his success with the Model T; the tractor was already transforming the farm when he began to tool up his River Rouge plant. As early as 1900 the southern plains witnessed the arrival of the monstrous Reeves machine—a miniature locomotive weighing several tons, chugging forward under steam power with a watertank and plow behind, severely compacting the earth but able to rip up more sod than dozens of yoked oxen could. The steam tractor, which had actually been around for fifty years before that date, was late in reaching the plains; not so its lighter, gasoline-powered replacement. By 1917 there were 200 companies manufacturing these new, small tractors, some of which had only 20-horsepower, 4-cylinder engines. Ford began producing his own Fordson version in that year, and when he gave up to his competitors a decade later, he had sold 650,000 of them. Out in the panhandle the most popular

Wheat king Simon Fishman (in coat and tie) and his employees breaking new land with disk plows. Greeley County, Kansas, 1925. (*Kansas State Historical Society*)

lines, selling as fast as they could be shipped out, were the McCormick-Deering 15-30 (made by International Harvester), the Farmall, the Case, and the bright green John Deere. Seated on one of these rumbling machines, small or large, the wheat farmer was a very different man from the old-style sodbuster. The tractor, argued one writer, changed him from "a clod into an operator; from a dumb brute into a mechanic."[17] Now he had a marvelous machine that could be used to break the land and hold it firmly under his control.

Another new mechanical innovation was the one-way disk plow, which resembled a series of concave plates set vertically on a beam. In the nineteenth century, Western farmers had used a moldboard plow to kill the grass. It dug deep, sliced through the roots, and laid the sod over practically unbroken. The new disk contraption did not go as far down into the earth; it moved along faster, chopped the ground up more roughly to increase water absorption, killed weeds efficiently, and, when used often enough, left a finely pulverized surface layer.[18] Under the dry-farming program, farmers were told to haul their disk plows out after every shower and stir up the dust for moisture conservation. But in droughty years they disked their fields so much that some observers blamed the dust storms of the 1930s on the misuse of this single implement.

There was one more apparatus that completed the industrialization of the grassland: the combined harvester-thresher, or, as it was called more simply, the combine. By the end of the twenties more than three-fourths of the farmers in the winter wheat section owned such a machine. Instead of hiring ten or twenty bindlestiffs—seasonal harvest laborers coming in on the railroad—who drank heavily, frightened the children, required the wife to feed them, and sometimes demanded higher wages, the farmer bought a combine that he and one or two others could manage. Pulled by a tractor, the combine could cut a 16-foot swath through the wheat, and in two weeks could harvest 500 acres.[19] The grain, threshed as it was cut, poured like a golden stream into the bed of a truck driven alongside; then off it went to the elevators and flour mills of the world.

Machines made money, but they cost money, too—far more than small farmers could afford. From 1910 to 1920 implements on the typical Kansas farm increased in value from $292 to $980, most of the jump due to tractor purchases. That was nothing compared with the thousands of dollars the typical farmer spent thereafter; buying a combine in the next decade, for instance, could add $3000 to one's investment. During the twenties the value of farm machinery in the Texas panhandle almost tripled, totaling $27 million. With a tractor, a Ford truck, a combine, and enough gasoline to run them all, the production costs there had jumped to about $4.00 an acre; if a farmer could raise 10 bushels of wheat per acre and sell them at 40 cents each, he could break even. Since the average price over the 1921-29 period was $1.03 a bushel on the southern plains, and the average wheat yields ranged from 8 to 18 bushels, it was, in most years, a paying proposition. But, as in every instance where new technology has entered, there were hidden, unanticipated effects, not least of them being, especially in the early twenties, a severe economic squeeze for many marginal farmers. The war left them with huge machinery debts to pay. For a while overseas markets remained good, prices stayed above $2.00, and there was no worry. But as the Europeans restored their own agriculture to full productivity, as old trade relations were reestablished, the Great Plains farmer lost some of his world outlet and found himself in a tighter and tighter bind. In every county there were those who could not survive the crunch and went under. On the other hand, as the survivors saw it, their salvation depended on more, not fewer, machines, so that they could achieve greater economies of scale.[20]

There were a few enterprising wheat farmers who welcomed the postwar competitive race to see who could mechanize fastest and shave their production costs to the lowest minimum. By the mid-twenties, as boom times returned, they raked in substantial fortunes. Ida Watkins, the "wheat queen" of Haskell County, Kansas, farmed 2000 acres, and in 1926 she made a profit of $75,000, which was more than President Coolidge's salary. Northwest of her, in Greeley County, was Simon Fishman, a Russian-Jewish immigrant who came to the frontier as a peddler and stayed to become one of the biggest wheat entrepreneurs in the state. Down in the Oklahoma panhandle there was J. H. Gruver, farming 4000 acres in 1928. And to Plainview, Texas, came the Hollywood mogul Hickman Price in 1929 to show the plainsmen what modern farming was really like. He preached the Henry Ford creed to anyone who would listen: "Only through large-scale, collective, group, special-

Wheat threshing as it was done before the coming of the combine. (*Kansas State Historical Society*)

ized, departmentalized activity has modern prosperity, with the accompanying high standards of living, become possible." His factory farm stretched over 54 square miles—34,500 acres—and required 25 combines at harvest time.[21] In every part of the plains there were pacesetters like these men and women who fervently believed that the methods of industrial capitalism were what the land needed. They were the largest and most successful; the less aggressive were forced to follow their lead.

The mobility of the new machines allowed not only large-scale enterprises, but also widely dispersed holdings. It was now possible to drive one's equipment to another county or even to another state, plant wheat, return home in a few weeks, and wait until the next spring before visiting the land again—it was possible, in other words, to become a "suitcase farmer." This was particularly attractive for wheat speculators, many of whom were city bankers, druggists, or teachers; they put in their seed, went back to their regular work, and waited to see what would happen to the Chicago grain futures. In a year of high prices they might make a killing, paying for an entire farm with one crop, then selling the land at a tidy sum to another fast-buck chaser. Not all suitcase farmers were looking for such quick returns; many of them were responsible men and women, concerned about their investment's long-range security, and technically proficient.[22] But the machine made possible, and common, an exploitative relationship with the earth: a bond that was strictly commercial, so that the land became nothing more than a form of capital that must be made to pay as much as possible.

All across the flat open spaces the tractors steadily plowed away, especially in the second half of the 1920s and on up until the very eve of the dust storms.

Occasionally they even worked at night, their headlights moving like fireflies in the grass. Near Perryton, Texas, H. B. Urban, an altogether typical wheat farmer of the day, arrived in 1929 and cranked up his two Internationals; each day he and his hired man broke out 20 acres, until virtually his whole section of land was stripped of its grama and buffalo grass. In thirteen southwestern Kansas counties, where there had been 2 million crop acres in 1925, there were 3 million in 1930. During the same period farmers tore up the native vegetation on 5,260,000 acres in the southern plains—an area nearly seven times as large as the state of Rhode Island. Most of the freshly plowed ground went into wheat, so that over the twenties decade the production of that cereal jumped 300 per cent, creating a severe glut by 1931. That was how men prepared for the days to come. When the black blizzards began to roll across the plains in 1935, one-third of the Dust Bowl region—33 million acres—lay naked, ungrassed, and vulnerable to the winds.[23] The new-style sodbusters now had their turn at facing disaster.

Throughout man's history he has now and then upset the ecological order, sometimes because he has had to do so in order to make a new home for himself, sometimes because he has been ignorant. Among all the earth's landscapes he has especially abused the grasslands, due to their climatic ambiguity and their fragility. It would be easy then, to dismiss the American experience on the plains as merely another case of human misjudgment, greed, innate aggression, or stupidity. Man has repeatedly fouled his own nest, some maintain; he is forever capable of considerable violence toward nature, he is everywhere materialistic, and he has never paid much attention to the environmental consequences of his deeds. The historian, though persuaded by such arguments to be realistic about human behavior, cannot be ready to let explanation rest there: it is, in the first place, too comprehensive— what explains all may explain nothing. It is also an excessively pessimistic way of thinking about man and the rest of nature, ignoring as it does the many examples of harmonious relations. The American plainsmen, it must be made clear, were as intelligent as the farmers of any part of the world. They were by no means the first to overrun the limits of their environment. But the reason they did so must be explained not by that vague entity "human nature," but rather by the peculiar culture that shaped their values and actions. It is the hand of culture that selects out innate human qualities and thereby gives variety to history. It was culture in the main that created the Dust Bowl.

The culture of modern, western man rests on the belief that he is autonomous in nature. He is confident that he is a sovereign creature, independent of the restraints that plague other species—not controlled as they are, but in control. That has not been the view of most people in world history, the American Indians being

Harvest time, late June 1924. The trucks and wagons are waiting to unload wheat, which the boxcars will carry to distant flour mills. (*Kansas State Historical Society*)

a proximate case. There has been no more important change in the human condition than the transition from a traditional sense of intimate dependence on the ecological community to the modern feeling of absolute free will and human autonomy. It is not too much to say that our entire industrial world was made possible by that change in outlook. We have no way of being absolutely precise about when and where the change took place, but we can be sure that as late as 200 or 300 years ago the dominant fact in man's life everywhere was his need to adapt to more powerful natural forces. Then, out of western culture, came a revolutionary impulse: a desire to throw off the restraining hand of nature and to assert in every way possible the contriving hand of humanity. If similar impulses occurred prior to that point, none of them was nearly so sweeping or so successful. The human species, it was now believed, stood liberated from a bondage to the earth that men of no previous era had been able to escape.

How can we account for this new, calculated indifference—a thoroughly rationalized and purposeful indifference—toward the natural order? We cannot begin with blanket condemnation, unless we are prepared to hold that absolutely no good came out of the shift in consciousness. But we can attempt to pinpoint the cultural roots of this search for autonomy. Since Americans were the foremost exponents of the new sense of environmental freedom, we are best advised to begin with our own culture. What produced in this nation so complete an alienation from the community—the interdependent life—of nature? What led the plains settlers to advocate and celebrate ecological aggression, as Charles Wilber did? Why did they take such pride in the name "sodbuster"? Why were they so peculiarly intent on "breaking the land"? What, in short, made them make a dust bowl?

One popular answer to some of these questions came in a 1936 film made for the Farm Security Administration by Pare Lorentz, "The Plow That Broke the Plains." Perhaps no other documentary work of the time had more impact, in its style, above all, but in its argument, too, on thinking about the Dust Bowl. Dorothea Lange, Archibald MacLeish, and John Steinbeck all picked up its images and cadences, and the film was shown in theaters across the nation, including those in the southern plains. It was Lorentz who first focused people's attention on technology as the instrument of destruction. Through newsreel-like camera footage and a rousing musical score by Virgil Thomson, he suggested that it was the machine—the unbridled, reckless force of modernity—that had made the dust storms. Great phalanxes of tractors were filmed, advancing on the land just as World War I tanks had moved across the smoke-shrouded battlefields. But given a new liberal government, Lorentz reassuringly concluded, the same machines could be turned to man's benefit; the conquest of the grassland would be more successful under the enlightened leadership of Franklin Roosevelt. When his cameramen, Paul Strand and Leo Hurwitz, refused to go along with this New Deal puffery, Lorentz stubbornly persisted: "They wanted it to be all about human greed," he said, "and how lousy our social system was. And I couldn't see what this had to do with dust storms."[24] It was the machine that got the blame, and yet, paradoxically, Lorentz argued that the New Dealers would make modern technology man's savior—so long as they could help drive the tractors. Despite its widespread influence, however, Lorentz's film did not begin to deal with the cultural sources of autonomy and aggression that lay behind the dust storms. As cinematic art, it was a triumph; as social analysis, it was wholly inadequate.

Explaining the plow that broke the plains requires one to explain the powerful expansionary and autonomous thrust of American society. The historian traces the origins of this extraordinarily determined push into the grassland to Jefferson's outward-moving democracy and to the shaping of American agriculture by an evolving capitalism. There was no sharp break between the two; both were expressions of the same self-minded, individualistic dynamism that ignored complex ecological realities. But the capitalist ethos was by far the more important, for it replaced man's attachments to the earth, which Jefferson still cherished, with an all-out dedication to cash, it replaced a rural economy aimed at sufficiency with one driving toward unlimited wealth. By the twentieth century American agriculture was moving rapidly into its industrialist phase, bringing Henry Fordism to the plains. Industrial capitalism, explained Thorstein Veblen, resulted from combining "the machine process and investment for a profit."[25] The productive powers unleashed by that amalgamation were stupendous, vastly unlike anything seen on the earth before. Whether it was shoes or automobiles, cattle or wheat, the new system of production turned out consumer goods in such quantities that it fairly took one's breath away. It led Americans and other societies out of scarcity into an age of enormous potential abundance—more, in fact, than they could consume at home without advertising campaigns and the creation of desires for goods. It was a well-organized and rationalistic system, supremely confident of its unending progress, unashamedly materialistic and utilitarian, critical of those who had failed in the race for spoils, and incredibly wasteful. The attitude of capitalism—industrial and pre-industrial—toward the earth was imperial and commercial; none of its ruling values taught environmental humility, reverence, or restraint. This was the cultural impetus that drove Americans into the grassland and determined the way they would use it.

The more humid parts of America—the pine forests of the Great Lakes and the coal-bearing mountains of Appalachia, for instance—already showed the traces of this economic culture, as Archibald MacLeish pointed out. But it was on the southern plains, where the grass had always struggled to hold the land against powerful winds and recurrent drought, that the self-seeking entrepreneur most clearly displayed his weaknesses. Here on the edges of the fertile earth man needed to summon all the cooperative, self-effacing, cautious elements in his nature to live successfully; Americans, however, because of their culture, found precisely those qualities hardest to nourish and express. It was easier for them to dismiss the grass as unproductive, unprofitable, and unnecessary, and to force the land to grow wheat instead. By the values they had been taught, they were justified in what they did; they were contributors, they assumed, to national growth and affluence. But as it turned out, the culture they had brought to the plains—the culture that had brought them there—was ecologically among the most unadaptive ever devised. That was the message written in darkened skies, shifting dunes of sand, and defeated faces.

Part III

CIMARRON COUNTY, OKLAHOMA

"Great bargains in real estate.
Bring your own container."

Sign in a Great Plains store window

Frontier

IN 1923, precisely thirty years after Frederick Jackson Turner delivered a retrospect on what the westward movement had meant to the national character, Oliver Baker of the Bureau of Agricultural Economics excitedly referred to the Great Plains as "the last frontier of agriculture."[1] There were many after Turner who thought they had come upon a further frontier. But by the traditional meaning of the term, Baker was right: the plains were a virgin land still to be exploited by farmers. After their plow-up there would be no new regions for agrarian conquest—no more great expanses of sod to bust. And after a final ten years of grab and boom, the plains would never again be the beckoning hope for thousands of new settlers. Future generations would have to change their notion of frontier if they were to keep the rhetoric and enthusiasm alive.

This fate of being the last agricultural frontier made the southern plains a peculiar place to be living in the 1930s. During that decade the nation suddenly had to face the fact that it was no longer a rural pioneering culture, always renewing its contact with fresh soil, a fresh wilderness. The new reality was grimly apparent: the city and the factory, which the Depression made more visible than ever, had become the characteristic American environments. Where did this shift in attention and identity leave the Dust Bowl? With bewildering speed it had been turned from a scene of grand, fevered adventure into an anachronism and a backwater, ravaged by the very forces of economic expansion it had symbolized. The plains had unexpectedly become a prime example of an older America that had failed. Caught in that sudden reversal of fortune and reputation, the people of the region passed through as profound a challenge to all their beliefs as they would ever face. How

Chapter Six

in Ruins

did they confront that challenge—how did they come to grips with their sudden slide downward from promise to defeat? What would henceforth be their perceived place in an urban America? Did federal aid and rehabilitation schemes significantly alter their purpose and direction? What was the prevailing mood of rural and village life in those dust-filled years? For answers to such questions we will select, as the Lynds did in Indiana, a community where we may gauge the full impact of those traumatic, dislocating experiences.

When the dust storms began to make headlines, two Farm Security Administration photographers—Arthur Rothstein and Dorothea Lange—converged on panhandle Oklahoma, particularly the westernmost county in that state, Cimarron. The photographers discovered that Cimarron was at the very center of the blow area; their pictures of its landscape, taken by the dozens and all of them emphasizing loss and incalculable ruin, became the quintessential regional image, especially the one by Rothstein showing a man and two boys scurrying through stinging dirt, heads down, to a shabby, forlorn outbuilding. Cimarron's widely respected county agent, William "Uncle Bill" Baker, confirmed the photographers' choice of locality. After extensive inspection, Baker had to admit that his county had been more severely and widely affected by wind erosion than any other on the southern plains.[2] If there was an archetypical Dust Bowl community—eroded, depopulated, broke, and on relief—it was Cimarron.

Stuck out on the very tip of the panhandle, Cimarron felt its remoteness acutely at times. It was the only county in the United States that bordered on four other states. One had to travel over 300 miles, most of them by graded dirt roads, to

Heading for an outbuilding in the face of a storm, 1936. (*Rothstein, Library of Congress*)

get to the state capital. All we get from Oklahoma City, some complained, are hunting licenses and auto tags; they don't even know how to pronounce our map names—Cimarron should end with "roan," and the county seat Boise City should rhyme with "voice." Some residents even wanted to secede and create with their neighboring counties a new, independent High Plains state. There was, in fact, a unique geography there, quite unlike the more congested remainder of Oklahoma. It was one of the largest counties in the state: a rectangle of 54 by 34 miles, almost 1.2 million acres in all, or 1832 full sections of land. In population, however, it was one of the state's smallest, counting only 5408 people in 1930, and only 3654 ten years later—a decline from three to slightly less than two inhabitants per square mile. Its principal town, Boise City, had 1256 residents in 1930 and 1144 in 1940.[3] Those were the dimensions of community on the southwestern flatlands: human bonds stretched like thin, spidery webs over a whelming void—a landscape ideally made for autonomy-seeking men and women, ideally suited to be ignored elsewhere.

Much of Cimarron is as level as a breadboard; as one goes west, the board tilts ever so slightly upward. But there are a few exceptions in this sameness. Two wide river channels wander across the terrain; the more important one, the Cimarron, carries water from the Rocky Mountain foothills year round, while the Beaver is an intermittent stream, in dry seasons exposing a sandy bottom out of which dunes and low hills are created along its banks, and a loose textured surface layer is spread more broadly from there. The exact line between these unstable lands and the "harder" soils is one that requires experience and restraint to discern. Over 40 per cent of the county's area consists of deep and medium-depth sandy brown soils with sandy subsoils for which wind erosion is always a serious hazard.[4] In the northwest quarter of the county the board-like surface begins to buckle and warp; stony breaks, caliche outcrops, knobs, mesas, and canyons erupt out of the monotone, anticipating the rugged piedmont farther west. The most impressive of these is Black Mesa, a tongue of lava that flowed from an ancient New Mexico volcano and now keeps the sandstone beneath it from eroding away; it stands almost a mile above sea level, 700 feet higher than the river at its base, with cedars and piñons growing along its top. Throughout this quarter of the county the soils are much too thin and rocky to plant to crops, discouraging even the most dogged plowman; consequently, cattle ranchers have held the breaks since they were first settled a hundred years ago.

In 1940 there were 84 agricultural units reporting at least 80 per cent of their income from livestock sold or traded: these were the major ranches in the county, mostly concentrated along the Beaver and Cimarron rivers and, in the northwest corner, around the town of Kenton. There were also 345 farms that depended just as heavily on raising field crops. (The remaining units were more diversified—usually smaller, near-subsistence operations.) Altogether there were

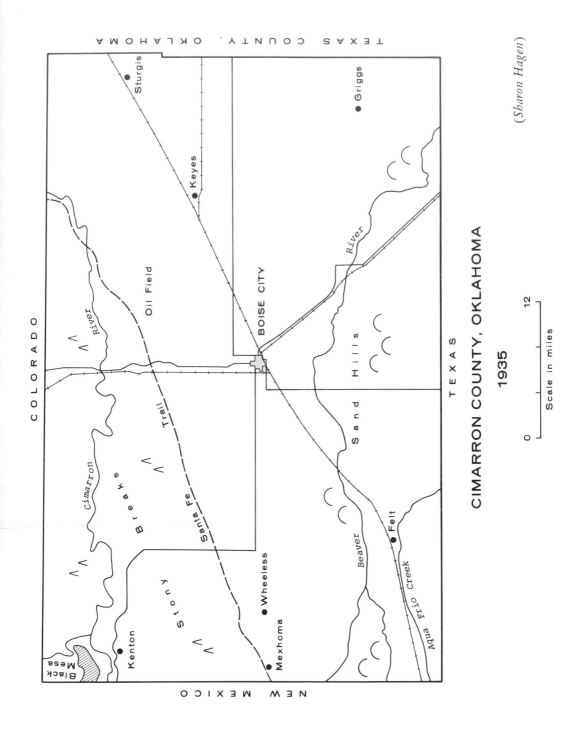

CIMARRON COUNTY, OKLAHOMA

1935

(*Sharon Hagen*)

605 farms and ranches in the county by the end of the decade, down by almost 40 per cent from a total of 975 in 1935, and from 887 in 1930. Most of the dirt farmers lived on the level plains, where the soils were the tight clayey loams that lay across the county like a dark-colored wedge, with its base the eastern boundary line and its apex jutting several miles west of Boise City. In the drought years those heavy soils blew badly at times, causing widespread farm abandonment. But the worst-struck area was the sand belt lying south of Boise City and southwest toward the small settlement of Felt.

When the rolling dusters appeared, Cimarron had been settled for little more than a half-century, its farming districts less than thirty years. The first people to come, after the Indians had been packed off to reservations, were Mexican sheepherders working for Don José Alvino Baca of New Mexico Territory; they set up their headquarters not far from present-day Mexhoma, where they could watch the last days of freighting on the Cimarron cutoff of the Santa Fe Trail. In the late 1870s cattlemen arrived, and they paid Baca $25,000 to take his sheep away. Along the Cimarron sprang up the 101 outfit, the OX, the ZH, and the Prairie Cattle Company. Cowboys found plenty of game to hunt in those days—wild turkey, mule deer, bears, mountain lions, along with a few desperadoes and cutthroats. Until 1890, when the panhandle was annexed to Oklahoma, this was "No Man's Land"; it had been somehow left out of all the surrounding political jurisdictions, and hence had no law but a .45-caliber Colt. When the nesters arrived looking for farmland, there was not even a land office where one could file on a homestead; it was make your own way by bluff and a quick trigger, or go someplace safer. Not until Oklahoma statehood in 1907, when the panhandle finally was divided into three counties and given more effective local governments, did farmers begin to settle here in substantial numbers, secure at last in their papers, if not in their hold on the land.[5]

That was the year when the French family came out from central Oklahoma to lay claim to their 160 acres of gambling ground. Bob French, who is today a well-to-do real-estate and oil broker, remembers that trip keenly; he was a small boy then, running alongside the two covered wagons that carried all their goods. For seventeen days they creaked westward, crossing a featureless unbroken plain, and at night they drew up close around the campfire and sang gospel songs—"the lonesomest people you ever saw." They were not really alone, however, in this last turning of wagon wheels, their ruts soon to be eclipsed by automobile roads; hundreds of other families also came to get the stake that had eluded them elsewhere. By 1910 the income from crops almost equaled that from livestock. In Boise City there was a new county seat, established by the usual frontier rogues and swindlers, and by 1920 the county had a population of more than 3400. Then, in the twenties, began the great scramble out of privation and hardship, remoteness and invisibility.

Santa Fe Railroad track in southern Cimarron County. (*Oklahoma Historical Society*)

The Santa Fe Railroad laid down tracks to Boise City in 1925 and on to Felt in 1927. Oil was struck in the same years, and the price of land skyrocketed. Bob French, newly designated land agent for an oil company, rode the boom to a personal wealth his parents had only dreamed of. Although the oil play fizzled out temporarily, Cimarron County, like the Frenches, had smelled a new kind of success—the smoky effluvia of the machine age—and was throwing the throttle wide open to get more of it.[6]

In a single year, 1926, one of the new Boise City farm implement dealers, Julius Cox, sold 65 tractors to Cimarron sodbusters.[7] With tractors and railroads at hand, the county became a wheat empire, at least for the next five years. There was, for the moment, enough rain to grow crops even on the loosest soils; from 1926 to 1930 Boise City averaged over 19 inches of precipitation annually, 2 inches above average and just enough to encourage agricultural expansion into the highest-risk, most marginal zones. By 1931 there were twice as many acres in wheat—305,000 in all—as there had been in 1925, the harvest reached almost 6 million bushels, and the average yield was a hefty 21.7 bushels per acre. But then the rain clouds failed to gather: in 1932 the total precipitation plummeted to 12 inches, and in 1934, to

Blown out, baked out, broke. (*Oklahoma Historical Society*)

less than nine. From 1931 to 1936 the yearly average was only 11.65 inches, and there were few fields that men bothered to combine. According to county agent Baker, annual wheat production per acre through the 1920s was 13.1 bushels; in the thirties, it was a miserable 0.9 bushels, not even enough in most seasons to provide seed for the next year's crop. Of 250,000 acres planted in fall 1936, "not a head of wheat matured in the entire county in 1937." By the spring of that latter year the winds had free play over the entire plowed-up area—one-third of the county. No wonder, then, that Cimarron became the focus of so many severe dusters. As one wag put it, "It's got so we get a half a day between the Spring Dust Storm and the Summer Dust Storm, and then we get a day and a half between the Summer Dusts and the Fall Dust."[8] Into a single generation this last frontier had telescoped all the environmental experience of the agricultural West: from a spirited home on the range where no discouraging words were heard, to a Santa Fe Chief carrying bounteous heaps of grain to Chicago, and, finally, to an empty shack where the dust had drifted as high as the eaves.

When the Cattle

EVEN IN BLOWN-OUT CIMARRON COUNTY, there was an area that survived the dust and drought years in reasonably good shape, thanks largely to a commitment to grass. This was the rangeland in the northwest corner: the dirt blew in here, too, but little blew out. Grama and buffalo grass died back to the roots in some places, but the soil held; it helped, of course, that there was less wind in the hilly country than out on the exposed plains. The thirties were, in some ways, placid times for ranchers here. Theirs was a world set a bit apart from many national and even regional troubles. In the tiny village of Kenton, where the old white frame general store with the single gas pump was the center of activity, a buckboard now and then rattled along, carrying a can of lard and a large sack of flour and another of sugar back to the ranch house. There were a few Dodges and Fords on the road, too, but this was still a horseman's country. Along the Cimarron and its tributaries, the North Carrizo and Texaquite, dark green cottonwoods leaned precariously over quiet pools of cool deep water, the sand banks as cleanly cut and smoothly vertical as a slab of cake. And at sunset, when the light grew soft and golden, the river valley was like an early Albert Bierstadt painting—a pastoral West, promising peace and contentment. When darkness fell, a million stars gleamed overhead and a knot of cowpunchers settled down in an isolated bunkhouse for a hand of blackjack.

But the ranchers of Cimarron County had their harsher ordeals to face, too, whether they lived in the breaks or on the rivers. One of the largest spreads in the area was the Kohler ranch, situated due north of Boise City on the Cimarron River and covering 13,000 acres. The ranch's founder, Julius Kohler, left Germany at age eighteen and came by train straight from New York to Meade, Kansas, where he

Chapter Seven

Ate Tumbleweeds

began working as a windmill repairman on the Anchor D ranch. In 1901 he struck out for himself, moving farther west and building, at the foot of Razor Blade Hill, a large adobe house that still serves as the Kohler headquarters. As near-by home-steaders gave up, he bought them out at a cheap price until he had the makings of a substantial cattle operation. All four of his sons grew up on and stayed with the ranch: they are still there today, managing it as a family enterprise. Robert is one of Julius's boys, now in his seventies but astonishingly robust—a large man, typically dressed in dirty boots and a Western shirt, his nose a dark-red maze of blood veins, his mouth continually at work on a chaw of tobacco, his manner unassuming and affable. He had only an eighth-grade education, but he has acquired something more important—the wisdom to be satisfied with a simple though demanding life. From his recollections—liberally punctuated with "You bet!" and a spit into his green plastic wastebasket—we may learn something of how plains ranch families struggled through the period.

In the spring of 1935 the Kohlers, unlike their neighbors, were temporarily running mostly sheep—5000 head of bleating ewes. With a federal land bank loan they had thrown a small dam across the river to divert irrigation water into an alfalfa field, but even so there was less and less feed for their animals. The dust storms that spring covered much of the grass, and thirty of their sheep suffocated in the corral. To save the flocks they drove them to Keyes, loaded them in boxcars, and shipped them to greener pastures in south-central Oklahoma, just as many cattlemen were doing, some taking their animals as far as Louisiana. It was a losing proposition, in any case; the markets for mutton and beef were far too low to justify the practice. The sheep therefore came home within a matter of months, and Julius had to sell most of them to the federal government for $2.00 a head, thereby earning enough to pay at least the interest on his loan, although nothing on the principal. Unlike the wheat farmer, the stockman could not store his product in a bin and wait for a better price; it was either sell off the sheep and cows for whatever you could get or keep feeding them somehow, someplace. Ranch families like the Kohlers, although they almost always hung onto their land and endured, did not have an easy choice between those two alternatives. As Robert Kohler recalls, they "didn't know where to better theirselves," so they stayed put.[1]

In those years the Kohlers ate plenty of pinto beans, which they raised down in the bottom land, and they had all the meat they wanted. In the winter they collected driftwood along the river to burn in their kitchen stove, as did people from all over the county. Now and again some hungry townsman would rustle one of their steers or lambs, and other free-enterprisers used their canyons or arroyos to set up illegal whiskey stills, some of which held 300 gallons. Those stills would pay the bills nicely until the sheriff ferreted them out. But no one on the ranch worried much about such infringements on their space. For entertainment the Kohler boys would join the hired men and ride their ponies over the state line to a dance in some Baca County farmhouse: if they made good speed they would be back home next morning in time for breakfast and a full day's work. The only labor-saving engine on the ranch was in Dad's old Ford; a team of Percherons did all the heavy hauling. But that was part of their salvation. With no machinery debts, with the land all long paid for, with a ready supply of food and fuel, with old-country thrift and management, and with less wind erosion to contend with, the Kohlers were in a better position to weather the decade, however grim some of their memories, than the average plainsmen.

Most of the other rural families in Cimarron County also kept some livestock, cattle generally, to sell or trade; in 1939 about 150 of them reported at least $1000 worth, and seven individuals had more than $10,000 worth. But over the decade the number of livestock fell drastically, and the income from them reached an all-time low. Like most plains counties, Cimarron had built back its cattle herds after the 1880s débacle to an unprecedented peak in 1920, then to a smaller peak in 1930, before it plunged downward again. The stockmen, like the wheat producers, consistently expanded their output beyond what the market would bear, so that by 1933 the price per hundredweight of beef was $2.05 below parity level. Nationally, federal agriculture officials estimated in the early thirties there was an oversupply of 6 to 7 million cows and heifers. In part the surplus was due not only to overexpansion but to declining beef consumption by Americans—a 20 per cent per capita drop from 1910-14 to 1928-32.[2] Ranchers like Julius Kohler then cut their Herefords back or shifted to sheep. But with drought and Depression that

Stock watering hole almost covered over by erosion. (*Rothstein, Library of Congress*)

retrenchment strategy became even more urgent on the plains. All over Cimarron in the thirties decade there was a livestock market squeeze, and it was followed by an even greater crisis of getting feed for starving animals.

The feed supply problem was most frequently linked to drought. In the terribly dry year of 1936 William Baker pointed out that on the 800,000 acres of pastureland in the county, the grass stand was only 30 to 40 per cent of normal. Rainfall, he was confident, would solve all the graziers' difficulties. But the Forest Service, in a report made that same year on the entire Western range, argued that the problem had a more serious and long-range source—the old, familiar pattern of overstocking and overgrazing, leaving the grass little resilience for bad years. Not more than 5 per cent of the American public range was rated in satisfactory condition, and the average depletion of normal vegetation was 52 per cent. On lands that had a carrying capacity of 10.8 million animal units (a unit being either one steer or five sheep), ranchers had crowded 17.3 million units. Cimarron County was largely private range mixed with a substantial chunk of public school lands leased out and loosely supervised by the state of Oklahoma. According to the Forest Service, such tenure did not make a difference in resource treatment; only 8 per cent of the private shortgrass range was in good or fairly good condition. "Forage in southeast Colorado," the report pointed out, "has lost 88 percent of its

Stuck on a county road in the Felt area. Tumbleweeds are caught in the fence; the house has been abandoned. (*National Archives*)

former value"—and this was only a few miles from the Kohler ranch. It would take a century of management to restore those pastures to their original capacity, and that would involve the eradication of useless weeds and the slow recovery of more nutritious cover. "There is perhaps no darker chapter nor greater tragedy in the history of land occupancy and use in the United States," maintained the report, "than the story of the western range."[3]

Among the weeds that had muscled into overgrazed and droughty pastures was the Russian (pronounced "Roo-shan," locally) thistle, also known as the tumbleweed. First introduced to the plains in 1906, it quickly became a pest. The worst feature of the tumbleweed was that it grew into a tough globular shape and, when broken free from its roots, would roll for miles before the wind, until it lodged finally in a barbed wire fence or alongside a house. But faced with gaunt cattle and empty trench silos, stockmen discovered a use for the plant; they began to feed their stock young, green tumbleweeds. When cut before it matured and developed sharp prickles, the thistle made a very nutritious diet, although it was highly laxative when the cattle were fed too much of it. In September 1934 the county proclaimed a "Russian Thistle Week" and sent all relief workers out to help stockraisers harvest them for winter feed.[4] Some ranchers also ground up soapweed (yucca) or burned the spines off prickly-pear cactus. For those who had cash there was cottonseed cake or alfalfa to ship in as a supplement, and in 1933 the federal government would lend an operator a maximum of $250 to pay for it. In the next year the government also convinced the area's railroads to reduce feed freight rates by almost two-thirds.

But the ranchers of Cimarron County and elsewhere on the plains were the most stubbornly independent agriculturists in the nation, quick to resent any government interference. "This is a job for God, not the New Deal," said Charles Collins, a Coloradan, and president of the National Livestock Association.[5] When the Agricultural Adjustment Administration (AAA) was organized in 1933, cattle growers voted down a program for their commodity. The AAA offered a system of income supplements in exchange for supervised cutbacks in production; the majority of ranchers, however, preferred to let free market forces determine their survival. But as the droughts grew worse and the laissez-faire noose tightened, they began to repent—first demanding that foreign beef be kept out (imports amounted to a little over 1 per cent of the total cattle slaughter) and then clamoring for any kind of temporary government aid. Legislation pushed through by Senator Tom Connally and Congressman Marvin Jones, both of Texas, authorized the Department of Agriculture to begin buying cattle in June 1934 and to distribute the meat free of charge to the unemployed. During that summer and the next fall, before the drought purchase program ended in early 1935, the government bought 8.3 million head and gave cattlemen $111.7 million. During the summer of 1934 no one in Washington had the slightest idea of how many animals the government would end up buying. Presumably, stockmen were offering only their culls—knock-kneed bags of bones barely able to stand on their feet, beyond hope of saving, hovering near starvation—but there was no way of knowing how many such creatures were staggering around on the Western range. There were also dairy cows to be bought in states like Wisconsin and Minnesota; altogether, the nation's milking herd shrank by more than 6 per cent under the program. But three-fourths of the purchases were made in the beef region—25 per cent of the total in Texas alone—and especially on the plains, which normally furnished almost half of America's hamburgers and steaks. Within an eight-month period, the entire oversupply of cattle was wiped out in a frenzy of buying and selling, leaving the government to dispose of the carcasses.[6]

The short-lived Drought Relief Service operated in this way: federal officers, often local veterinarians, inspected the cattle or sheep a rancher wanted the government to buy and calculated the payment. Those unfit for consumption were shot on the spot and buried; the rest were shipped to a packing house or, if there was a backlog, to pastures outside of the drought area, where they awaited their turn on the chopping block. In Oklahoma 18 per cent of the purchased cattle had to be condemned because they could not survive a train trip; in Kansas less than 3 per cent were in such pitiful straits. Needy families in Boise City could go to a cattle kill and cart home the meat that was not diseased, although it might be tough eating. Ross Labrier, who now owns his father's 101 Ranch, remembers herding a hundred of their old, scrawny steers up into a canyon where they were killed by government-hired marksmen, after which townspeople poked among the bodies to salvage whatever was safe.[7] Most of the animals, however, left Cimarron for the

Kansas City or Fort Worth stockyards. By 1935 Washington had become the largest cattle owner in the world, the poor had more canned meat on their tables, and
lying in warehouses were 2 million hides that nobody quite knew what to do with.

The livestock purchase program was a relief measure, not intended to be a
guarantee of profit on investment. The Kohlers, as mentioned, took the flat government rate for their sheep—two bucks apiece. Cattle prices were higher and more
complicated, broken down as they were into a benefit payment that went to the
stockman, provided he was willing to cooperate in future production control programs, and a purchase payment that went to the owner, whether it was the same
stockman or someone who held a mortgage on the animals. The combined price paid
for calves was $4.00 to $5.00, depending upon their condition; for yearlings, $10
to $15; and for cattle two years and older, $12 to $20. Considering the emaciated
creatures the government was getting, animals that could not be sold to any other
buyer, it was a low but fair price schedule, although there were predictable protests
that the bureaucrats were too stingy with the public monies when they came to farm
subsidies. Some of the more suspicious were worried that the drought purchase program was an invitation to government regulation—even though subsequent federal
policy toward cattlemen was always more carrot than stick. Under the agricultural
programs of 1936 and 1938, ranchers could get further government payments for
following commonsense practices such as deferred grazing on damaged pastures,
better water management, and herd stabilization: innocuous but useful aids in
bringing order to a recurrent chaos. But once the emergency was past even such
minimal inducements could provoke violent attacks on "dictatorial" politicians, and
the cattlemen were allowed to preserve their self-reliant posture.[8]

At the beginning of the thirties Cimarron County tallied 37,590 cattle, including calves. During 1934 the government purchased 12,499 head, for which they
paid $164,449, plus another $2100 for sheep. There were, in addition, 58 feed loans
that year, amounting to $4560—making a total of over $170,000 in federal aid for
local stockmen. Other near-by counties received higher amounts: Baca, over a quarter of a million dollars; Dallam, Ochiltree, Hall, and Deaf Smith in Texas, even
more. The money saved ranchers from one of their worst crises, and the declines
in the herds boosted prices at the commercial packing plants. Once the reduction
in livestock began, the momentum carried through after the purchase program
ended: fewer cows meant fewer calves. By 1935 there were 25,518 cattle in Cimarron; by 1940, only 14,876. Beef prices had risen from $4.14 a hundredweight in
1933 to $7.76 in 1939. "Government emergency programs," writes historian John
Schlebecker, "literally saved the cattlemen."[9] For ranch families such as the Kohlers
or Labriers that statement may be an exaggeration; their plight was never as severe
as that of the wheat farmers trying to get crops to grow on baked hardpan. But the
500 head of cattle that Henry Labrier was able to sell to federal buyers meant a nice

Farmer raising his fence to keep pace with the dirt drifts. (*Rothstein, Library of Congress*)

bit of cash in the bank—enough to pay taxes and, more, to maintain that sense of apartness, however illusory, from a noisy, desperate world. Few distressed families in Depression America made out so well.

The average agricultural unit in Cimarron County was large—1204 acres in 1930 and 1536 in 1940, as small fry were eaten up by big snappers. The many ranchers, of course, made that average especially high; in the early years of the Depression the typical southern plains ranch sprawled over 6300 acres.[10] Even more than in wheat farming, giant-scale units ruled the range industry, producing, in many cases, private regimes that were almost feudal in their autarchical mentality. These big, premechanized cattle spreads required much paid labor, and there were thus living in the county in 1935 about 130 hired hands, most of them cowboys, hovering near the very bottom of the social scale. If federal relief saved the ranchers, or at least eased them over a rough spot, it also preserved the even more precarious jobs of those wage employees, whose skills elsewhere would have been about as useful as those of a chimneysweep. Improvident by tradition, the ranch hand was eminently vulnerable to economic slump, even where an employer took a paternalistic attitude toward his "boys."

As with people everywhere who live obscurely, the cowboy in thirties America is a forgotten, inaccessible figure. A few numbers in the census reports are all he has left behind—and numbers can be almost worse than nothing, so impersonal and abstract are they. But perhaps the memories of one cowboy can be made to speak for many. Joe Garza, now retired and living in Boise City, spent most of his adult life riding in the saddle for someone else, and from that vantage he saw the Dust Bowl. "I herded sheep, I herded cattle, I do everything I could do," he says, "in order not to rob a bank, do something like a white man do, you know." Born in 1900, he grew up in the Spanish-speaking area around Mexhoma, where at an early age he went to work for Juan Cruz Lujan, one of Don Baca's sheepherders who stayed on to become a substantial rancher. But in the first half of the decade Garza hired out to Anglo cattleman Red Moore for $35 a month and keep. Every morning he would get up at four o'clock, eat a stack of flapjacks, feed the cows, hitch up the mules, and mount a pony for the day's duration. When the pastures got bad, Moore sent him over to New Mexico with a herd, then at last let him go with pay still owed him. Once more Lujan gave him a chance—this time shooting coyotes that were preying on the sheep: Garza sold their hides for $3.00 each, and it was a long time before he could kill enough to afford a new pair of boots. After a year of that catch-as-catch-can life Garza was ready to jump at a job with Rufus Wright, branding and castrating calves at spring roundup, then doing more range work. Black Sunday, April 1935, found him in the breaks riding herd on a small bunch of whitefaced steers. The dark blizzard hit just as he was driving his wagon (fitted out with a small cabin, where he lived) across a dry creek bed. He got bogged down in the middle. In the sudden midnight he stumbled against the horses and wagon tongue, found his way into his kitchen, lit his lantern, and then yelled out the door to guide his companion to shelter. Today there is no remembered fear in that story, nothing more than amusement in his seamed brown face and quick black eyes. "I was never scared to die," he adds simply, "because that's why I was born." Perhaps it took that kind of stoicism, as well as a tenacious attachment to ranching life, to stay on with Wright through more dust, more sweaty labor, and more low pay for a dozen years.[11]

Down in Boise City townspeople crowded into the Palace Theater to see the new talking and singing Westerns: Hoot Gibson, Ken Maynard, Gene Autry, Zane Grey's *Thundering Herd,* Randolph Scott in *The Last Round-Up,* Errol Flynn swaggering through *Dodge City.* But it is safe to say that few people in the Cimarron community paid much attention to the real, every-day cowboys in their midst, a large number of whom were Mexican-Americans with names like Archuleta, Martinez, Castanada, and Gonzales, names that were never represented in respectable cafés like the Silver Moon or Mrs. Skaggs's. Some of these cowpunchers gave up fighting range dust and took WPA jobs in town, so many that there were loud complaints about "our best citizens"—whites, that is—being "cut off from work and a crew of Mexicans kept on."[12] The gulf between Western reality and Western mythology was summed up in those social facts of Cimarron County: there was, on one hand, an intense appetite among the better-off citizens for Hollywood's version of their past, in which tall, well-turned-out gents—unmistakably Anglo, even to the point of having English accents—used their two fists on a threatening world while, in contrast, there were the real Dust Bowl cowhands, who were usually small, insecure men, knocked about by hard times like everyone else, and who in some cases were a despised minority—always needed but seldom welcomed. Joe Garza never made it to the picture show in those years; and today, living as he does beyond the paved streets and green lawns in a wretched duplex with the smell of dog manure thick in the air and a defunct Mercury coming apart in the front yard, his only income a Social Security check, he is even further removed from the fantasy cowboy who once strode across the movie screens of the region.

In the thirties there was considerable talk about turning most, or even all, of the High Plains back to livestock. More ranches, fewer farms, was the remedy many espoused, especially those who were already in the cattle business. If northwest Cimarron County can be taken as a model, clearly there was much to be said for that proposal. Even overgrazed, native grass was a better check against wind than the less hardy wheat. The rancher and his cowhands could carry on, in some ways, at least, as if theirs were a world suspended in time, independent of an industrial culture breaking down. There were also many genuine satisfactions they could derive from a constant intimacy with animals and with a land less altered by humans than it was elsewhere in the county. But all the same, America did not need more ranches, more cows, more meat—nor more Robert Kohlers and Joe Garzas. The emergency drought purchase demonstrated that fact conclusively, and it also demonstrated how limited the rangeman's independence really was by the fourth decade of the twentieth century. And the chancy working life of the hired ranch hand, often with nothing at its end but calluses and empty pockets, was no pattern worth extending. The decade of the 1930s laid some of these problems bare for the first time, reducing the ranching ideal from a panacea, from an Owen Wister idyll, to a man-nature relation that had much to be set right.

Hard Times

LIKE A ROCK FALLING into placid waters, the Depression sent circles of adversity spreading across the nation. Cimarron County, out on the edges of the agitation, was not tossed and pitched about as other communities were. Tied as it was to national markets and to the factory system, the county inevitably felt something of the economic shock waves. But it was possible here to view the turmoil of industrial America with a measure of detachment, not to say indifference. Had there been no dust storms, the panhandle would have been a pleasant enough place to live during the thirties—more secure at least than Detroit or Muncie. Blowing dirt turned that advantage upside down, multiplying Cimarron's problems beyond what other regions had to bear. On the other hand, the dusters, because their causes were less clearly cultural to many people, did not challenge traditional assumptions, as could shutdowns or layoffs. The economic values of panhandle residents were indeed shaken—but not hard enough to come loose. By the end of the decade things were nearly back to normal, and normal emphatically meant the old style of pushing toward unlimited profits.

Several months after the stock market crash, the *Cimarron News* (its name was later changed to the *Boise City News*) marveled that "the panhandle has felt very little of the destitution felt throughout the nation." All through 1930, in fact, the local future looked even more gleaming than it had in the "New Era" days of Calvin Coolidge. In January the editor promised his readers that "Our Ship is coming in!—loaded with something for each of us. . . . When Cimarron's ship comes to dock, be one of the gang to meet it—have something to trade." The vessel hoving in sight was the Santa Fe railroad, busy building new lines that would link Boise n the Panhandle

City to Los Angeles, Denver, and Houston; all of those connections would "release the shackles" on the community and thrust it headlong into the "competitive struggle of progress." In February and March business leaders inserted a series of newspaper ads intended to inspire a consensus of energy in this struggle:

> THERE IS NO STANDING STILL—WE MUST MOVE FORWARD—OR, WE MOVE BACKWARD. A town cannot be bigger until it is better, and it cannot be better until it is bigger. Let us remember that it is natural and normal for a community to grow—unless there is something wrong—something lacking.

The commercial imagination soared even higher in June, when Cimarron celebrated the hundredth anniversary of merchants first traveling the Santa Fe Trail. From that distant time, when Missouri trader Josiah Gregg had encamped at Flag Springs, the course of history had been, as the proprietor of the Foxworth-Galbraith Lumber Company put it, a saga of "Progress and Prosperity." The iconography of this giddy, if somewhat contrived, celebration suggested the anticipated shape of the coming decade: not once, but on three separate pages newspaper ads portrayed an elaborately Gothic Manhattan skyline suspended in the clouds over flat prairies, humble cabins, and Indians on horseback, while Grecian goddesses wreathed in ivy beamed down on Cimarron with the obvious promise, "Soon you will have your own Empire State Building, right across from Kirby's Kash Grocery."[1]

Three years later, due to sand storms and drought, there was virtually no wheat harvested on several hundred thousand Cimarron acres. Two banks in the

Boise City, Oklahoma, in a dust storm. April 1936. (*Rothstein, Library of Congress*)

county had failed, and the remaining one had jolted everyone further by closing its doors during the national bank holiday, thus surviving the panic.[2] Boise City delegates to a conference in Guymon reported that $5 million in emergency federal aid would be requested for the panhandle. Thirty-one local businesses signed National Recovery Act agreements to put a floor under shaky employee wages, and the Blue Eagle was now part of the Cimarron fauna. A prominent doctor, deranged by heavy losses on the Kansas City board of trade, killed his wife and then himself with a .38-caliber revolver. On the front page of the *News* appeared a cartoon showing the "Big Business Man" knocked off his pedestal; the caption read, "One thing that will not go up again soon."[3]

By almost every economic indicator Cimarron County was reeling on the ropes in 1933, with the onset of drought and before the worst of the black blizzards. It went steadily downhill from there. Fundamentally, the collapse was agricultural; everyone in the community, from schoolteachers to implement dealers, from railroad workers to dentists, depended ultimately on the farmer and his crops, and he was in deep trouble. The wheat harvest in 1930 had a market value of $700,000, and in 1931 almost $1.2 million. But in 1933 the value was a paltry $7000, spread among 800 wheat growers. The next year 200,000 planted acres produced nothing but erosion.[4] By 1939 the value of all crops harvested and sold—wheat, corn, hay, and feed grains—was one-fifth of what it had been ten years earlier. One consequence of crop failure was that the average Cimarron farm, according to the federal agricultural census, declined in worth from $16,600 at the outset of the decade, to $10,700 at midpoint, and to $9200 at the end. Still another measure of rural deterioration was the ten-year jump in the proportion of tenant farmers, from 35 to 43 per cent, as the more vulnerable operators had to sell out, rent someone else's property, and watch their opportunity to rise on the land fade away. In the face of that reversal all the dreams of imperial grandeur had to be temporarily set aside.

In the late 1920s the key to unlock the wealth of the Great Plains dangled from a creditor's chain, but it was not until the thirties that farmers realized how short that chain was. When the expectation of ever larger crops turned out to be a false hope, Cimarron growers were left with substantial mortgages that had to be paid, whether there was income or not. In 1934 the total rural debt in the county amounted to $4,750,000, or about $5500 per farm, an increase from a third of the average farm's land and buildings value in 1929 to a half five years later. Since only one in four agricultural units remained mortgage-free, the actual level of debt among those owing money was even higher. It was mainly the wheat entrepreneurs who had put so much of their land in hock, borrowing from anyone who would lend them cash in the days of easy credit in order to expand their operations, and now worrying about how those land debts could be met. Their first impulse was to plow up still more ground, raise an even bigger crop, and thereby keep the wolf from the door. By 1935, despite successive wheat failures, a larger acreage than ever before had been stripped of its protective grass cover.[5] When that strategy made the dust blow all the harder, farmers began to give up—parked their tractors and went to town, hanging about the streets in angry uncertainty.

But land debt was only one of their burdens. Under Oklahoma law it was possible to take out a chattel mortgage on crops not yet planted, and most Cimarron wheat farmers found somebody willing to share that gamble with them, usually an implement manufacturer. A farmer near Keyes, for instance, signed away his 1934 crop to pay for a new tractor, lister, cream separator, and Chevrolet roadster. Over all the county in that same year there was a total lien on wheat of $603,000, and all the harvests of 1932-34 would have been required to satisfy it. Some of the individual crop mortgages went as high as $4000, though more commonly they ranged from $100 to $1000. There were, in addition, machinery bills going back several years: in 1929 local farmers purchased on credit a million dollars' worth of equipment; five years later only one-fourth of that sum had been paid back.[6] Panhandle people were no more profligate than Americans who lived in other regions—no more hooked on credit-based affluence. But in their hunger for instant "progress and prosperity" they had thrown caution to the winds. For literally hundreds of Cimarron rural families there was no way out of the mid-thirties squeeze but to retreat, surrender, or take a beating.

Many farmers, staggering hopelessly under these debts, declared bankruptcy and put all their possessions on the auction block. Others simply loaded what they could into a car and drove off in the night, telling no one, least of all their creditors, where they were going. For a farmer who hunted for a buyer for his farm, prospects were grim: in most cases there were several potential customers around, but they did not feel obliged to give anything near what he had originally paid for the land. Real-estate dealer Bob French recalls arranging a sale just west of Boise City at

Farm near Boise City, 1938. (*Lange, Library of Congress*)

$3.50 an acre; $5.00, he told his clients then, was a good price to get, considering the condition of the country. In one extreme case a 160-acre farm went for $25, plus overdue taxes. "I didn't sell out back there," complained a California-bound man; "I *give* out." For those who for one reason or another still had cash, on the other hand, the pickings were easy, although it required considerable faith to see much value in the creeping desert. Roy Nall, a schoolteacher, was one of those who spied his chance through the dust; out of his and his wife's small income he bought parcel after parcel until, in the 1940s, when the rains returned, he could give up teaching and become a full-time, and very wealthy, farmer. Another buyer was an out-of-county Elk City, Oklahoma, man who acquired over 100 full sections of Cimarron land (64,000 acres plus); "he could see something," French points out, "beyond the Dust Bowl." There were perhaps a dozen people who stood ready to make their fortune—or augment it—in the midst of distress.[7] But the loss of 370 farms from the 1935 to the 1940 census (from 975 down to 605) strongly suggests how much more frequent was the experience of economic ruin.

Through the decade the *Boise City News* carried notices of sheriff's sales of farm property almost every week: Prudential Insurance owed by Laura and William Clayton $2098.66; Kansas City Life owed by L. Z. and Neva Pierson $1044.45; Central Life Assurance of Des Moines owed by Dory and Cora Ward $4169.80. Typically, the arrangement was that Sheriff Jake Allison would stand at the front door of the courthouse at 10:00 a.m. to accept bids on the property. In almost every case it was the mortgage holder or his representative who was there to make the only bid—someone from the First State Bank across the street, a local physician, or an agent for a distant insurance company or a federal office. In 1933, farm foreclosures such as these reached a national as well as a state and county high. Over 5 per cent of the farms across the United States were subject to forced sales that year —more than $3 billion worth of property. For every 1000 farms in Oklahoma, 45 went up for bids, which was near the average for the ten Great Plains states; in Kansas, the proportion was 53, in South Dakota, 79. Although foreclosures were nothing new in this unstable region, the 1933 figures were three times as high as they had been in 1929.[8] "Forced sales" may be too strong a phrase to describe all of these cases; often the Cimarron debtors put up no resistance, were in fact relieved to see the matter settled, and sometimes were already living far off in another state. Jacob Harman is a case in point: his 12,000-acre ranch (there were few ranch sales in the paper) had been left idle for several years after Harman had retired to eastern Kansas, too old to want to struggle any longer. He owed a whopping $60,000 on the property; a Peoria, Illinois, insurance company held the mortgage and acquired full title for $35,000—thenceforth it was their headache.[9]

A foreclosed farm usually meant that another Cimarron family was moving, or had moved, away. There was no kind of work to be had in Boise City, even when rural people were willing and ready to make the shift to a town job. Some kind of agricultural employment elsewhere was what most hoped for. So they usually became Okies—panhandle versions of the Joads. No John Steinbeck appeared to publicize their story, though many of its details, especially the destitution and trekking west, were accurately described in *The Grapes of Wrath*. As real-life individuals, however, the Cimarron exodusters are lost to history. Ask a farmer who survived down in the Felt area: Who left here back in the thirties? Where did they go? What happened to them? And he remembers nothing. Even as they were packing up, the migrants were ignored; their names never appeared in the newspaper except in the legal columns, although if a successful businessman left it was front-page news or if the Baptist church had a sale of baked goods all the details were written up. A few of those who stayed behind did correspond for a year or two with a departed neighbor, living, it might be, near Phoenix or Fresno or Little Rock, then stopped. Cimarron, which had never been a close-knit community, regrouped quickly, parceled out the land among the more wealthy, and went on as before—as if the departed had never existed. Only the census books carry the record of the exodusters' existence (as they do the cowboys'). During the decade the county's population outside Boise City dropped from 4152 to 2510, a loss of 1642 residents, almost all of them small farmers. That is a *forty per cent* decline. And it is today all anonymous, faceless, invisible, forgotten.

There were government programs, to be sure, that were intended to save farmers from forced sale and migration. But so discouraged and indifferent were many of the people that those programs had only a limited impact. In June 1933 the Farm Credit Administration was established in Washington to refinance farm mortgages and, through a system of regional offices, to make production and marketing loans—to become, in short, rural America's bank. Nothing could have been more radical, unless it were the collectivization of the farms themselves, than this essentially socialist institution of government banking, which made loans at a modest 5 per cent interest, effectively wiping out most private competition. The FCA also helped organize debt adjustment committees in many counties, including Cimarron, that attempted to scale down farm debts to payable levels, on the assumption that most creditors would rather have money than a string of properties needing rescue.[10] In the three years following its birth, the FCA loaned more than $600 million nationally, and the plains received a disproportionate share by far. By 1936 it was getting hard to find a farm mortgage in the panhandle that did not have a government official's name on it. Cimarron used almost all of its first-year land bank loans to refinance existing debts, substituting a more patient but bureaucratic creditor for an importuning town lawyer or Prudential agent knocking on the door.[11] All the same, the substitution was no panacea if one was fed up with trying to raise a crop in the dust belt.

Down in the worst of the blow area, around Felt, not even the federal bankers would make loans after August 1934. They, like the commercial lenders, wanted to see the money repaid on schedule, and in that sandy, drifted-over country there was little chance it would happen. "Some white-collared official probably drove through here and got a speck of dirt in his eye, and rushed back and made his report," snorted the *News* editor. But in the next spring he too was admitting the unprofitability of agriculture in the southwestern part of the county; as many as 100 families may have left farms there in April 1935 alone. Not until 1937, however, did anyone put forward a solution for the sandy country, and again it came from the federal government. In the Felt high school auditorium James Foster of the Bureau of Agricultural Economics' Land Use Planning Division offered the farmers in his audience a chance to sell out to Washington. The Tri-State Land Utilization and Conservation Project, under Felix Neff, had been set up to buy problem lands, to put them into permanent vegetative cover, and to keep them perpetually under federal stewardship—180,000 acres were authorized in Dallam, Union, and Cimarron counties. Although some diehards refused to sell, the federal purchase agents were generally successful in enticing people off the rolling dunes so that a stabilization effort could get started. In most cases the owners were desperate to find a buyer and leave.[12]

Sand drifted against outbuildings. (*Rothstein, Library of Congress*)

Even where a farm was debt-free, the rural people could feel their grip on the land being pried loose. In some Junes, when the wheat harvest garnered no more than a bushel per acre, and when that bushel could be sold for only 50 cents to $1.00, there might be nothing in the till next fall with which to try again. A man needed at least $1300 a year to keep going on the average-sized farm: $900 of that sum for machinery and gasoline, the rest for wages, livestock feed, and building materials. Then there were taxes to be paid—about 8 cents an acre for real-estate levies in 1939, one-half of what they had been a decade earlier. At that reduced rate the owner of a 1500-acre farm paid less than $150 in land taxes, plus a personal property assessment of perhaps $15. Not much, it would seem by more recent standards, but in the depressed thirties it was enough to break the farmer's back. County taxes in 1929 reached an aggregate of $248,000, and 84 per cent of them were paid on time, without penalty. By 1933, although taxes had been cut to only $138,000, 41 per cent of individual bills were in arrears. Every year thereafter delinquencies, listed by the newspaper in column after column, remained about half the total levy. Edwin Henson, federal coordinator for the southern plains, made it clear that Cimarron was not unique; it was the pattern for the entire region and by decade's end had been so long enough to become a tradition. Most of the delinquent land, Henson revealed, "belongs to residents; absentee owners normally keep their taxes paid."[13] Even some of the more well-to-do Cimarron families made the news-

Hard hit by tax cuts and delinquency. (*National Archives*)

paper lists year after year, apparently finding it more acceptable now to pay at their leisure. After an individual had been delinquent for three years, the county began to take offense; in especially recalcitrant cases the county commissioners seized farms and sold them at open auction to collect their levies.

Whether in fact they could not pay, or whether they chose to put social needs last in their priorities, delinquent taxpayers threw local government into disarray. Cimarron schools, in particular, were hard hit, and teachers, already paid little by national standards, often found themselves teetering on the edge of bankruptcy. In the 23 one-room schoolhouses across the county, teachers made $700 a year; in the Boise City high school, $1045. Eventually, to cover these salaries, school districts began to issue warrants—paper promises to pay when the taxes came in—instead of checks. A promise would not buy many groceries, especially after the First State Bank refused to risk its deposits by cashing any warrants. Some teachers found a rich benefactor who would buy these promissory notes—at a ten per cent discount. But the common attitude among farmers and townspeople alike was that public employees ought to share in the uncertainty and decline rather than expect a steady income, although in the boom years there had been no readiness to raise their salaries or spread the growing wealth around. On balance, teachers and other tax-supported workers probably made out better than most dirt farmers, and the warrants were finally all paid off. But education—which had never been interesting to most Cimarron citizens—along with other public services fared badly in the 1930s, not only because of tax delinquency, but also because of taxpayer leagues that organized throughout the Dust Bowl to protest what the people saw as excessive waste and to beat back further their property assessments.[14]

Left to its own resources, Cimarron County would have lost more ground than it did—far more people would have left, far more schools would have been closed, far more Boise City merchants would have boarded up their windows. What saved the community from scraping absolute bottom was an awakened social conscience in the rest of the nation and an influx of federal money. Besides the listing payments, the cattle purchase scheme, the Farm Credit Administration, and the Land Utilization Project, there was, for the special relief of farmers, the Agricultural Adjustment program, which paid wheat growers for not planting their crops. During 1934, the county's farmers began to receive sizable quantities of help from Washington:[15]

1290 AAA wheat contracts	$642,637
286 " corn-hog "	48,216
12,499 cattle purchased	164,449
1050 sheep "	2,100
68 spring crop loans	10,345
251 summer fallow loans	51,080
58 feed loans	4560
	$923,387

Nearly a million dollars in twelve months, most of which did not have to be paid back—a munificent gift from taxpayers living elsewhere. So it went year after year: in 1938, for example, a redesigned AAA mailed $505,000 worth of checks to Cimarron, $18 million to all of Oklahoma. Other federal agencies sprouted, flourished, and died away, leaving behind substantial contributions to the community's finances. All told, from 1933 to 1939 Western states collected more than $300 per capita. Storm-wracked places like Cimarron did much better than that—an average of $4000 per farm by 1937.[16] Such aid could not build skyscrapers on the plains or fulfill all the grandiose ambitions of earlier days, but it did keep the county from reverting to another kind of "no-man's-land."

When the government checks began to arrive, creditors were usually waiting at the mailbox. High-pressure bill collectors, smelling new cash, came into the panhandle to try to get something out of the farmers; in most cases they represented John Deere, J. I. Case, or the like. Immediately south, in Dallam County, Texas, a few such collectors met with violent resistance: one was chased by a farmer armed with a razor, another had part of one ear bitten off in a fight, and a third scurried away from a load of birdshot. Cimarron's county agent, Bill Baker, was so outraged by creditor tactics, which usually included some arm-twisting and threats to get part or all of an AAA check, that he wrote an open letter to the Boise City newspaper, warning that such practices would not be countenanced.[17] Congress, he maintained, had intended the money to be used by farmers primarily to stay in business—to pay taxes, buy clothes, and plant a new crop, as well as to settle implement debts. But wherever the money went, it led to no dramatic turnaround in Cimarron's condition; the most it could do was allow a momentary stay against disaster, a breathing spell during which farmers could, if they chose, search for more permanent reorganization of their lives.

Ultimately, the problems of the community were caused by ecological breakdown and land misuse; they required an extensive and enduring program of conservation to be solved. Such a program in turn implied political action that might violate traditional panhandle autonomy. As this fact became more obvious, the *Boise City News* reprinted on its front page, in March 1936, an editorial from a California newspaper. It was entitled "Dust Storms Show the Way toward National Planning." By this timid strategy of quoting someone else's ideas, the local editor could float a trial balloon while disclaiming all responsibility if it got punctured. The borrowed and somewhat vague message ran thus:

> With all this talk of rugged individualism, of unwarranted government in
> terference in economic matters, we are reminded again by bitter black
> headlines that there are some problems that must be solved by a socially
> conscious Federal government, or they will not be solved at all. And among
> these are problems upon the solution of which depends the very future of
> American civilization.

Soil erosion on the southern plains, the California writer argued, was one of those problems.[18] The people of Cimarron knew better than anyone else the magnitude of erosion and misfortune. Having taken one long step away from pioneer self-reliance toward widespread acceptance of federal aid, they now were confronted with a greater challenge: what would they need to do to stop the dusters—the source of their woes? Could they themselves devise an effective conservation program and enforce it, or would Washington have to do the work here, too? Most important, could any land-use program, local or federal, succeed where the dominant values supported "the competitive struggle for progress" and the "bigger is better" attitudes? Neither the *News* nor any other leader in the community was quite bold enough to tackle that question.

The main thing Cimarron needed, in the view of most residents, was neither national planning nor permanent government land regulation, but simply "relief." People in the cities who were unable to find work because of glutted factories got relief. Why, then, should not a family in the panhandle expect the same? "Relief" was, by and large, a positive word; it implied a succoring and comforting of those overwhelmed by powerful enemies, it meant rushing in reinforcements for those on the front line of battle. To be relieved was an honor, in fact, for no one questioned that you had done your duty well and now deserved a break. Although a few farmers and townspeople in the county scorned government aid as an admission of personal weakness, most of those who really needed help asked for and received it. Intense pride in themselves and their achievements, which is the natural emotion of a frontier community, nonetheless required that the asking be severely constrained: there was to be no confession of failure; work was infinitely preferable to the dole; relief was to be only a temporary arrangement.

The distance from sufficiency to need was remarkably short forty years ago. Despite their swollen aspirations, the actual standard of living in Cimarron was still close to the bone. To be impoverished, therefore, meant a loss that even small-scale assistance could remedy. More than two-thirds of the population lived in the countryside or in hamlets so small that their life style was essentially rural. As late as 1940 only one in four farms had electric lights, and even fewer had refrigerators, vacuum cleaners, or washing machines; a Delco home generating plant explained the cases that did. The same small percentage had telephones. Cooking was done with bottled gas, with coal, or, in a few cases, with riverbank wood. Only one-half of the farmers had water piped inside their dwellings; the rest of the people fetched it in buckets from the well every day. Indoor toilets were found only in town, and there were not many even there. A 1936 housing survey of the county rated the vast majority of occupied structures as "fair" or "poor"—only 30 per cent as "good."[19] Virtually every farmer had an automobile and a tractor, and roughly half kept a truck, although by the end of the period those vehicles were six or more years old. The people of the county were land- and machinery-rich, for these were their precious capital. But in other respects they were closer to the sod-house era than to our own, or, for that matter, than to the metropolitan level of the thirties.

At least 29 people died of starvation in New York City in 1933, while in the Oklahoma state capital so many were digging through restaurant garbage that a public official proposed, incredible to say, that the stuff be *sold*—no one should get anything free.[20] Nowhere among Cimarron residents was the problem so severe, although the dust spoiled many dinners. They may not have had city conveniences, but they did have a more reliable access to food. Those who had turned to store-bought bread and beans could revert to raising their own again. In the five years after 1934, the value of vegetables grown for home use on the county's farms edged up from $4700 to $5400. Storm cellars were filled with potatoes, onions, squash, canned tomatoes, and fruit. Milk cows required feed that was hard to come by in some of those years; consequently, average herds dropped from ten or fifteen ani-

Pioneer woman in a patched-over adobe house. (*Rothstein, Library of Congress*)

mals to only three or four by 1937, then began to increase as hay and grain became cheaper. In the face of crop failure, many farm families had to survive solely on milk, butter, and cheese, which they sold in town to the creamery agent or bartered at the grocery for salt, coffee, and flour. Chickens were another backyard asset—200,000 dozen eggs were produced a year, providing the petty cash that often saved a family's pride. In the 1920s some observers had warned farmers not to forsake "the cow, the sow, and the hen," a bit of wisdom that the hard times of the 1930s drove home. The third member of that homestead economy, the sow, contributed bacon, ham, ears, knuckles, head cheese—everything, it was said, but the curl in the tail. Hog butchering was always done in cold weather so the meat would keep, and the carcass was left to hang for weeks from the windmill. Or sometimes neighbors would gather with picnic baskets when a hog was to be killed; the meat was then divided up and canned, as quart after quart of it was taken from the pressure cooker. With such homegrown resources, a family of six plus a hired man in Sherman County, Texas, could shave their monthly food bill to $10, all of which went for the staples they could not raise themselves.[21] In Cimarron, too, a few hundred dollars a year was all that was required, besides money for taxes and mortgages, to last out the dusters.

When that minimal cash was lacking, however, the first recourse was to ask the Keyes or Boise City storekeeper for credit. Not the banker, but the grocer—especially those who were old-timers, who knew too many families too well to say no—made most of the local loans in the thirties. In Boise City people often went to Roy Godown and his wife, who ran a grocery and dry goods emporium. At one point they offered 5 cents a dozen for eggs, 7 cents if one "traded out"—took store goods instead of cash. A few eggs or some lard and cracklings would not swap for much, even at deflated shelf prices: beef roast cost 8 cents a pound in 1933, two pounds of bacon was 25 cents, a dozen oranges only 19 cents, men's overalls 79 cents, a suit $13.75. Unable to meet even these charges, some families, generally those in town who had less to sell and more to buy than farmers did, ran up their credit to $50, even to $300. The Godowns knew that they would never collect in several cases, but neither could they deny potatoes to a man or woman with four or five children to feed, whatever their prospects. Others, they were sure, would settle their debts as soon as possible, although they might need nudging. Gently, almost apologetically, Godown took Bob French aside one day: "Bob, can you pay a little on your bill?" He got his money in that case, and a dividend of gratitude, too. Not every creditor in Cimarron was a Shylock, and it was the likes of the Godowns who allowed the institution of credit to work as an ad hoc, neighborly relief system for the hard-pressed.[22]

But neither homegrown food nor store credit, nor, for that matter, AAA checks, proved sufficient to keep all of Cimarron's people from going over the near edge of desperation. What more was needed came from the federal government again, in the form of surplus commodities and make-work relief for the unemployed. During 1934 the county received and distributed free of charge more than 2 tons of smoked pork, 16 tons of beef, 17 of flour, 33 of coal, and—for feeding poultry and livestock—250 tons of corn and 100 of oats, as well as 4000 bales of hay. The poor commonly refused to accept these commodities as an outright gift; they preferred to have a price set on them and to be given enough hours of work so they could earn them. Three hundred and six household heads were drawing direct government relief in June 1934: 60 of them were paid entirely in commodities, the rest mostly in cash. If there were four people in each of these families, as one sampling indicated, then more than 1200 individuals—one-fourth of the county's population—depended to some extent on public work. Other Dust Bowl counties had as high or higher percentages of their populations on relief in 1934-35; in Baca, Colorado, it was 45 per cent; in Dumas, Texas, 24; and in Curry, New Mexico, 22, all of which were above national urban levels. When President Roosevelt met with E. W. Marland, Oklahoma's governor, in Des Moines in September 1936, Marland claimed that almost 90 per cent of his state's farmers were getting or needed public work or grants, and Rexford Tugwell, Roosevelt's aide, admitted that

A Cimarron family on relief, 1934. This is their home. Three children are away, one in reform school. The mother hoped to take in washing to help with their living expenses, but received none. (*National Archives*)

"this is our biggest relief state." Two months after the Des Moines conference and after the national elections, 40,000 Oklahomans were cut from relief jobs, 150 of them in Cimarron, to reduce Roosevelt's budget deficits. Federal assistance turned out to be a shaky crutch to lean on; no one could ever be sure when it would be pulled away. But whenever it was offered, the number of qualified applicants always exceeded the assigned quotas.[23]

Work relief was an idea assiduously promoted in Washington by Harry Hopkins, head of the Federal Emergency Relief Administration and its successor, the Works Progress Administration, as an alternative to a degenerating cash dole. Building permanent public works was a slightly different idea, urged with equal tenacity by Harold Ickes, Secretary of the Interior and chief of the Public Works Administration. In the New Deal there was room for both men and their programs; they carried on a running, not always amiable, competition for funds that, fortunately, had little effect on Cimarron. There were a few of Ickes's projects there: notably a new grade school handsomely constructed of local stone and an "airport" that was little more than a faint runway. Then there was a more expensive scheme, a dam across the Cimarron River near Kenton, that was never approved by Congress despite considerable cajoling and foot-stamping. But the county did not have the skilled labor, other than a small number of Mexican-American stonemasons, needed for most PWA-type projects. Hopkins's work relief program, which involved using unskilled people on less demanding assignments, was far better suited to a needy population that in most cases had only farming experience. In those pre-asphalt and pre-Caterpillar days, grading new roads or spreading gravel on old ones was a simple, manageable undertaking, and it was indisputably useful in a county so large and so sparsely settled. A gang of men with shovels, horse teams, and a back scraper or two at work on the highway, or a circle of women gathered in the sewing room at the high school—those were "made work" in the panhandle. In 1933 the funds came from the FERA's special drought appropriation and from beefed-up federal and state highway funds (Cimarron spent $300,000 on its roads in that year, twice as much as in the previous 9 years); by 1935, when erosion had become severe and relief needs had mushroomed, the money came from the new WPA. In the view of Debs Baker, a farmer who was a WPA worker off and on, "Them jobs made all the difference for me. It was a *rough go*—they ain't no way to understand it without you was here then."[24]

Those who got work relief in this southern plains community were, overwhelmingly, farmers. A 1934 government survey found that 111 individuals out of a sample of 147 were from the open country, and later that number rose to as many as 118, or 80 per cent. Crop failure caused by drought and blowing dirt, as well as heavy mortgages contracted in more hopeful days, were what usually brought men to the relief office, not town unemployment. In other regions farmers seldom took government relief: only 3 per cent of them did in California, 1 per cent in New Hampshire and New York, 9 per cent nationally during June 1935. But in the Dust Bowl one out of every three or four farmers was the norm, with tenants represented most heavily and smaller operators more common than large ones. The man shoveling sand drifts from a highway or patching up a bridge was most likely to be thirty to forty years old, the father of two to four children, sole breadwinner in his family, a Cimarron resident for at least ten years, and without even a full grade-school education. At the relief office case workers drew up a budget for him and then tried to find enough public work to help him meet it—always remaining well under the prescribed maximum of 36 hours per week. Thirty cents an hour was the standard rate, double that if you brought a team. Individual work relief income during one month in 1934 averaged $22, of which $21 was cash, while the remaining dollar was given out as surplus commodities. A few of the most impoverished families got an extra $8.00 grant.[25] On such pittances did the people of the panhandle survive; they were the Okies who stayed behind—better fed than the Joad family, to be sure, and more protected from exploitation, but never very far from walking on their uppers.

To administer so fluid a federal relief system locally required a great deal of patience and improvisation. No one in Cimarron was quite prepared for the job, and no one brought in from the outside stayed very long at it. First there was T. H. Smith, who in January 1933 undertook the office of superintendent of direct relief and county supervisor of social services; he was an area resident appointed by the governor to his posts. Twelve months later a non-resident took his place, and so the process of turnover went for the rest of the decade. Salaries were decent enough, higher, at least, than what WPA workers made, and too high in the eyes of some irate citizens; county relief directors earned $115 to $125 a month, and the three case workers in Cimarron, $110 each.[26] Crowded into a small room on the first floor of the courthouse, they wrestled with ever-changing federal and state regulations, voluminous report forms, and hundreds of family budgets, which, in the preponderance of cases, there were never enough public funds to meet. In addition to these burdens, there were the new county welfare responsibilities suddenly taking form and being thrust upon them.

In the first year of the decade Cimarron hardly knew what public charity meant. A mere $250 was the county's appropriation in that category; compared with the $12,000 spent on paving Boise City streets it was a token acknowledgment that poverty existed in their midst. The thirties, however, stirred the commissioners to greater generosity. Within a year their charity budget jumped to $1500, about half the amount paid in bounties on crows and other animals, and only a little under the county attorney's salary. In July 1933 the charity fund more than doubled, to $3600, widows and orphans getting $1100 of this, the miscellaneous poor who could not qualify for federal work relief requiring the rest. So large had welfare expenses become, and so worrisome to taxpayers, that names of all recipients and the amounts they received appeared in the newspaper for the edification of "those who are supporting this work"—there was little privacy for the poor. In the 1931-35 period Cimarron spent a total of $2.29 per capita on charity, only slightly over the state average, but well above the 5 cents paid out in the poor-white Ozark county of LeFlore. Subsequent welfare budgets reached a rough plateau after 1935: $5320, $6020, and $5410 were representative. With the passage of the Social Security Act in 1935, the county at last began to keep records of its relief efforts, organizing cases under "old age assistance," "aid to the blind," and, after 1938, "aid to families with dependent children." Applications approved for these separate categories totaled 243 from 1936 to 1940, all but ten of them for old-age payments.[27] Considering the condition of the county and the difficulty of collecting public monies, these sizable increases in the welfare program are impressive. That the coming of the black blizzards did not force the county's charity down suggests that the people had decided to accept the necessity of helping the helpless—a resolution from which they would never be able to retreat.

The Dust Bowl relief mosaic, if one stood too close, was a confused scattering of pieces, most of them federal, but mixed with county initiatives and also those of the Red Cross, the American Legion, the Ladies' Aid Society, and the Gloom Chasers Club. Backing off, one could perceive a more coherent, though hastily

Panhandle wheat farmer at a crossroads service station. (*Lange, Library of Congress*)

drawn, picture with several qualities that were found nowhere else in the nation. A sunburned man in bib overalls with his wife and children occupied its center—they were the primary concern of those who gave the aid. Able-bodied, the owner of a tractor, an erstwhile farmer on the make, he was, in his own mind, emphatically not a social parasite, but a hard-working and self-reliant citizen, down on his luck but not on his knees. All he asked was a little something to tide him over—and a lttile rain to settle the dust. Given some help, he would be eager to go about his business again. Toward that end the various relief agencies came into being. Back in the 1890s, when little outside assistance had existed, the southern plains settler had learned that he either had to adapt to nature or leave. The generation that came to plow in the twenties and ate their own dust in the thirties evaded much of that earlier ecological disciplining. They lived in a more humane and protective age that was reluctant to see the poor marginal farmer suffer so grievously for the sins of all. But the aid that came to Cimarron also had a less carefully targeted, less constructive effect. Bolstered by the AAA, WPA, FERA, and the rest (and there was hardly a soul who did not accept something from one of these), the farmer could emerge from his ordeals without having been forced to ask what he and his neighbors had done wrong. Large-scale relief was an unprecedented development, forming a watershed of sorts in the history of the southern plains. It was an advance toward a more organic social order. But it did not produce a turning point in basic economic values; perhaps it even worked against that change.

Roy Butterbaugh, the local newspaper editor, expressed as succinctly as anyone the economic ethos of Cimarron: "We are hard-boiled capitalists." That was the community's message to the world in 1930, and a decade of dust storms and Depression tempered but did not materially alter that self-definition. Panhandle capitalism, to be sure, was from the beginning tinged with a suspicion of big-city financiers and businessmen and a populist defense of small-farmer virtues, but its goal was nonetheless to transform the county's little men—or at least some of them—into great tycoons by and by. As the ambition got buried in the dirt, residents thankfully grabbed whatever aid was dealt out by the federal government; it was time to get some better cards, they decided, if they were to stay in the game. In the 1932 election F.D.R. collected 1887 votes here, Hoover 569. (Hoover, the paper said, "never did offer anything to the common man.") Four years later F.D.R. was still immensely popular in the county, winning, for the second time, 71 per cent of the vote. But almost immediately thereafter Cimarron began its retreat from the moderately leftist New Deal back toward its bedrock, business-centered inclinations. When the voters went to the polls in 1940, they gave Roosevelt 989, Wendell Willkie, 841—a Democratic victory margin of 54 per cent, which was 1 per cent less than the national tally.[28] From being one of Roosevelt's more enthusiastic counties, by the later thirties Cimarron had moved to a lukewarm, sometimes even hostile, position. Once its own crisis of survival began to ease, the Dust Bowl community had little use for social reconstruction at home or anywhere else. Its people began to resent the expensive federal programs that went to other regions and the intrusion of more and more land-use planners in their own lives. The same government that had thrown them a lifeline had become an unwanted impediment to their free enterprise.

In truth, during the thirties there had never been any profound reappraisal of the county's bourgeois values. Only one group in the community openly challenged even a few of the ruling economic ideas—the Townsendites. In May 1935 a group of Boise City elders organized a club to propagate the panacea of California physician Francis Townsend: a 2 per cent "transaction tax" on big businesses that supposedly would finance a "revolving pension fund," giving everyone over sixty years of age $200 a month. Every week the club gathered to hear Ole Showalter's band struggle through a few Christian hymns and John Philip Sousa's marching songs, to play checkers, and to plan together how they would spend their expected pensions—not a likely atmosphere for radical criticism. But when the *News* ran an editorial attack on the club's ideas, arguing that they were a threat to American capitalism, several club members shot back surprisingly fierce letters. "The Old Capital system had reduced us to what we are now," wrote one man; "Do you like it?" The Depression, he argued, had been brought on by "the greed of gain," and so far all the government had done was to save the banks and railroads from self-destruction. Other Townsendites made it clear that they intended to "rejuvenate" the economic system rather than do away with it, but nonetheless theirs were angry voices that stirred up considerable debate on the front page of the newspaper for several months. In the words of the club's president, "the masses have been exploited by the privileged class for the past 100 years." To which the paper's pseudonymous "Slats" replied: "We think Townsendism is a disease that will vanish from among us in a short while." With the coming of the Social Security system, that was precisely what happened; Ole Showalter packed away his trombone and the Townsendites disbanded, content after all to draw their government checks rather than actually repudiate the Cimarron, and American, commitment to private gain.[29]

By 1937, with no one around to argue another view, the *News* began to carry, almost every week, nationally syndicated cartoons portraying politicians as thieves and pickpockets, labor union leaders as nasty thugs, and farmers and small businessmen as victims of both. The old creed of "hard-boiled capitalism" was still in the ascendancy, but apparently it now required more defense. "What is responsible for our world supremacy in the workers' standard of living?" editor Butterbaugh urged his readers to ask. "You can answer that in three words—the capitalist system, which encourages private enterprise." In one cartoon an ugly, barbaric Russian looked enviously at the Americans and their creature comforts. Never mind the soup kitchens, exodusters, and rising tenantry; the United States, it was suggested, enjoyed the good life that its enemies wanted to wreck. The cartoon's congratulatory message was reinforced by these sententious words:

> No more opposite philosophies exist than Communism and Democracy. The guiding principle of the former is rigid state control over the individual under a political dictatorship. Democracy, on the other hand, insures to a free people the free play of individual initiative and rewards commensurate with ability.[30]

When this editorial appeared dust was still blowing across the southern plains, but for the editor the winds of radical ideas had begun to howl more loudly. There was a more important threat appearing than what had happened to the panhandle's soil: a Soviet-style police state that just might be lurking in the United States—even in Oklahoma—under the guise of higher taxes, more government restrictions on farming and business, lowered respect for individual initiative, and utopian social planners. Butterbaugh spoke for the Boise City merchants in particular, but there is no reason to suppose that the surviving county farmers saw things differently. To salvage and defend the old economic order took precedence over all other social aims, including a safer way of using the land.

By the last years of the decade, with better rainfall and less erosion in 1938 and 1940, Cimarron residents congratulated themselves on having handled the disaster so well. Rationalizations of the experience, and a few mythologies, began to be elaborated. Those who had left the area became misfits and ne'er-do-wells—good riddance, some maintained. Losing half of the population had turned out to be a blessing, others said, as there was now more land to go around. Dust Bowl survivors believed that, thanks to their own resoluteness, they were set to enjoy another glorious period of agricultural and commercial growth. But this time around it would be forever: "This new era of prosperity," said the newspaper in 1939, "is working toward its own perpetuation." Grocer Godown believed that "the people who built this country up are still here and expect to stay here and make a go of it. Cimarron County is still the garden spot of the country." As far as the farmers' role in creating, or intensifying, the dusters was concerned, Bill Baker made an indignant retort that echoed a common feeling: the storms had occurred, he insisted, through no real fault of the Cimarron sodbusters, but through the freakish accident of droughty weather. Like tornadoes, dusters were primarily "acts of God," unlikely to strike the same place twice, and the sensible response was to go right back and rebuild what had been torn down.[31] In other words, the millions of dollars this county had cost the federal treasury were all to be charged to nature. Baker's easy sliding over the ecological failure of panhandle agriculture made it clear that the dirty thirties had passed too quickly to produce either a full admission of human responsibility for the black blizzards or a major cultural foundation for a substantially new man-nature relationship. Perhaps that was inevitable: the values a people hold, their notion of success and their way of achieving it, are among the first things to be formed, the last to be reformed. In the midst of disaster the altogether human reaction is to cling even more tightly to those values until there is simply no other choice but to let go or perish. Seven years of Dust Bowl life were evidently not enough to force that last-ditch change. As the forties rolled around, the Cimarron farmer was sure he would soon have the earth back in hand, and he was ready once again to extract from it a long desired, long postponed wealth—to collect a deferred payment on his dreams.

Part IV

HASKELL COUNTY, KANSAS

"Is land in Kansas one-generation land?"

L. E. Willoughby, Kansas
State Agricultural College

Unsettled

GEORGE TATON, who looks at least ten years younger than the seventy-odd he is, still raises wheat on the farmstead his grandfather bought long ago in Haskell County in the southwest corner of Kansas. As he sits at the kitchen table toying with his Prince Albert can, the thought occurs to him: "If everybody had just folded up and stopped trying to plant, Mother Nature would have taken care of settling the dust in about half the time they took to do it."[1] Sunflowers and thistles would have covered the bare earth and held it in place until grass could spread back over its old domain. The $2 billion plus that the federal government had spent on the Great Plains would have gone elsewhere. But then so would Taton, and so would the townspeople who depended upon him. That, he is quick to add, was an unacceptable price to pay to end the storms. It was slower and harder work, and considerably more expensive in tax dollars, to save fields that people were still plowing—to salvage, in other words, the community along with the land. In earlier droughts and economic busts no one had stepped in to try that difficult task. The thirties, however, were a different story, primarily because the government had become more concerned about rural welfare and stability, but also because many plainsmen were not so willing to leave this time.

With the large exception of the exodusters, for whom there was no choice—real or apparent—but to migrate, people in the region had become less mobile than they had been a decade or two earlier. Except in extreme hardship cases, the economic insecurity of the times discouraged their old footloose ways. They feared there was no longer anyplace to go in Depression America for a new start; if there were greener pastures elsewhere, they belonged to somebody else already. And

Chapter Nine

Ground

farmers like Taton, as they jog their memories now, recall feeling an urgent need to achieve permanence in their lives, a desire to stay put rather than go on roaming around in quest of something better. Recovery in human terms, therefore, came to involve not merely restoring the vegetation, but also giving people a chance to hold on. Greater financial security was obviously a major part of that chance, but it was only a part. Recovery also required that a more secure, lasting social order be created, which would come from a larger commitment to place and neighborhood—and in the Dust Bowl that was not going to be easy.

For Cimarron County, in the persistent center of the wind-erosion area and with a massive outflow of residents, the chances of conserving some semblance of social order were low, of course. But in a second tier of counties, forming a kind of ring around the Dust Bowl's center, there ought to have been a more promising situation. In fact, however, community cohesion was difficult to achieve there, too. Haskell County, Kansas, is a case in point. Its main town, Sublette, is a hundred miles northeast of Boise City, putting the county just outside the worst-hit zone. A smaller proportion of its people left in the decade than did in Cimarron. Haskell's agricultural settlement had begun twenty years before the panhandle's had, so that both children and grandchildren had been born here, and in many cases they wanted to remain. There was little cattle ranching left in Haskell by the 1930s; it was almost the pure essence of wheat country, which, it might seem, would have given it, through a more unified economic base, greater social coherence. Notwithstanding all those qualities, this Kansas community was a most unstable place. The reason for this was essentially the kind of farming the county followed, and would not

The main street of Sublette, Kansas, in 1941. (*Irving Rusinow, National Archives*)

give up: a cash-crop system that had proved to be not only destructive to the land, but to the communal order as well. Nowhere on the southern plains was commercial farming more advanced than here. And nowhere, for that matter, were the problems associated with non-resident, speculative ownership, factory monoculture, or self-seeking values more entrenched. Haskell, then, might be taken as indicative of the social distress which that agriculture had created, and of the change, and lack of change, it experienced in those years.

Whatever its yearnings for a place to stand, Haskell County was in a terribly precarious condition, so much so that on two occasions it was selected for federally sponsored research. In the first instance, A. D. Edwards came out to undertake a sociological survey for the Farm Security Administration and Bureau of Agricultural Economics. That survey was published in 1939. Then, in 1942, appeared the second study, written by Earl Bell, also the BAE. Along with the photographer Irving Rusinow, Bell had been sent out to Haskell by Carl Taylor, the BAE's noted rural sociologist, who had chosen it as one of six farm communities to survey. At the top of his list was the Old Order Amish settlement of Lancaster County, Pennsylvania, representing the most firmly rooted of American agricultural groups, and at the bottom was Haskell, included as an example of the extremely unstable communities found in the wheat belt. The combination of drought, dust storms, Depression, and, above all, on-the-make ambitiousness had created in this Kansas county an almost pathological state. Haskell may have had fewer exodusters loading up their jalopies with kettles and blankets than Cimarron did, but in the 1930s there were plenty of other disintegrative elements in its midst.

Nothing of this social instability, however, nor the countervailing urgency to achieve equilibrium, was apparent on the Haskell County map. On the contrary, the geographical dimensions shown there suggested a world of perfect equanimity and control. The county had carved out of the grasslands a perfect box for itself—exactly 24 miles on each side—and inside that box were 580 smaller boxes, all of them full 640-acre sections of land, divided and subdivided into smaller and smaller boxes. Along most of the section lines ran bare dirt roads, as straight as a surveyor could make them on a round earth. This Haskell landscape was the perfected paradigm of the traditional American gridiron, which had been slapped down by land officials over most of the nation west of the Alleghenies.[2] The origins of that system of dividing the country into neat geometrical squares lay in the late eighteenth century's rationalism and its neo-classical ideal of abstract, timeless order. But, ironically, the pattern had always served quite a different array of values— those involved in the rapid turnover of land demanded by a mobile, acquisitive society. It was much easier to buy and sell land when it was conveniently laid out in uniform, interchangeable boxes. To further this process of exchange, every parcel became an arithmetical abstraction, a quantity identified by a number instead of a personality or history: "T 28-S, R 32-W, sw ¼," for example, instead of "the old Briggs place" or "Maidenstone Farm." In Haskell County a farm often was merely a 160-acre expanse of soil, and by that definition a man might be said to operate six or seven farms, none of them carrying any special identity or allowing much emotional attachment. Such a relation was bound to be extremely impermanent, as farmers continually swapped and sold or rented land, always trying to get a more advantageous arrangement to work next year. The very shape of Haskell County, therefore, contained a crucial contradiction. Its regular fence lines and roads conveyed the reassuring message, "Everything is in order here. Man is fully in charge, and his dominion over nature is complete to the point of monotony. All human eccentricities have, like those of the land, been smoothed away, and peace reigns unbroken." Yet all the while the ground underfoot had become in fact a revolving wheel of fortune—affording no place to settle on, no real peace.

It is always a bit jarring to come upon the gridiron plat in a rugged mountain valley or on a river delta. But in southwestern Kansas the squaring impulse of American settlement seems at home, if only because the land here has so little intrinsic order apparent to the eye. At last the will to dominate has come to a place that offers no resistance. As a real-estate ad promised in the 1920s: "A tractor can be driven in a straight line from corner to corner of the county"—or at least it could until the fences went up. The only irregularities in the county's surface are the low sand hills along the Cimarron River in the far southwest corner and those along the northern border that are part of the Arkansas River valley, although the Arkansas itself is almost twenty miles away. So flat is Haskell that there is hardly any drainage, and after heavy downpours the water stands in shallow sinks and depressions. The deep soils that blanket this tableland are among the most fertile in the entire region; 70 per cent of the country is covered by the Richfield-Ulysses soil association—friable silt loams on the surface that are easily cultivated and, at the subsoil level, silty clay loams underlaid by loess.[3] Water erosion can never be

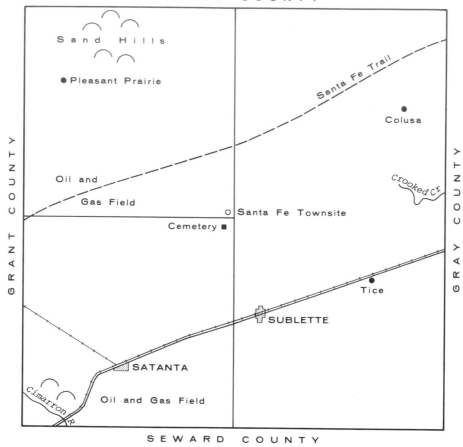

FINNEY COUNTY

Sand Hills

● Pleasant Prairie

Santa Fe Trail

● Colusa

GRANT COUNTY

Oil and

Gas Field

Crooked Cr

GRAY COUNTY

○ Santa Fe Townsite

Cemetery ■

Tice ●

✠ SUBLETTE

▨ SATANTA

Cimarron R

Oil and Gas Field

SEWARD COUNTY

HASKELL COUNTY, KANSAS

1935

0   12

Scale in miles

(Sharon Hagen)

much of a problem here, as it is in more irregular terrain, but the wind blows hard and without stint, always ready to pick up the loose brown earth. In the 1930s Haskell's fields generally did not erode as severely as the sandier areas of Cimarron County did; there was nevertheless considerable wind erosion even of these heavier soils. On some days, in fact, the rigid, man-made pattern of roads and wheat fields disappeared under swirling dirt, and the landscape became a featureless plain, running loose from man's control.

Before it was settled and squared off, the Haskell territory had been one of the most dreaded parts of the "Great American Desert." It was a pathless sea to travel, yet there was no water to drink.[4] However, the land hunger of the home-steaders, who began arriving in 1885, proved to be stronger than their thirst. Within a couple of years 2841 people were living here, nearly all the public domain had been taken up in homesteads, and a new county, named after a state legislator from the area, had been authorized. The earliest wave of settlers came from other parts of Kansas, predominantly, but also from Illinois, Missouri, Ohio, and Indiana, and, in a few cases, from Germany, Canada, and Poland.[5] Instability plagued Haskell from its beginning, as many of the first homesteaders, especially the native-born Americans, began to feel the itch to move not long after they arrived. For instance, the Leander Clifts (one born in Ohio, the other in West Virginia) showed up in late November 1886, and within a month they had constructed a 16-by-22-foot sod house with a board floor and three windows, along with a sod stable for their two mules, horse, cow, and hog. Their only other possessions were a stove and cooking utensils, beds and bedding, a table and chairs, a wagon, a plow, a harrow, and a few small tools. In March 1887 twin boys were born, with a midwife in attendance, and there were then six children altogether. During their one and a half years on the homestead it never rained, and the Clifts hauled water from a well seven miles away, dumped it in their cistern, and, after using it to wash, carefully poured it over the garden, bucketful by bucketful. By the time their land patent had been processed and signed by the President, the Clifts had already moved away, looking for a more rewarding life somewhere else. First they went to Anthony, Kansas, then to Oklahoma in the 1889 land rush, then out to the panhandle, and finally to Washington State, where the father died in 1934.[6]

The wanderings of another old-timer, Pat Murphy, were more circular, beginning in Haskell County and ending there after he too had seen a large chunk of the American West. His parents had come from Missouri to live with a brother on a claim; it was on that farm that Pat was born and lived the first four years of his life. Then the family rolled on to San Diego, California, and there they stayed for two years. At the age of seven Pat lost his mother, and, with his younger brother, he was sent off on the long road back to Haskell, where he lived with his grandmother. Come winter, he was trundled off to LaJunta, Colorado, to go to school. So went the pattern of his youth—yo-yoing back and forth across the plains. Meanwhile, the homestead cabin in which he had been born passed through the hands of one owner after another until it fell apart. By the 1930s Pat Murphy at last knew where he belonged: he had become one of the more solid citizens of Sublette —cashier at the bank, proprietor of a filling station. But even after he had achieved position and comfort he still found it hard to hang his hat in one place for very long. In his mature, settled years he built and lived in three different residences in the town. Out of such restless, rambling pasts Haskell's town fathers came.[7]

Whole towns, as well as homesteaders and their dwellings, appeared and vanished during the early years, like snow melting under the High Plains' sun. All across the region stood the remnants of once hopeful, thriving centers: a darkly weathered hotel left to scampering mice, a tumbledown brick shell that had held calico and harness for sale, or, in many cases, nothing but the ghostly outlines of foundations—former house sites clustered in a pasture. Haskell County sprouted a number of short-lived hamlets—Dalton, Lockport, Colusa, Stowe, Ivanhoe, Santa Fe —none of which survived into the thirties as anything more than a lonely school-house or a memory. At one point, however, Santa Fe, promoted in the usual fashion by speculators, swelled to a town of 1000 inhabitants and waged fierce battle against its rival, Ivanhoe, in a county seat election. So violent ran the emotions that Ivanhoe brought in Bat Masterson and his cronies from Dodge City to keep order. Santa Fe nonetheless won the election and over the next few decades thoroughly eclipsed all its competitors (the town of Ivanhoe was sold to a farmer for $10). Then in 1912, the railroad came through the county, cutting diagonally across the boxes with no respect for symmetry, no regard for Santa Fe's triumph. Eight years later an-other county seat election had to be held, and Sublette, the railroad center, displaced Santa Fe. Entire buildings, along with their inhabitants, migrated southward by wagon, until the old county seat was left with nothing but a gas pump along the highway and wheat growing in its streets. By the beginning of the 1930s the popu-lation of Sublette had grown to 673, although by the end of the decade it had fallen back to 582. The only other town in the county during those years was Sa-tanta, likewise established as a shipping point along the train tracks; it had 508 residents in 1930, only 345 in 1940. Thus, Haskell's two trade centers were as new as any towns in the United States; they were places especially created to service a railroad corporation and to send farm products to distant grain companies. As it turned out, Sublette and Satanta survived where the others had failed, although with nothing like the splendor that had been expected of them.[8]

In 1935, one of the worst years of the black blizzards, there were 2465 peo-ple in the county, slightly less than there had been fifty years earlier. It is a decep-tively static figure. In the first place, the population of the county had experienced a volatile up and down movement over those decades, declining sharply to 434 in 1899, then rising to a high of 2804 in 1930. Moreover, many of the 1935 residents were newcomers; in each of the first few decades of Haskell's history the turnover rate had exceeded one family in every two, and a large number of those on hand in the thirties had only recently chugged into the county from points east. Of the 461 farm operators in the county in 1930, 200 had arrived within the preceding five years. Most of them were not impoverished Leander Clifts, but people of means, bringing with them bundles of cash to buy land and machines. But after the pros-perous years were left behind, the turnover rate diminished. Fewer people left and far fewer came in. Haskell lost slightly over 700 people in the thirties, or one-

Santa Fe depot at Satanta, built in the mid-1930s. The grain elevators are more recent. (*Author*)

quarter of its 1930 population. Admittedly, it was a substantial outflow. But it was not so massive as it had been in that other time of pinch and squeeze, the 1890s, nor was it so turbulent a mobility as that of the latter half of the flush 1920s, when three times as many farmers entered the county as had in the first half of the 1930s and a higher number (28 per cent) had left.[9]

In the dust years, after struggling through an unsteady past, Haskell County's citizens were drifting toward an even more unpredictable future. In the majority of cases they responded with a determination to last it out—or, as one man put it, to stay around simply to see what would happen. Some of them, chastened and wearied by adversity, wanted nothing more than to hold onto their homes and live modestly in them. By itself, this yearning for stability or permanence could not rescue the Kansas community from nine inches of rainfall a year or from dirt-laden winds that cut the tops off the young wheat. Under such circumstances, that conserving mood required a substantial supplement of federal aid before it could begin to be truly effective. Nonetheless, it was potentially a valuable resource, and in the long run it was one of the most important ingredients needed for establishing man-nature harmony on the plains. The question was whether in Haskell or anywhere else in the region there was a sufficient supply of this kind of thinking to do the job. Was there enough of a conserving interest to overcome the strong de-stabilizing traits in Haskell's culture? According to sociologist Earl Bell, who spent many months observing the county, the answer was no. "People who had come solely to exploit the land of its wealth," he wrote, "had not put down the strong roots of land ownership, long occupation, and community stability."[10] That description covered most of the county's residents; it summed up succinctly the underlying problem in this Dust Bowl community. There was here, from the beginning of settlement until the thirties, a transient, exploitative relation with the land that tore loose every attachment that appeared. Haskell could not have it both ways. Its people could not keep up forever the drive for expanding and getting ahead and still expect to find a settled place on the earth.

The Wheat Farmer

IN THE LONG SHADOW of a grain elevator Haskell County conducted its business. Trucks lined up at harvest time to have their loads of wheat weighed on the elevator scales, then augered into the waiting silos. For the rest of the year the place was quiet, almost deserted, save now and then a farmer would stop by in his idle months for a friendly chat, or a few boxcars would fill up with wheat destined for a flour mill. But after harvest, in the silent part of the year, the grain dealer would sit in his office at the foot of the drab gray cylinders and play the most important game of all—watching for the right moment to sell, for the few pennies' increase on which Haskell's solvency might depend. In other rural communities of the world farmers plowed and buyers haggled in the shadow of silver-roofed cathedrals or gilded pagodas. But in Haskell, trade, not religion, dominated the skyline. The soaring elevator, visible against the horizon well before any other human structure came into view, told the visitor immediately what this county believed in and worked for—"cash grains." Grain as cash, grain as the link to a money-based economy, an international web of commerce, an urban-industrial world's needs and rewards. The stark, functional lines of the wheat elevator, barren of all whimsy or ornament, were the purest symbols of an agriculture run on modern business lines.[1]

There were seven elevators in Haskell County by 1931, some of them constructed of concrete and others of tin, all of them snuggled against the railroad tracks at Sublette, Satanta, and Tice, the last of which was no more than the elevator itself. In that same year every one of those storage facilities was full, and excess wheat lay heaped along the tracks and in farmyards. Forty-nine per cent of

and the Welfare State

the county's land produced wheat that year—181,525 acres, a thousandfold increase over the 184 acres cultivated in 1888. There were 3.5 million bushels to sell. It would have been a veritable bonanza, had not every other wheat-producing county in America, and foreign producers, too, increased their output simultaneously. And had not consumers decided they wanted to eat more fruit and vegetables and less bread. Instead of enjoying dazzling profits, Haskell's farmers faced a glut of disastrous proportions. The bushel price plunged to less than 25 cents immediately after harvest and averaged only 33 cents over the year, the lowest in the county's history, and well under the $1.48 it had been when the great plow-up began in 1925. Wheat-growers talked of "strike"—of withholding their crops from market, or feeding them to hogs, until the price rose back to at least the break-even point.[2]

Only two years later the elevators stood almost empty. In 1933, because of the onset of drought and blowing dust, Haskell produced a mere 89,500 bushels: only 5 per cent of the county's total area had a stand of wheat and only 24 per cent had any crop at all. The price of wheat climbed to 71 cents a bushel, but farmers without a crop were no better off than when they had had to pile a surplus on the ground. Either situation was a threat to financial and community stability. In the past the rapid movement of people in and out had been Haskell's major social problem; now it was the extreme oscillation of yields, markets, and prices, a condition due in some part to a capricious environment, in larger part to aggressive agricultural expansion and consequent land misuse. For the Dust Bowl period the extent of the county's crop failure and loss of income appears in Table I. Some of the effects of these barren years on Haskell farms are suggested by Table II's data.[3]

Closed by drought and depression. Windows are covered with glasscloth to keep out the dust. (*National Archives*)

Haskell farmers felt an attraction for wheat, as Table I illustrates, that a mere decade of adversity could not overcome. When the drought broke in 1941 they were once more queuing up at the elevators to sell their grain, this time getting better prices. Some field-crop diversification occurred in 1932, 1933, 1935, and 1936, when more acres were put to the hardy sorghums than wheat, but it did not last. No pronounced shift toward a livestock economy took place, either; the number of beef cattle flipflopped from over 4000 in 1931 to a low of 1894 in 1936 back to almost 5000 in 1939. The county remained a wheat empire simply because, when the conditions were right, wheat paid a higher return per acre than anything else, and because Haskell's farmers remained at heart gamblers willing to risk all for that one good roll of the dice. For the pure cash-grain operator a row crop like sorghum, although a safer bet year after year, not only did not pay enough, it also required too much work, plus an implement or two he did not have. So firm was his preference for wheat that, in the words of Earl Bell, the farmer would plant that seed "regardless of how satisfactory the moisture may be and how unlikely the chance of a crop"—and then expect a miracle.[4]

Over most of the southern two-thirds of Haskell County, specialized commercial wheat growing was the dominant pattern, and it remained so. But in the sandier soils of the north lived a few farm families who diversified. Wheat was their chief interest, too; however, they also raised sweet and grain sorghums or Sudan grass to feed the Herefords they kept. While the all-out wheat specialist despised chickens and a milking herd, these northern farmers did not, perhaps be-

Table I: Crops Income

	Precipitation at Sublette	Winter Wheat Harvested	Total Yield	Wheat Market Value	Other Field Crops	Animal Products	Total Farm Income*
	in.	acres	bu.				
1930	24.29	171,280	1,712,800	$1,061,936	$138,202	$210,890	$1,411,028
1931	12.47	181,525	3,448,975	1,034,693	59,016	185,646	1,279,355
1932	16.54	47,552	332,864	99,859	103,455	127,122	330,436
1933	11.24	17,900	89,500	71,600	241,025	107,480	420,105
1934	11.05	78,997	394,985	343,637	57,309	112,444	513,390
1935	12.01	47,390	189,560	181,978	179,629	188,150	549,757
1936	12.82	34,215	171,075	181,340	123,931	115,973	421,244
1937	11.24	70,500	282,000	298,900	62,077	174,484	535,461
1938	18.34	82,320	510,400	285,900	66,540	135,287	487,727
1939	9.68	107,000	449,000	305,300	29,144	306,620	641,064
1940	11.21	113,000	746,000	462,500	190,830	207,980	861,310
1941	25.63	160,600	2,040,000	1,917,600	155,855	487,550	2,561,005

* Excluding government payments.

Table II: Changes in Farm Units

	Number of Farms*	Average Size	Farms with Beef Cattle	Average Farm Value	Tenant Operators	Tractors
1930	461	672 acres	286	$25,770	213 (46%)	423
1935	429	692	318	16,009	201 (47%)	486
1940	423	748	254	13,728	210 (50%)	401

* "Farm" has its traditional meaning here: all the land in the county under the management and/or ownership of a single individual or corporation.

cause they had so much at stake. They were most likely to be owners of the land they worked, and residents on it, whereas the cash-crop man rented some or all of his fields, often lived a long way off from them, and developed little attachment to a particular piece of earth. Four or five quarters was generally understood to be the optimum for managing a diversified unit, but the wheat specialist had no upper limit on his land hunger, except that imposed by the available machinery. One was an older and often less prosperous style of agriculture that had evolved slowly out of the pioneer era; the other was the newer system of mass production for high profits. In the thirties it was clear which type of farming was better adapted to the region's cycles—which kind of operator had fewer debts accumulated, could more readily pay his taxes, feed his children without government relief, keep the soil in place, hold the community together. "The diversified farmer," observed Bell, "is more steady, remains at home more, attends meetings more frequently, is more co-operative, more neighborly, and much less speculative."[5] It was a lesson, however, that other federal agents, not to mention the county's own inhabitants, in the end ignored.

One of the major obstacles to farmstead diversification was the high percentage of non-resident operators in Haskell—people who lived too far away to carry on the daily, year-round tasks of milking, cultivating row crops, and turning cattle out into the young wheat to graze. Almost one-third of the farm units were operated by people who did not live in the county, and usually had never lived here. It was not as large a percentage as in Greeley or Morton counties, but it was large enough to have a powerful impact on local practices. About a dozen Haskell farmers did not even live in the state of Kansas: they were all operators, not mere owners, who had to plant and harvest every year, and list against the prevailing winds in dry springs and summers. Ninety more non-residents lived within the state, but they might live 50 miles to the northeast, in Dodge City, or almost 200 miles east, in Wichita. More often than not, these suitcase farmers were big landowners who used the most mechanized methods they could find; a Garden City man farmed 49 quarters, and the Collingwood Corporation worked hundreds of quarters in Haskell and elsewhere in the southwestern corner of the state. Altogether, non-residents owned *two-thirds* of Haskell's land area. They had a plausible defense in economic terms. Almost all of them had other sources of income, so that they could fail in Haskell wheat but could still make a living from a bank, an auto-repair shop, or another farm outside of the Dust Bowl. But unquestionably, this kind of risk-spreading diversification divided rather than consolidated their loyalties to the land and the community. To a lesser extent this was also true among operators who lived in Sublette or Satanta—"sidewalk farmers," they were called—numbering about 60 in the latter part of the decade. The majority of this second class of non-residents also ran town businesses; for example, Frank McCoy, who owned a large elevator, also farmed many thousands of acres over the county. For both types of non-residents—out-of-county and town farmers—a more balanced, cautious agriculture that de-emphasized wheat was out of the question. Virtually none of them was interested in land as a home for themselves and their children; to them it was solely an instrument to make cash.[6]

No one had worried much about this increase in specialized one-crop farming, and its non-residency correlative, during plush times. But when the fields began to drift and there was no one there to stop them, when one out of every three farmers could seldom attend county meetings, Haskell began to reconsider its economic direction. Perhaps there had been too much enthusiasm for the busi-

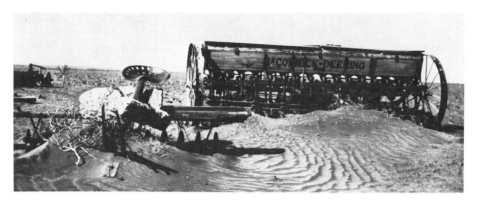

Mechanized farming in the spring of 1935. (*Kansas State Historical Society*)

nesslike approach to farming and too little concern for safeguarding traditional community values. The *Sublette Monitor* (which in 1933 was judged the best weekly newspaper in Kansas) put those second thoughts into print:

> Farms have become [*sic*] to be considered too much as business ventures, yielding good and easy returns. Mass and mechanized farming loomed like an ogre over the homely virtues and gratifications that legendarily belonged to the farm. Drive the tractor day and night! Buy more land because machinery can be financed to farm it! But it's different today. . . . Profits will be welcome, of course, but this is not the day to put profits ahead of home.

A return to the old style of families living on their land and caring for the fate of their community, the paper argued, would give Haskell a more secure base. Later the *Monitor* repeated State Extension Director Harry Umberger's warning that agriculture had a social side that had been widely neglected in the great plow-up: "the farm," according to Umberger, "is more than a factory for food and fiber."[7] Whether the mere expression of such sentiments showed a genuine change in plains agriculture is, of course, open to question. Historically, some of the nation's most outspoken advocates of progressive business farming had also repeatedly praised the moral qualities of a disappearing rural life. One can at least say that in the 1930s there was in southwestern Kansas a deepening sense of conflict between those two ideals. And one can find examples where the conflict was resolved in favor of saving the old way, as when the Kansas legislature in 1931 forbade the further chartering of farm corporations in the state—an action that would have been thought "bolshevist" in any other part of the economy.[8] But the change to an impersonal, commercialized relation with the earth, and its attendant social consequences, did not depend exclusively on the corporate farm. As yet there were only a score of farm corporations in the state, but there were plenty of people who operated on similar assumptions and by similar methods. These capitalist-minded individuals were still permitted the freedom to live where they chose, to own as much land as they liked, to plant whatever they wanted, and to pursue gain without much hindrance. De-emphasizing the business spirit in farming required, along with the right sentiments, sweeping changes in private property rights—a more determined assertion of communal control over how the land was held and how it was used. And despite many misgivings and complaints, by 1940 Haskell had shown itself to be unable—and unwilling—to make those changes.

Although this Dust Bowl community did not reverse the commercial drift, it did accept other changes that made farming a very different enterprise from what it had been before the thirties. These other developments came from the federal government, and in their sum they amounted to a new welfare-state existence for the Haskell farmer, whether he was big or small, market-oriented or semisubsistent. The welfare state, created in the main by Roosevelt's New Deal, basically was a government that used its power and resources to protect people from getting trampled in the competitive jungle of free enterprise—the aged, the unemployed, the migrant workers. Farmers all over the country claimed, often justifiably, that they had much in common with those hapless victims and that Washington ought to be giving them a helping hand, too, so they themselves would not be ground under. So attentive were New Deal planners, as well as the President and Congress, to this plea that agriculture became one of the welfare state's most important concerns. In fact, saving the American farmer was, to many officials, the key to saving the entire society from Depression and injustice—"agricultural fundamentalism," the stance was termed, meaning help the farmers first and everyone would be better off.[9] The people of Haskell County thoroughly agreed with that sense of priorities. Accepting the welfare state's support, however, involved a partial but significant substitution of the government office for the grain elevator and marketplace in the county's life.

It may seem ironic that wheat farmers in Kansas, who had become so fully a part of the economic system, would want protection from its penalties for failure. But the experiences of overproduction and dust storms were sufficiently traumatic to produce a revised maxim for business farming in the decade: do not interfere with us when we are making money, but rescue us when we are going bankrupt. To be sure, they were not alone in their fear of the root-hog-or-die ethic. As Undersecretary of Agriculture M. L. Wilson observed, "Underlying all the wants and needs of people today is an overwhelming desire for security"—which in translation read, put no ceiling over our heads, but build an income floor under our feet.[10] Americans had tasted just enough affluence not to want to lose it, even where they were most devoted to a gambling way of life. The public cost of economic security, however, came high, in the case of agriculture amounting to about $1.4 billion a year by

1940. It was at that time the largest single item in the federal budget. That amount of various kinds of government assistance to the nation's farmers added, by A. Whitney Griswold's calculations, 10 per cent to the consumer's grocery bill.[11] Clearly, farmers proved to be immensely successful in persuading the rest of the nation to pay for their protection, while, in the case of wheat entrepreneurs, preserving their self-aggrandizing ideology intact.

New Deal agriculture was the composite of too many individuals and programs to have a single end in view. For a large number of USDA bureaucrats the main goal was, as it had been since the 1920s, simply to enable the commercial farm sector to compete more successfully with manufacturing—to achieve the old parity level of rural purchasing power. To this circle, "agriculture" tended to become a monolithic abstraction; in their view all farmers, regardless of their size or assets, ought to be aided by subsidies, because all farmers labored at a disadvantage compared with their better organized industrial counterparts. In contrast, there were other officials who concentrated on the rural poor, of whom there were millions, and called for more directly targeted programs to help them survive. There was no end of conflict between the two groups. But running through much of the New Deal's agricultural thinking, as it did through Haskell County's, was a more unifying, if ambiguous, theme: the image and ideal of the family farm. An overwhelming majority of the country's 6 million farms were still family operations, although some of those families were considerably wealthier than others. A central ambition in the Roosevelt program was to keep as many families on the land as possible. The motives in that effort were, of course, not only undiscriminating, but parochial—to halt in this one area of the economy the movement toward concentration of power. Although the twentieth-century family farm was usually not the subsistence unit it had been in an earlier age, it still represented old hopes for preserving a virtuous, small-scale, decentralized society. New Dealers evoked a warm response from Americans whenever they talked of saving family-based agriculture, even if it meant, as M. L. Wilson admitted it might, the sacrifice of "maximum commercial productiveness." But that painful choice, he and others were confident, would not be required; the family farm could both operate as a modern, efficient business and also remain the country's chief defense against the corporate, industrial takeover. On the safeguarding of this traditional yet modernized agricultural institution, then, the welfare state expended much of its energy and imagination.[12]

The defense was not limited to rhetorical flourishes; out in Haskell County many family farmers were indeed rescued from quicksand by government programs. The most important hands extended were those of the AAA and the rural rehabilitation campaign. In scale and community impact the Agricultural Adjustment Administration dwarfed everything else Washington did for the region. It was not designed specifically for the Dust Bowl; in fact, it aimed to do for the nation precisely what the southern plains through most of the thirties did *not* need to have done—cut back crop production instead of increasing it. Yet the AAA above all was a source of money, and plainsmen found that they could get it as readily as anyone.

After 1931, outside the drought states, American farmers continued to grow more wheat, corn, hogs, tobacco, and cotton than the markets could absorb, either at home or abroad; consequently, commodity prices sagged below operating expenses and stayed there. That ill-fed and ill-clothed people existed in the world, unable to enter the marketplace and bid on these products, was obvious. The AAA solution, however, was to concentrate on the producer's plight, not the would-be consumer's, by a plan of systematic, federally supervised decreases in leading commodities until supply matched "effective" (which is to say, backed up with cash) demand. "Planned scarcity," its critics called it—and they were absolutely right. But not being ready to restructure drastically the distribution of wealth in the United States, let alone in the world, Roosevelt's advisers decided that only a retrenchment policy could stave off a merciless economic war from which some Standard Oil of agriculture would emerge victorious, with power to control production and set prices wherever it chose. Established in the spring of 1933 to prevent that from happening, the AAA proved to be so immensely popular among farmers that something very like it had to be kept in action not only through the decade, but over the next forty years.[13]

Although a cutback program was on the face of it absurd in a region where not much was growing, Haskell farmers did not waste time laughing. The government did not care whether your prospects for a crop were good or bad, so long as you agreed not to plant some of your fields. Haskell farmers therefore signed up *en masse;* 99 per cent of the county's operators—and in five townships it was 100 per cent—made contracts with the AAA by mid-September 1933. Under the terms of the contract they agreed to plant that fall, and for the next two years, only the acreage allowed them by Secretary of Agriculture Henry Wallace. In the first year the maximum permitted was 85 per cent of the base acreage each farmer had been assigned, which was an average of what he had been seeding in the preceding 3 years, 1930-32. For instance, if a farmer had planted 300 acres in each of those years, that amount would again be his base acreage under the contract, and he could plant only 255 acres of wheat this time around. Only those who had seeded wheat in one or all of the preceding years could qualify for the program. In exchange for leaving some of his ground idle, or putting it to some other use, the farmer earned a payment from Washington. But that was calculated according to the number of bushels of wheat he would probably harvest the next summer, a figure again derived from earlier yields. If the farmer had been raising an average of 15 bushels to the acre in the boom years, then his 1934 yield on the reduced acreage was projected to be 3825 bushels. Now came the higher mathematics: every wheat farmer was granted an allotment or share of the domestic market, which was 54 per cent of the recent nationwide production. The AAA would pay only for these allotment bushels—that part of the harvest which would be consumed in the United States. Haskell's benefit payments were set in the 1933 contracts at 28 cents for each allotment bushel. In our hypothetical case, where the 54 per cent allotment would equal 2066 bushels, the payment would come to $578. All of the farmer's wheat could be sold at the elevator, while at the same time he could draw this income supplement on the allotted bushels.[14]

In a year like 1935, when 700 Haskell farmers harvested only 47,000 acres, or 67 acres apiece, there was a super-abundance of land on each farm that could be set aside, and little chance that anyone would try to work it surreptitiously. Nevertheless, committees that were appointed in each township traveled about to check on the accuracy of all allotments and acreages so that no one could defraud the government by reaping where, supposedly, he had not planted. The quantities of money involved made some kind of supervision necessary. During the first two years of AAA, Haskell collected just under $1 million in government wheat checks ("do not fold, perforate, or deface," they read), and in 1936 the average benefit received was $812 per operator. It was a tidy sum of cash for not doing a thing—more money, in fact, than millions of Americans could scrape together to live on each year, more money than a Haskell schoolteacher or minister might make. No wonder the county's farmers were outraged in January 1936, when the Supreme Court declared that the AAA's financing method—a tax imposed on food processors—was unconstitutional. It was "the greatest economic disillusionment in the history of the county," complained the *Sublette Monitor*. Roosevelt immediately rushed through a replacement program, the Soil Conservation and Domestic Allotment Act, which paid farmers out of general revenues for following soil-building practices on surplus acreage instead of planting wheat or cotton. The AAA label, however, was too popular to abandon; in 1938 Congress passed a new Agricultural Adjustment Act with more complex acreage restrictions and benefit payments than ever, although the benefits were still paid directly by the federal treasury. Under the first of these two replacement programs Haskell County did not do as well as it had done, getting only $340,000 in 1937. But the sign-up rate was again 99 per cent in that year. Sensing that his constituents had abruptly opted for federal assistance, the Republican Congressman from the area, Clifford Hope, who had voted against the original AAA, leaped on the New Deal farm wagon with remarkable agility. With his help in redrawing the subsidies, the Haskell farmers took in $670,983 during 1939—compared with $641,064 they earned in the marketplace.[15]

The subsidy-paying public assumed that for its money it was getting substantial crop reduction, but in fact the AAA and its successors—like the New Deal generally—did not go far enough to achieve its own goals. In 1933 Kansas cut its total wheat acreage not 15 per cent, but only 11.4. While almost all of the southwestern

Kansas farmers signed contracts and followed them, those in the eastern part of the state saw that they would have a better chance if they stayed out of the federal programs. They had not been planting enough wheat in past years to qualify for high base acreages and allotments; now, with their competitors under restriction, they rushed in, hoping to grab the market. By 1936 Kansas had more wheat planted than it had had at any time in its history.[16] Nationally, the wheat crop was temporarily reduced in the thirties, but that was due more to environmental distress than the government's measures. When those adverse conditions eased in 1938, wheat production soared to 962 million bushels, the second largest crop ever, and prices slid down again.[17] Nor did all the New Deal subsidies really improve most farmers' position in the economy: in 1938 farm people constituted 25 per cent of the population, but they received, after several years of public assistance, only 8 per cent of the national income, and as a whole they were slipping further behind each year.[18] The AAA approach, whether right or wrong in what it attempted, fell far short of success. It did not improve the lot of the large number of poor, marginal farmers, nor did it control effectively the big, well-capitalized growers.

Although within Haskell County the AAA was easily the most important stabilizing force in the decade, giving family after family the chance to stay on the farm and in the community, farmers had some legitimate complaints about the program's design and administration. Most important, the AAA amounted simply to freezing the economic status quo. Those who were large-scale operators got large-scale benefits, while small-scale farmers who risked going to the poorhouse got very little. The president of the Santa Fe State Bank in Sublette, for example, raked in $4270 on his 1933 contract, while a Mennonite man living on a 160-acre farm got $23.[19] Part of the gap was due to a difference in holdings; but it was also the result of the AAA formula, which, following its 1930-32 base acreage clause, paid the one-crop wheat specialist, who had always put most of his land in cash grain, more than the diversified farmer. Therefore, those who had been most devoted to all-out commercial production were rewarded, not penalized, by this government program, including, especially, the non-resident entrepreneurs. And to keep the benefits coming, one had to stay in the wheat business—keep planting that crop regardless of what it did to the land. A western Kansan, galled by this continuing discrimination against small-scale operators who commonly followed diversified management, wrote to Senator Arthur Capper in 1939:

> I don't think it is fair that the big speculator has so much land to farm and the small farmer has to curtail production until he scarcely has a living left. . . . Why can't the little fellow on the family sized farm who has no other means of making a living receive a nice benefit payment if he curtails production and let the big speculator work out his own salvation.[20]

It was indeed a strange program that sought to keep families on the land and safe from predatory competition, yet helped most those who least needed it. Without question, much more could have been accomplished for Haskell's social and ecological welfare if the same amount of money had been given only to those who actually lived in the county, left part of their land in grass, and were in genuine danger of failing.

That poor rural families got inadequate help from the AAA was manifested in the local work relief rolls, where the names of many farmers could be found. Beginning in November 1934, the Kansas Emergency Relief Administration, following federal advice, paid some of those farmers a subsistence grant to work on their own places and showed them how, with additional loan money, to improve their fields, houses, and equipment. It was part of a national rehabilitation campaign "to assist destitute farm families and other families residing in rural areas to become self-supporting and independent of emergency relief aid." Within a few months 85 Haskell farmers were getting such attention.[21] In April 1935 a new Resettlement Administration, with Rexford Tugwell at its head, was created to bring all state rehabilitation programs under a more unified federal direction. Tugwell at first envisioned a sweeping land reform that would remove poorer families from submarginal regions and set them up on better farms elsewhere—an idea that hardly anyone liked, especially the big farmers, who feared new competition. Under constant attack for his alleged radicalism, "Rexford the Red" left the government, and in 1937 Congress established, under the Farm Tenant Act, a replacement agency for the RA—the Farm Security Administration, whose job it was to find a cure for rural poverty that would neither cost much money nor disturb the peace. The FSA, modest though it was, lasted only a decade before its political enemies finally got enough muscle to axe it. Unlike the AAA, special welfare for the bottom class of farmers was as popular as ants at a picnic.[22]

Receiving a government wheat check was soon accepted in Haskell County as a legitimate right—an overdue subsidy owed to farmers in compensation for all the swag collected by railroads and manufacturers. To accept any kind of loan from the FSA, on the other hand, was viewed as slightly undesirable—a sign of incompetence.[23] The simple reason for the distinction was that while almost every farmer got a wheat payment, only a minority took FSA help. Some in that minority were tenants trying to buy their own farms but unable to obtain credit even from the Federal Land Bank. As Fred Hammer, who applied for a loan to purchase some land near Satanta, explained: "I feel a man with a family should have a permanent home to build to. I feel as long as I am a tenant there is a moving day ahead."[24] Fifty per cent of Haskell's resident operators were tenants by 1940, although it must be added that many of them preferred that status over ownership, which had its burdens. A tenant in southwestern Kansas might be a desperately poor man hanging on

Daughter of a tenant farmer. (*Rusinow, National Archives*)

to a living by the skin of his teeth, or he might be a wheat speculator who liked to put his capital into tractors and combines rather than land. For someone in the first category renting was a one-way road down, until the FSA and its 3 per cent loans came along. It was by no means a large enough program to change American tenure patterns; nationally, in 1940 only 2 of every 100 tenants had an FSA purchase loan. But it was the government's first effort to reverse a long-term trend toward a two-class agriculture. And it was, among other farmers and the general public, the most acceptable part of the FSA's work.

More sharply criticized—because it made competition for the already successful—was the rural rehabilitation program, with its special southern plains addendum, unit reorganization. It was here the government entered more completely into a family's life and, unavoidably, marked them as not quite competent to manage their own affairs. Along with an operating loan of $200 to $600, and perhaps an emergency cash grant of $20 now and then, the FSA gave technical instruction to its clients: how to farm more efficiently, what crops to plant and when, how to make clothes for the children—all useful information—as part of a farm plan drawn up by government advisers. Easily the most successful part of the average plan was a "live-at-home" scheme for raising more of the family's food and producing some cream and eggs for sale. During 1937 over 8000 farmers in the Dust Bowl participated in rural rehabilitation; in Haskell County that year it was as high as one in every five resident farm families.[25] For a much smaller number, and more in some other counties than in Haskell, FSA supervisors reorganized farms to give them a larger, diversified base. Typically, a dusted-out farmer who normally kept his section or two in wheat would be loaned enough to get long-term leases on surrounding fields, bringing his total unit up to 2000 or more acres; most of this then would be regrassed to support a herd of cattle. It was, in the view of Roy Kimmel, federal coordinator for the southern plains region, an effort to move away from the wheat fixation and back toward John Wesley Powell's "pasturage farm" ideal. By 1940 there were 400 reorganized FSA units in the region—over half of them in southeastern Colorado.[26] Though often stigmatized as charity cases, these rehabilitation clients now had a more secure hold on the land than before and a better understanding of the land's capabilities than many of their heavily AAA-subsidized neighbors.

The entry of these rural welfare programs into Haskell's life brought into being, in some ways, a new kind of agriculture. Every resident farmer became, under the pressure of circumstances, a unionist of sorts, working with those around him to keep afloat. All over the county there were new committees inspecting farms, disbursing funds, and writing reports. A branch of the American Farm Bureau Federation, which represented commercial growers politically, was formed, and it had 261 charter members. In 1934 the county had to hire its first extension agent to explain and administer federal programs. Many balked at all the advice and restrictions they suddenly had to submit to; it was often farm wives who proved most receptive to the changes and dragged their reluctant husbands to meetings. But community action and involvement among local farmers, although not an unfamiliar experience, took a big step forward during the 1930s, even if it largely amounted to pressure-group organizing.[27]

As for saving the family farm, upon which Haskell rested so much of its hope, there was a mixed result. The names on the mailboxes, where there had been any, remained by and large the same through all the black blizzards and crop disasters. By decade's end the Snellbachers, Moores, Tatons, Preedys, and Blairs were still working the land as families, and they would go on doing so for some time to

A jackrabbit drive employing chickenwire and clubs. Often several thousand animals were killed on such drives—brutal, bloody affairs that were necessary, farmers argued, to save their meager crops. (*Kansas State Historical Society*)

come. Haskell, therefore, had weathered, with outside support, its most trying years and had emerged with more continuity and stability than ever before. This time there would be no new influx of settlers who had neither a well-developed commitment to the place nor any experience with wresting a living from its peculiar environment. In these regards the family base of the community had survived better than anyone had dared expect.

But there was a negative outcome too, which on balance was decisive. The threat to Haskell's social order came from something more than dust and drought: namely, all the disintegrative forces—attitudes as well as institutions—associated with commercial farming. In this frantic, hardscrabble period, when salvage, not expansion, was all that could be expected, the advance of large-scale business agriculture had come to a halt. But its underlying ethos—in particular, its devotion to extracting higher and higher profits out of the plains—merely lay dormant, ready to spring to life when the rains fell again. During this dormancy it was easier to talk about merging the business notion of success with the family farm ideal, but afterward such an amalgamation became far more problematic.

The Haskell farmer, observed Earl Bell in 1942, "believes himself to be as much a businessman as a manufacturer is."[28] Yet somehow the farmer also expected to avoid the fate of family-owned and family-operated enterprises in the manufacturing world. Nothing in the AAA, which was government's major agricultural program, encouraged him to think differently. Nothing helped him to confront his basic dilemma: whether a business-run farm was truly compatible with traditional small-scale communal values. Nothing in any of the federal activities altered much the system of non-resident tenure, factory-like monoculture, and market speculation that had dominated the county. Not only did it fail to induce these changes, the emerging welfare state actually prevented their occurring. In the main it propped up an agricultural economy that had proved itself to be socially and ecologically erosive.

MAN'S ADAPTATION to nature is never merely a matter of technical understanding and inventiveness. If it were, then the most highly advanced cultures in terms of science and machinery would also be the most well fitted to their environments. In fact, those cultures are among the least well adapted in the world; their prowess encourages a disregard of natural limits more than the qualities of respect and restraint do. Living within the ecological order requires knowledge, of course, and appropriate technology, but more important is the capacity to feel deeply the contours of that order and one's part in it. When both the identity of self and of community become indistinguishable from that of the land and its fabric of life, adaptation follows almost instinctively, like a pronghorn moving through sagebrush. Houses and fields, tools and traditions, grow out of the earth with all the fitness of grass; they belong in their place as surely as any part of nature does. This is genuine adaptation, and it implies much more than shallow managerial skill. It comes from having a sense of place, which is at once a perception of what makes a piece of land function as it does and a feeling of belonging to and sharing in its uniqueness. Because man is a social animal, that sense is a group faculty as well as an individual one—indeed, it is the community that is the principal adaptive unit. The sense of place, therefore, is a complex adaptiveness in which the self reflects the community and the community reflects the natural system, and out of these interdependencies emerges a peculiar cultural ecology.

The movement of dust on the southern plains in the thirties argued forcibly that the people of the region had not achieved that sense of place and the environmental adaptation it produces. There had not been enough time for those things to

Chapter Eleven

of Place

develop—for a slow absorption into the landscape to be completed—and there never would be. From the beginning communities such as Haskell had been wide open to all the uprooting influences of modernizing America, including its mobility, its drive toward affluence, and its enthusiasm for technological change. Haskell's openness to those external influences had created an amazingly cosmopolitan rural mind that took considerable pride in its progressiveness and lack of provinciality. But in looking so eagerly to other places for guidance Haskell's inhabitants failed to pay much attention to the earth under their feet. It was not simply that they brought with them Eastern notions of how to handle their new farms, thereby failing to adjust themselves to the semiarid plains.[1] More important was the fact that they had their sights fixed on an urban world of markets, fashions, and living standards. By the 1920s they were firmly caught up in that distant whirligig; they paced much of their lives by its rhythms, not by the self-contained, self-generated rhythms of their own community. This outward-looking stance was part and parcel of the highly commercialized agriculture they adopted. Since the Dust Bowl years did not bring a change in that economic base, there could be no escape from the magnetic, disruptive influences of America's metropolitan culture.

Walking along the streets of Sublette during the thirties, one could have felt those external magnets pulling on every hand. At the north end of the main avenue, Inman Street, sat the new Santa Fe railroad depot, where passengers waited for the train to Kansas City or Chicago, and boxcars, loaded with fresh fruit and vegetables, Post Toasties and Postum, factory-made work shoes and tractor tires, waited to be emptied. Across the highway intersection was a Mobil station, pumping

Haskell County's cemetery. (*Rusinow, National Archives*)

gas refined in east Texas. Cars and trucks buzzed up and down Inman the day long: farmers coming to the courthouse to pick up their wheat checks, housewives heading for the IGA store, a delivery truck rattling its Coca-Cola bottles. Chain stores, franchised dealers, and advertising slogans all testified to the dependent role Sublette had come to play in the national economy. Like other communities, large and small, it was convinced it had to have all the products the external world offered for sale; there was not much inner resistance to the magnets. Consequently, by the thirties very little that was for sale in the town was produced at home. Even much of the bread that the people of Sublette ate came from outside, made from wheat raised in some other place.

Sublette thus had an astonishingly urban way of life, although according to federal census standards neither it nor Satanta counted enough population to qualify as an urban place. The minimum required was 2500—many times more than either settlement could muster. Both were therefore technically classified as agricultural villages, serving as nuclei for the rural community around them and basing their economy strictly on that function.[2] Their fate, unlike that of Wichita or New York City, was immediately tied to the land. Sunburned farmers sitting in Murph's Café eating chicken-fried steak and coleslaw were a constant reminder of why Sublette existed. So were the fields that lay on every side, wherever the white frame bungalows and Chinese elms came to an abrupt end. But although "agricultural village" properly describes the importance of the land here, it is a rather misleading term, associated as it usually is with pre-modern places that have little in common with

Sublette or Satanta. A Cotswold village in England, for example, undoubtedly took its dependence on the land much more to heart in the thirties. Even today an Old World village of that sort maintains a greater aura of isolation and self-sufficiency; typically, its buildings are made of its own native stone, its architecture follows an ancient folk tradition, and its highly diversified farm products are, in large measure, consumed locally. There is, despite many new counterforces, a powerful sense of place in such villages, where, over the centuries, nature and man together have contrived a special identity—a stable, enduring relationship.[3] In size only did Sublette of the 1930s resemble Old World villages of that type. Otherwise it played an entirely different role, due to the kind of agriculture practiced around it and the intrusion of an outside consumer culture. It looked to the land, as all agricultural villages do, but only for cash to buy goods and services from urban America. Once it had that cash it looked to other places to spend it.

Haskell's trade centers, moreover, were manufactured out of whole cloth, not organically grown in place, as most Old World villages were. When Sublette was laid out in 1912 by railroad promoters, the streets, along with the town itself, were named after Western frontier heroes, many of whom had never seen the area—including Inman, Pike, Carson, Cody, Lalande, and Choteau. Like suburban developers packaging dreary new row housing as "Laurel Hills" or "Brentwood Village," Sublette gave itself an instant, and meaningless, identity. At the same time down the tracks Satanta was getting its name from a Kiowa chief who had been driven to alcoholism by defeat and had died in a federal penetentiary. The promoters applied the same thoughtless gimmickry to its checkerboard of wide, dusty avenues: Sequoyah was the main commercial street, after which came Apache, Comanche, Kiowa, and so on. Over the next two decades the names of businesses carried the pattern to quaint extremes—the Big Chief Garage, the Pocahontas Theater, the Hotel Modoc, and, not least, the Wigwam Meat Market. However colorful as merchandizing strategies, names such as these, borrowed wholesale from an alien past, could not disguise the true identities of the towns. In reality, both Sublette and Satanta were ready-made versions of Main Street. They were not significantly different from the thousands of other small towns and villages scattered from Ohio and Wisconsin westward—all standardized, first by the American passion for redundancy in the landscape and second by the machine age's mass-produced artifacts, and all aspiring to urban status and wealth. From the red brick Methodist church on the corner to the granite bank whose cornice was emblazoned with a date and founder's name to the stuccoed Ford showroom with the dark blue and white sign over the door, Sublette was a study in national clichés. The effect of so much replication was to give the entire place an impersonal, anonymous tone—like a blank page upon which men and women had not yet begun to write about what was really there.

Thanks to the automobile, a citizen living in Sublette or on a farm was in weekly touch with the other Main Streets of western Kansas, taking home from them a continually blurred sense of place. In 1931 there were 527 automobiles in the county—one for every 5.3 persons. Nothing was more welcome to the wide open spaces, where families lived painfully far from each other, than this invention. Yet, paradoxically, although it facilitated the gathering of rural neighbors for an ice cream social, it also loosened the bonds that had held people together in a single community and had nurtured their devotion to place. Because of the automobile, observed Earl Bell, "the individual is now the center and looks about him in all directions."[4] His life had been broken into many segments and lay scattered over a fifty-mile radius. The Haskell County farm resident might go to Sublette to see the county agent, to Garden City or Liberal for groceries or hardware or a movie, to Dodge City for a doctor or clothes, to somewhere else for his social life. Many families drove their cars over 25,000 miles a year. Each week the *Sublette Monitor*'s social news items illustrated the automobile's centrifugal impact: "Mrs. Frank Mc-Coy and Mrs. Orlando Miller were in Liberal Friday afternoon," or "The Arthur Vails motored last weekend to Pueblo, Colorado, to see their son Everett." During the late twenties local churches frequently complained of the distractive influence of the auto, and merchants worried about their declining patronage.[5] Then, for a while, people began coming back to local institutions. In the early thirties there was a temporary fall off in new car sales; the $500 charged for a Ford V-8 amounted to a great deal of 25-cent wheat. There was less money for gas, too, so men spent more time playing dominoes at the Sublette pool hall, women shopped exclusively in town, and both sexes went to church more regularly. But when the AAA money began to flow, car sales picked up, as did gasoline comsumption and out-of-county travel. Haskell was not going to give up its mobility for very long, nor its pursuit of individual freedom.

The automobile's pervasive presence in Sublette, Satanta, and the countryside was, along with the grain elevator beside the tracks, the most important indication of the community's attraction toward the outside world. It was also a clue to what that outside world had become, and hence what Haskell had become. Well before the Depression the automobile had made almost all of America over into a mass society: a culture dominated from coast to coast by the techniques of mass production, mass-media advertising, and mass consumption. Those techniques developed along with the auto, especially Henry Ford's Model T, and then passed into virtually every other aspect of the nation's life—its clothing, food, entertainment, hair styles, house designs. The rows of shiny black roadsters parked on thousands of Main Streets were only the most obvious evidence of this invasion by mass culture, giving town after town a more homogeneous appearance than ever before. Other evidence was the sound of radios in the summer night, drowning out

Sublette's pool hall. It and the drug store were the only local recreation centers. There was a domino game going on here almost every night. Beer was legal but liquor was not, although the town had its bootleggers. (*Rusinow, National Archives*)

the music of crickets and frogs with the Pepsodent or Eskimo Pie jingle or, every Wednesday in every corner of the nation, the Hit Parade. The forces behind the radio, the automobile, and the can of Burma Shave were the same as those behind America's business farming; mass culture was the latest stage in the evolution of the capitalist economy. Now there was added to that order a sophisticated ability not only to produce goods in staggering quantities, but also to manipulate consumers and create larger and larger markets. As one businessman pointed out, "Man's desires can be developed so that they will greatly overshadow his needs."[6] That was precisely the thinking that made the mass culture thrive, and its outcome was to transform the older American penchant for repeatability into a national compulsion to buy whatever someone somewhere else had—producing a continent-wide chain reaction of desire bouncing off desire. Although it was a thousand miles and more away from the mass culture centers, Haskell was jerked and pulled by their magnets in unison with every other southern plains community.

One of the results of the mass culture's dominance has been suggested: the breakdown of a local group identity (never well developed) for the individual and the substituting of a more impersonal identity based on a national duty to consume. There was an illusory sense of freedom that went with this change—illusory because the mass society had its own subtle methods of enforcing conformity. In addition to this social effect there were momentous ecological consequences following Haskell's invasion by the outside world. Money, and more money, was needed for participation in that world. The county had no factories to produce its own goods; its only possible solution was to sell whatever it could take from the earth. Thus farmers and townspeople alike—and there was not much difference in their resistance to the magnets—conspired to plant wheat wherever they could. Every *Monitor* ad for a new car, every radio interview with a Hollywood star, every traveler's report of a new automatic gadget for automatic living argued for keeping the land in that single crop, even when there was serious danger of a dust storm. Given the manipulative and far-reaching power of the mass culture, there was no longer any possibility that this remote county could live to itself or remain content with its natural needs. From this point forward there was no opportunity for an indigenous culture to take firm root here or for man and nature to find a stable equilibrium. Ecological adaptation was perforce shoved to a secondary level of concern. How the land would be used would always be determined not by what its own well-being required nor by local people's self-derived requirements, but by unrelenting pressures from the urban hucksters.

Pitted against the magnetic outward pull of the mass consumer society were a number of social groups and institutions in Haskell County. It was their function to stabilize the local scene—to draw people back into the community and keep them there, and to remind them of their own homemade identity. The tug of war was not a complete mismatch, for the local forces were often strong and determined. Economic and environmental adversity helped them, as it always does, to demonstrate their value; after every dust storm, for example, church interest crept upward for a while—a phenomenon that prompted the Nazarenes at one point to hold a revival campaign with newspaper ads for it reading, "Get the dust out of your eyes and make the closing services a time of soul saving." The Easter following Black Sunday in April 1935 saw the Methodists, Christians, and Nazarenes in Sublette all set attendance records.[7] Fraternal and civic lodges, along with the

4-H Club and the Farm Bureau, were active, too, offering support to distressed individuals throughout the decade. On a more informal level, neighbors turned to and aided each other, particularly in the countryside—plowing a sick man's fields or collecting clothes for a family with no crop. So long as they were battered by hard times, Haskell residents clustered together more tightly, just as they had often done in frontier days, and in so doing they set up a potent countervailing influence, capable of checking some of their communal disintegration.

The most common of these local counterforces was the family. Throughout Haskell's turbulent history that institution had been by far the most important force against instability, excessive individualism, and outside influence. In the thirties it once again assumed responsibility for that conserving task. It also proved to be an economic asset, as fathers and sons pooled their equipment and farmed their land in partnership, mothers and daughters together prepared food and made over children's garments. On Sunday afternoons two or three generations, now with no money to spend on the movies, gathered for visits in homes all over the county. To be sure, families in Haskell as elsewhere in America were getting smaller and more dispersed. Among the older settlers four children was the nuclear family norm, while among the Sublette business people the average number was two.[8] But whatever its size, the family is remembered even today as easing people through those desperate years. Helen and Lawrence Meairs, for example, had seven children. Lawrence was the county's probate judge as well as a farmer living in the country, while Helen took over the child-rearing—and a heavy burden it must have been, especially in the dirt-filled thirties, but not one she at all regrets. "I never thought we had too many hardships," she recalls, "we were very happy because we had that big family."[9] It was not, however, dust storms and poverty alone that the institution fought; there were also the psychic ills on which the hucksters depended. Loneliness, insecurity, and deprivation were all problems that the mass society first created and then sought to cure by more and newer possessions. A well-knit family like the Meairses, on the other hand, could prevent those ills from ever developing. It could also encourage its members to stay put and work not only for their own welfare on the land, but for the next generation's. In Haskell County the family did all those things, at least well enough that divorce, juvenile delinquency, and severe parent-child conflict—the major manifestations of a family's failure—were almost nonexistent. But all the same, despite some successes, the family was being steadily forced into a subordinate position. Madison Avenue increasingly claimed the function of educating the young and providing self-esteem and direction. Without serious economic change on a national level, the private Haskell family had a most demanding and essentially defensive task on its hands.

The family was primarily the women's concern. It was they who were commonly expected to build up the social fabric, while men (and a few wheat queens

A farm couple canning fresh pork from a hog they raised and butchered. (*Rusinow, National Archives*)

like Ida Watkins) carried out the more competitive, individualistic task of farming or selling implements. Haskell women took their assignment seriously—in the home, first of all, but also in the community. Town women, particularly, were joiners and organizers; in Satanta they formed the Owaissa, Sequoyah, and Santee social clubs, while in Sublette there were the Sosuntee, Read-a-Book, T.N.T., Social Neighbors, I Delta Dek, Modern Priscilla, Bible Study, and Social Hour groups, with memberships ranging from ten to thirty.[10] Once a week or once a month each club would meet in a member's house for refreshments, conversation, and usually a program or a card game. Men, in contrast, had fewer organizations open to them and less interest in clubs. But important changes were occurring in Haskell women's groups that increasingly made them facilitators for, rather than defenders against, the urban culture's appeal. Few of the groups in the 1930s could be called traditional in their interests. Most of the newer ones were bridge clubs, bringing to covered-wagon pioneers and their daughters the fads and refinements of city ways. In other groups, where there were weekly programs, the topics were often self-consciously "modern"—as when Cora Cave, hostess of the Social Hour Club, served, with the coffee and sandwiches, a short talk on "Lon Chaney in

The Ladies Club in the Colusa area meeting in a member's house. (*Rusinow, National Archives*)

Movieland." A few months later the same group held a debate on whether modern women were as well off as their grandmothers had been. A few complained of the materialism that had crept into their lives. But Mrs. Snavely, according to the gossip column's report, carried the day with her peroration: "We are just as happy as our grandmothers. We certainly are living in much more of a whirl." They were indeed most fortunate, it was generally agreed, to be exposed to a glamour-peddling media, to be offered so many electrical devices for their kitchens, to see such sweeping changes occurring in their community.[11] The role of most Haskell clubs thus was to put local women in the national mainstream and to encourage them to accept and adjust to it all—not to resist the mass culture's enticements, but to embrace them. Although the clubs provided a valuable network of social relationships outside the home, they usually stimulated discontent rather than satisfaction with Haskell's older, more simple way of life.

There was one group of women, however, which was adamantly against I Delta Dek, Lon Chaney, and against interest in the rise and fall of hemlines—the Mennonites. For them, social clubs were worldly and frivolous, and they stayed well away from such goings-on. Though not hostile toward the rest of the com-

Mennonite mother and daughters planting their farm garden. (*Rusinow, National Archives*)

munity, the Mennonites, both women and men, held a conspicuously different set of values and stood out as an island of plain, old-fashioned people living in the rising sea of mass culture. They believed in staying together and to themselves, the sons and daughters living just down the road from the parents or often on the same farm, and socializing mainly with their own kin. Most of them were clustered in the northeast corner of the county near the one-room schoolhouse that was all that remained of Colusa town. Across the road from the school was the Salem church, where one of the two Mennonite congregations in the county, numbering about ninety members, met. This tribalistic concentration, with their interconnected fields and farmsteads, was undoubtedly one of the factors that gave them a stronger resistance to the outside urban world than the rest of Haskell had. Another was the fact that these were all residential, diversified farm people—indeed, a most successful model of that declining agricultural order. In their communalism, their stability, their careful husbandry, and their high degree of self-sufficiency, they presented some alternative answers to the challenges of the Dust Bowl thirties.[12]

The first Mennonite people had come to Kansas in 1873 from the Ukrainian steppes of south Russia. During the previous three centuries they had been a farming folk as well as a religious sect, emigrating from Holland and Switzerland to

Prussia and then, in the 1780s, at the invitation of Catherine the Great, to the banks of the Dnieper. Another branch sailed to America and settled in Pennsylvania. But it was the Russian-German group who, much later, were the settlers of the Western plains. When Czar Alexander II revoked their exemption from military service, these pacifist farmers sold their land, often at a heavy loss, and came across the sea and by railroad to Kansas, Nebraska, the Dakotas, and Manitoba—18,000 of them by 1883. It was they who introduced the Turkey Red winter wheat that made the region a breadbasket; they also pioneered in large-scale grain farming.[13] In Europe the Mennonites had long been known to be astute businessmen, industrious laborers, and experimental agriculturists. Max Weber might well have used them instead of Benjamin Franklin to exemplify the early Protestant ethic of hard work, rationalism, accumulative drive, and asceticism—the foundations of the capitalist spirit.[14] But at the same time they were an intensely conservative folk, firmly bound to a simple life on the land. While the economic culture around them moved on to factories, cities, and exuberant consumption, they clung to most of the old ways. Although the Mennonites of Kansas were quick to buy cars, tractors, and other industrial products as these became available, they remained aloof from much of what other Americans regarded as progress, and cautious. Their sometimes unhappy history had taught them the virtue of keeping their doors closed until they knew who was knocking and what they wanted.

Yet the Mennonites of Haskell County were, and are, a friendly, hospitable people, not unwilling, after an initial reservedness, to talk to a strange "Gentile" about how they got through the 1930s and what they learned from that experience. Wallace and Bertha Schmidt were among those living in the Salem-Colusa area during the dust storms. They lived just one mile south of the church and still live there today; there have been Schmidts on that land since 1919. Their home is an old but immaculate white cottage surrounded by what on the plains amounts to a veritable forest of elm, mulberry, and Russian olive trees, with red-orange marigolds blooming in the kitchen garden. A few feet away from the cottage stands a tiny adobe cabin, the only one of its kind left in Haskell, carefully preserved by the Schmidts over the years—this was where they began their married life in 1934. Bertha is a large woman who wears a black cap, her hair pulled tightly back, her face shaped like the moon and her eyes oriental slits when she laughs. She remembers without rancor those years when there was seldom a dollar bill riding in her husband's pocket and her own dresses had to be cut out of chicken-feed sacks. "It did us a lot of good," she says. "We learnt to save. We learnt to survive with what we had—make do, you know." Wallace, smoothing his whiskers and still speaking with a slight German accent, agrees that those were not such bad times, what with a few dirt-clogged engines to overhaul for neighbors, AAA benefits, and dozens of relatives around for aid and comfort. A few of his Mennonite brethren made

out less well and were forced to move to Idaho and California, but it was a far
less common fate among these people than among those who lived elsewhere in
the county. The Schmidts, Koops, Unruhs, Reimers, and Doerksens were not as a
rule wheat speculators, heavy borrowers, or tenants if they could avoid it. Their
plain economy, in which desires were clearly distinguished from needs and were
tightly controlled, required less cash income than the average Haskell standard.
Above all, they were more determined than almost anyone to stick it out "if the
Lord would let us," and they would farm in whatever way would best assure that
they could remain.[15]

The Mennonites' greater immunity to the disintegrating mass-market pressures was a quality found, although to a lesser extent, in some non-Mennonite
rural folk, too, especially those who lived around the Colusa school and the
Pleasant Prairie Church of God. Again, these were diversified family farmers who
belonged to highly cohesive neighborhoods that had their origins in pre-wheat
days. Keeping to themselves much of the time, as did the Mennonites, with their
own food supplies at hand and little reason to frequent Sublette or other towns,
people in these northern corners of the county presented to the rest of Haskell a
second model of stability—developing a sense of place to anchor a wind-blown
culture. Warren Moore, who is still one of the most socially active men in the
Colusa district, remembers the cooperative spirit that existed in his area in the
thirties:

> I have some nostalgic memories of the dirty thirties because, now you go see
> people, about half of them've got some damned show on that thing [tele-
> vision set] and they want to see it so you can't visit with them. Nobody here
> had any money then—*practically* no one did, there was a few who happened
> to inherit a bunch of it and doing all right, or else maybe they was farming
> with family backing from the central part of the state. But we had a literary
> society—we met every two weeks—and by gum we just had fun. You'd go
> over some evening to somebody's place and maybe they'd butchered and
> they had home-cured bacon, and somebody else'd bring eggs and we'd have
> us a waffle fry.

Moore and his neighbors were free to make their own world in those days—freer,
at least, than they are today. There were no clear economic distinctions to divide
them from each other, and little migration in and out to break the bonds of community. Some of the families living here had known each other for fifty years. It
helped too that they saw themselves twice over as a beseiged minority: first threatened by competition from the big wheat growers in the county and, second, by
the near-by cluster of Mennonites. The latter group they sometimes poked fun at:
their dress, their moral scruples, their refusal to send their children to high school.

In more hostile moments these non-Mennonites even referred to themselves as "whites"—that familiar flag of self-respect the "Old American" so often flaunts before strangers, whatever their complexion—and they treated these unassimilated, foreign-looking people around them with contempt. This was the shabby side of their communal spirit, a danger every group risks when it struggles to preserve its own coherence against perceived threats. But far more common was a congenial attitude. Mennonites and "Gentiles" generally lived alongside each other in peace, cooperating on many projects and demonstrating to the region some of the social qualities needed for equilibrium.[16]

The southern part of Haskell County, however, ignored these indigenous models of stability. There was not enough money in them, nor enough contact with the outside "age of whirl," to make them attractive alternatives. Even in the thirties the main thrust of Haskellites' thinking was to measure the county by more distant standards of success—purchasing power, return on investment, and urban tastes—rather than by local needs of community and ecological harmony. After a few moments' pause to pay homage to these latter qualities and to insist on their primacy, Haskell quickly went back to the slogans of ever greater progress and gain. This was the reaction of Rolland Jacquart, editor of the *Monitor*. There was a short period when he had a few misgivings about the commercial, consumer values of metropolitan America, which in the pre-dust-storm years had become dominant; during the summer of 1933, as failure struck hard, he admitted that "our vision was a little blurred by the shortsightedness of success" and that the people of Haskell had allowed themselves to be too preoccupied with the "tawdry glory" of a money-chasing life. But by the end of 1936 he had made it his task to repeatedly reaffirm those shortsighted values by strenuously encouraging the county's go-getter temperament once more. "We have natural gas and oceans of water under these prairies," he wrote, "that hold riches beyond our dreams." One day soon, when these underground resources were mined, when the land was put under a more scientifically advanced control, when Haskell had plenty of everything to sell, its people would all live in regal splendor, journeying to Europe regularly and buying all they desired from the world's marketplaces. Jacquart's vision of the future involved not less, but more dependence on external standards, more mobility, more participation in the narrow cosmopolitanism of an aspiring bourgeoisie whose notion it was to consume rather than create culture. All this was, in addition, assumed to be the natural and inevitable direction of Haskell's history. "The country is working back to normalcy which means prosperity," Jacquart reassured his readers.[17]

There was only one area of its life that Haskell as a whole struggled to preserve from outside contagion—its puritanism. In their newspaper local residents read of gun battles between Chicago mobsters, of Sally Rand dancing nude at the

New York World's Fair, and of the drinking sprees of a nation freed from Prohibition. The amount of space devoted to such affairs suggests that the county found them as titillating as people elsewhere did. But all the same, Haskell maintained a confident tone of superiority over such depravities. They would readily discuss planting barley for brewers, but they voted overwhelmingly to keep Kansas dry.[18] They would read all about the infidelities of movie stars and chuckle knowingly at Mae West's "come and up and see me sometime," but they enforced a strict code of sexual conduct at home. Puritanism, the exaggerated and often hypocritical effort to repress moral deviance, was Haskell's chief defense against the external world and the hedonism of its mass culture. The more they purchased (or, in the 1930s, desired to purchase) autos, radios, and cosmetics, the more they insisted on their adherence to old codes of behavior, the more their preachers thundered against a corrupt world. And the more they found themselves living by an untenable contradiction. Neither dances nor cocktail lounges were allowed in Haskell County, but it was all right to indulge vicariously in those pleasures at the Satanta or Garden City theater. Confusion and self-deception were the inescapable outcome of Haskell's moral stance. Unlike the Mennonites, whose strictures on dress and amusements were part of a larger asceticism toward the outside world, the other county residents embraced that world tightly and then tried to back off in one small area of their lives. Nurtured by itself, a moral rigidity toward booze and sexual freedom—and that was essentially all puritanism here meant—was not equivalent to a genuine indigenous cultural base. It contributed nothing to environmental adaptation, nothing to a sense of place. In fact, it worked to mask the extent to which those things were lacking.

Puritanism was another evidence that this was an outward-looking community—but it was also proof that Haskell County felt itself very much on the defensive, very much in an inferior position, striving to reassert its intrinsic worth. Under its air of self-congratulation the county clearly felt, and sometimes admitted it felt, dreadfully inferior to the world of the urban hucksters. This was the worry behind Rolland Jacquart's utopian promises and all the reassurances of a return to "normalcy" and progress: that perhaps they were destined after all to be a perennial problem area—another Appalachia rather than a grand seat of empire, or, at best, a dull, obscure place scorned by the centers of value. Where they had once been part of an advancing region with an unlimited and glorious future, they now found themselves shoved aside as other Main Streets had been, becoming one of the boondocks, slipping into a parasitical dependence on external aid and ideas. Then the dust storms added a powerful new reason to be defensive. Suddenly the national media were pointing their accusing fingers at the county's residents and describing them as living in a barren desert that was no one's idea of Paradise. But instead of turning its back on external notions of success, Haskell shuffled

The interior of a basement or semi-subterranean house. (*Rusinow, National Archives*)

along after them all the more determinedly. Somehow, they told themselves, they would get all the goods and services for sale without losing, thanks to their superior moral values, their souls. They would show the rest of the world that they were better than anyone thought.[19]

Toward the land itself Haskell's people developed an ambivalent attitude that revealed as well as anything how inchoate was their sense of place. On the one hand they accepted the land as a positive presence in their lives. With the *Monitor,* they could celebrate their proximity to nature as making them superior to urban Americans: "We walk on the earth rather than pavement. We see the unsmoked skies and hear the call of birds throughout the day. Wildflowers bloom almost on our doorstep. . . . At night there is the peace that soothes man's soul."[20] On the other hand, they would sell all this, whenever they had the chance, to be a part of the far-off mass society. They had done just that in the great plow-up of the late twenties; the ground consequently had become in truth a pavement-like crust, the skies were filled with dirt, the wildflowers had disappeared with the sod, and there was little peace. Worse yet, the people had come to see their land as an inferior one—something to be apologized for. If it could not produce wealth, what good was it? After several decades of settlement all they felt genuinely worthy of attention was the technology they had purchased that someday would make of this area a garden after all. "Southwestern Kansas," argued editor Jacquart, "offers more than monotonous prairies plagued by wind storms, prairie dogs, drouth"; it could more impressively show the world hordes of tractors and "combines thick on the prairie" to an extent no other region could boast.[21] In those counterpoised identities was summed up what most of the people of Haskell thought of their land and what they considered more attractive—what they had to consider so, as long as their criteria of worth were derived from somewhere else. They had come, as Earl Bell said, to exploit the land and turn it into cash. By the end of the thirties they found themselves still unable to accept their part of nature on its own terms, to regard its limits without apology, and to shape their culture by its imperatives and not by those of capitalist-consumer drives. Their eyes were still on the far horizon, and their feet were not planted firmly on the ground.

Part V

A NEW DEAL
FOR THE LAND

"The land may bloom again if man once
more makes his peace with Nature."

The Future of the Great Plains

Facing up

FROM THE MOMENT the first tobacco planter began clearing the Tidewater forest on the East Coast, all-out production was a part of the New World way to farm. It was on this continent that the creed of maximization developed furthest, until it came eventually to dominate and characterize the American response to the land. By the twentieth century there was no major agricultural region in the country that did not live by that creed: the people of the cotton South, the timbered North, the corn and hog country of the Midwest, the fruit and vegetable area of the Southwest, the sheep-raising high country, the wheat-growing plains—all were believers. Product specialization and division of labor were their modes, as they are in Adam Smith's famous pin factory. For each environment a cash crop had to be found and then every effort applied to its unlimited increase. What constantly forced the nation's agriculture toward ever greater output was a growing hunger in the American belly—not only for food and fiber, but for what they would buy. With the profits from its land the nation acquired some of the capital to create an enormous industrial apparatus, turning out its own cornucopian delights. Still there was no satisfying the demand. Produce, produce, produce—was there ever a culture so tirelessly driven by that single idea?

Time and again in the decades after the Civil War farmers harvested more than the nation's own population could consume. New immigrants and new overseas markets had always appeared to eat away the surplus, and farmers had had to buy more machines to restore it. By the 1930s, however, the problem of glut was more serious than it had ever been before. Immigration had been severely cut back in the xenophobic twenties, while higher trade barriers around the world ruined the prospects for international expansion. Then demographers brought further bad news: the population of the United States had gone up by 2 million in 1920, but only by 1 million in 1930. Within 30 more years, warned Nils Olsen, chief of the Bureau of the Agricultural Economics, the population would reach a maximum of 145 million, then begin to decline. Although his prognosis turned out to be false, too quickly assuming, as it did, that the temporary birthrate decline of the early Depression would be permanent, it offered a dismal outlook to the people of the farm sector, who believed that providing food for more and more bellies was their happy, decreed lot. Added to these developments was the fact that the adoption of tractors had dropped the horse and mule population by 10 million, releasing the 30 million acres of cropland once needed to produce their feed.[1] In a rational economy that released land would have been a blessing—a margin of safety for the future. But American farmers, suffering from a compulsion to plow and plant every available parcel of ground, quickly used the land to grow more crops for a saturated market.

That there were hungry people in the world who could have taken up part of this slack was indisputable. Virtually no one in thirties America, however, had a workable scheme for exporting the surplus food supply abroad; the times were too autarchical for that kind of global thinking. Moreover, all the continents except Europe were net exporters of cereals in the decade. It was only after the post-World War II population explosion began that Asians and others began to ask for outside food aid. As far as the American poor were concerned, most observers in the Depression years, if they thought about the problem at all, believed that those unmet nutritional needs would be satisfied by more equitable distribution, not by increased production. Fruit had rotted in orchards, baby pigs had been slaughtered, cotton had been plowed under—the total stock of American agriculture, like that of manufacturing, apparently was abundant to the point of decay. Overproduction, in fact, had helped create the thirties débacle; more production could not set things right again. It was time now, many believed, to talk about the distributive process, about the concentration of wealth, about institutional changes, and about adjustments of output to real national needs.

Disillusionment with the all-out production creed was frequently expressed at the National Conference on Land Utilization, which met in Chicago in 1931. Over the preceding ten years agricultural leaders had often talked about the need for such a meeting, but it was not until late in the Hoover administration that it was held. The keynote theme of the Chicago conference was tersely expressed by Secretary of Agriculture Arthur Hyde: "Boomer days are over." Representatives from different sections repeated a melancholy refrain of farm abandonment—farms worn out by soil mining, farms no longer needed by the nation. Out of this unprecedented discussion emerged a National Land Use Planning Committee, which later, under President Roosevelt's uncertain regime, became successively the National Planning Board, the National Resources Board, the National Resources Committee, and then the National Resource Planning Board. In 1934 this board attempted to predict American land needs over the next twenty-five years; it was the first such coordinated effort ever made. As nearly as the experts could guess, harvested crop land would have to increase only 1.4 per cent in that time, to 20.3 per cent of the total United States land area, and all of that increase could come from plowable pasture in existing farms. Moreover, there were another 55 million acres in farms that would not be required in the future and therefore could be used for towns, roads, wildlife refuges, parks, grasslands, and forests. The old beliefs that the land was wasted unless it was farmed and that increased output from the soil would always be demanded no longer made much sense. It was necessary now to confront the fact that America was a "matured" economy. At long last this nation had to accept some limits to its expansionary urges—in agriculture primarily, but perhaps in other sectors as well. These were the brave new themes of the thirties' land-use planners.[2]

The discovery of expansionary limits has recurred in modern American history, like the experience of a runner pausing for breath along his course. Each time he rests he is in a different place, sees a new terrain, assesses his reserves by what lies ahead—and then goes on to run again. Those moments when the nation has paused have been filled with mixed feelings about the race to get somewhere: doubt as to whether it has been worth the effort so far, determination to run the next leg more wisely. "Conservation" is the word that sums up these disparate

attitudes; it has meant for some a rejection of the race itself, for others a preparation to plunge ahead. But the very fact that the nation has now and then paused
suggests an occasional awareness of limits—a need to reevaluate its resources for
the route chosen and to rest an overtaxed body before it collapses.

The Depression–Dust Bowl decade was a long and important pausing point,
when the country earnestly considered not only the idea of limits, but the idea of
conservation. It had done so once before on a nationwide scale, during the Progressive presidency of Theodore Roosevelt (1901-8). Franklin Roosevelt, following his cousin's example, also devoted much of his own energy to devising a natural
resources policy, with emphasis again on government intervention in the economy,
more scientific management of the land, and public over private welfare in its uses.[3]
Unlike that earlier rest stop, however, the New Deal found itself ministering to a
nation in the throes of ruinous unemployment and income loss; the runner had
suddenly fallen, exhausted. It was nothing less than a medical emergency, and it
produced cries, many of them pathetic, of "Recovery!" and "Get us back on our
feet!" And yet, ironically, it also created some dissatisfaction with staying on the
unending course and even a desire to quit, or at least to go on at a slow walk.
Instead of Teddy Roosevelt's exhortations toward a more strenuous effort lest the
United States lose its world standing, conservationists in the 1930s frequently maintained that it was too much strenuousness, not too little, that had put the country
on its back.

New Deal conservation could be more questioning and more radical than
that of the Progressives had been. Some of its leaders spoke of the need to reor-
ganize such basic institutions as capitalism, commercial agriculture, and factory
farming. Those leaders were especially to be found among the new breed of land-
use planners, who were eager for a chance to bring discipline and order to the
economy. For them, public planning was a strategy that would do just that; it
would also challenge the laissez-faire hegemony of business—under which deci-
sions about natural resources always reflected private needs, seldom the general
welfare—without threatening the basic structure of property ownership. Although
the idea of a planned society was primarily a remedy for boom and bust cycles in
the industrial sector, these planners saw implications in it for the land as well.
Land-use specialists would assume responsibility for forecasting resource demands
and resolving conflicts, deciding on the most efficient and most conserving ways to
meet those needs, and suggesting how government might see that their recommendations were followed on private as well as public lands. All of this, although
it was hardly revolutionary, went a great deal further than the first conservation
crusade had. It was based, moreover, on a different understanding of what limits
meant: limits in the thirties were restraints to be imposed on an overexpanded
economy, at least insofar as land use was concerned, rather than being shortages

to be overcome. Among the earlier conservationists there had been a Malthusian fear of running out of resources to fuel the nation's future—timber scarcity was the most publicized worry. Although the New Dealers also talked of a closed frontier and of husbanding depleted resources such as the soil, they were at the same time faced with too little economic demand for the available production, not too much. Famines and failures were occurring in the wake of plenty, and they required an unprecedented kind of conservation. Consequently, by the 1930s a new theme in land use had appeared: America as an *overdeveloped* country, violently pressing on the earth's marginal lands to make greater profits, while already producing enough food to go around if it were not wasted or hogged by a few. This was the principal justification for land-use planning as an economic reform.

There was another difference between New Deal and Progressive conservation, one that led back to the planned economy idea. Teddy Roosevelt and his fellow crusaders, particularly Gifford Pinchot, the forester, tried to prevent public lands from falling into the clutches of interests who would tear from them their trees and minerals, then leave them and go on to fresh pickings elsewhere. The Progressive crusaders' strategy had been to hold back some of the public domain from settlement and manage it more carefully, with government supervision, for sustained productivity. In the thirties, on the other hand, the conspicuous need was for agricultural conservation. The new task involved safeguarding, with public power, privately owned and privately worked land. It demanded, according to the planners, fresh thinking about traditional property rights of the individual where they threatened the community's welfare. Among the goals of this new agricultural conservation were removing excess and marginal acreage from crop production, preventing soil erosion through improved agronomic practices, rural zoning and other grassroots regulatory action, solving chronic farm poverty, and bringing the science of ecology into resource management. Obviously, this was a complicated program, lacking the philosophical clarity of the Progressive crusade and resembling a bundle of assorted sticks hastily gathered up. The agronomy stick in particular did not readily align with the rest of the planners' program to control production. But it can be said that, with an important exception or two, agricultural conservationists' aims in the thirties were not based on scarcity thinking. They shared, to varying degrees, a conviction best expressed by Lewis Mumford at the time: "The Era of Expansion . . . has come to an end; the era of settlement has taken its place. . . . Instead of exploitation by mere spread and plunder, a stable and orderly culture of the earth and its resources will take its place."[4]

No doubt it ran against the American grain to talk that way. Even the slightest hint that unlimited growth in every enterprise was not necessarily natural or wholly beneficial was a heretical idea to many, and invariably it set the scarcity howlers going. "The philosophy on which this country was developed into a great country [was] the philosophy of plenty," thundered a *Saturday Evening Post* writer, and America had not yet had enough of plenty —it never would. The new emphasis on the limits of expansion brought the loudest protests from Western agriculturists. Much of the unmarketable farm output came from their side of the Mississippi; during the 1920s the area in harvested crops east of the river fell by 19 million acres, while in the West it jumped by 20 million. Most of the Western acreage increase came from the plow-up of the Great Plains, although the more impressive per-acre yields were produced on newly irrigated land in Arizona and California. Those increases had been supported enthusiastically by the earlier generation of Progressive conservationists; it had been their ambition to see the West curled into another horn of plenty. The Reclamation Act of 1902 had been a keystone in their crusade to vanquish the specter of want. Once begun, however, the westward march of agricultural empire became a stampede. Among Kansas newspaper editors, Colorado ranchers, and California fruit merchants there were now vociferous constituencies that promoted farming in those regions. Opposed to them were a few critics, usually living in the East, for whom the dust storms were a good reason, besides the commodity surpluses, to make at least one part of the West off-limits to cropping. They also pointed out to Westerners that nearly two-thirds of the reclamation districts were in serious financial straits due to overly optimistic planning. But neither Franklin Roosevelt nor most other political leaders dared to challenge head on the agricultural development of the West. Reclamation therefore continued apace in the thirties and the plains remained extensively under the plow, while elsewhere conservationists talked urgently about curtailing farm output.[5]

The new conservationists of the 1930s were in much the same unhappy position that John Wesley Powell had occupied a half-century before, and they looked to him more than to the Progressives as their spiritual forebear, especially on matters pertaining to the West. Powell was out of the picture by the time Theodore Roosevelt and Gifford Pinchot came to power; although he had sought to contain as they later did, the laissez-faire exploitation of resources, he had been worried less than they about impending scarcity and more concerned about respecting the natural limits to agrarian development. Agriculture, he had told an unappreciative nation, must adapt to its environment. It must make its way forward cautiously, scientifically, and democratically. In its success or failure in demonstrating these qualities the future of the westward movement depended. Although in his own time Powell was an advocate of reclamation, he would have been quick to agree with the critics of the thirties that the dam builders had gotten out of hand and that Western boosters had become carried away by extravagant expansionary dreams. In John Wesley Powell, then, the New Deal land planners found their principal hero, though the stance he had taken was by and large still a difficult, thankless, and unpopular one to assume.

The Department of Agriculture, where this post-Progressive conservationism found a home of sorts, was traditionally and sometimes fanatically devoted to increasing crop production. Most of its employees came out of agricultural colleges, or at least they shared the attitude instilled there of using every means available—machines, fertilizers, pesticides, improved seed—to get more out of the earth. Business-oriented farmers, who typically were the quickest to adopt those means, naturally received the USDA's most solicitous interest. Temporary acreage cutbacks with attractive subsidies for the commercial operators was as far as most old-time department officials would go toward a philosophy of retrenchment. But then the land-use planners began coming into the department, and they argued that more was needed than solutions of the AAA type. During the first half of the New Deal years they formed a sizable coterie of reformers concerned with a more comprehensive kind of agricultural adjustment, and for a while they had a chance to influence departmental policy. Prominent among them were Rexford Tugwell, Lewis Gray, M. L. Wilson, Erich Kraemer, Oliver Baker, Howard Tolley, John Bennett, Ernest Wiecking, and, off and on, even Secretary Wallace. They commonly approached farming as a social as well as an economic problem—as a valued way of life, not merely another "industry." In their view, this rural culture was threatened by overproduction and overexpansion among its commercial elements, by squalor among its subsistence families, and by inadequate protection of the land. To remedy these problems, the reformers sought to de-emphasize the commercial bias of their department and to make conservation planning a priority. During the decade, although they managed to shake many USDA trees, they never gained a permanent, reliable hold on agricultural policy. Tugwell recalled the struggle with some bitterness in later years:

> One of the disagreeable experiences graven most deeply on my memory, I think, is the complete scorn with which our arguments for better land use were met in the Congressional Committees to whom we appealed for support. They let us know that this was a fancy idea devised by intellectuals. It was wholly impractical; and they refused to have anything to do with it.

In truth, Tugwell and the rest were more successful in reorienting the Department of Agriculture toward their new conservation ideas than his remarks indicate. But it was indeed an uphill fight, as it had been for John Wesley Powell, and many of the gains were only temporary.[6]

Representative of the new breed, although he had been around for a long time, was Lewis Cecil Gray. No one in the New Deal played a more influential role than he in trying to reform the USDA mission, and no one was more important in launching the new agricultural conservation. Born near Kansas City in 1881, he earned a doctorate in economics at the University of Wisconsin, where he studied under Progressive, production-directed economists Henry Taylor and Richard Ely. Twenty-two years later, in 1933, his thesis was published in two volumes: it was a magisterial survey of antebellum Southern agriculture as a capitalist system. In 1919, after teaching at colleges in Oklahoma, Tennessee, and Saskatchewan, Gray was appointed head of the Land Economics Division of the Bureau of Agricultural Economics, where he remained until late 1935, when he was named Rexford Tugwell's assistant in the Resettlement Administration. Due in large measure to Dr. Gray's prompting, the National Conference on Land Utilization was convened. Later he served as director of the National Resources Board's land-use section and was architect of its anti-expansionary recommendations. Then, as if all this were not enough, it was Lewis Gray again who in the main prepared the influential report on farm tenancy and an equally important document, *The Future of the Great Plains,* which laid out a social and conservation strategy for the Dust Bowl's recovery. Following a cerebral hemorrhage at age sixty, he retired from public life, leaving behind an impressive legacy of reformist programs for the rural poor and the environment.[7]

Most of the problems in American land use, Gray believed, were the outgrowth of an unrestrained capitalism, which he understood, broadly, to be an order founded on the ideals of personal economic freedom and unlimited acquisitiveness. In Europe, where those ideals had first appeared, there had also occurred an important "social or collectivist" countermovement to correct their excesses. Germany, for example, had instituted, as had Denmark, France, and England, new, strict controls over private property rights in agriculture: one law required owners to live on their farms and work them personally, another allowed the state to appoint a trustee to manage misused land, and another placed limits on the subdivision and sale of farm property to prevent speculation. Under those laws land was no longer to be regarded as a mere "commodity to be exploited at the whim of the current proprietor." In the United States, however, the countermovement had yet to be carried out. It was not Gray's intention, nor other New Dealers', to repudiate completely the classical liberal values. Rather, to him agricultural conservation and land-use planning would be "an attempt of the American people to find an intermediate ground between laissez-faire capitalism and socialism." It required a shift away from the traditional policy of disposing of the public domain as fast as possible for rapid economic development; it also involved a policy of "securing conservative use of privately owned lands" by government regulation. As Gray's environmental thinking took shape, it proved to be, when compared with the European precedents, decidedly moderate; his "intermediate ground" still gave individuals more freedom to pursue their own gain than the people of Germany had. It was also more a set of intentions, often vague in particulars, than an elaborate national reform program. But it was his hope to help bring America around, bit by bit, to what other "economically mature" societies had long since accepted as necessary if they were to endure.[8]

Insofar as he had a program, Gray's conservation came in three stages, each more innovative and sweeping than the last.

The first stage was most clearly derived from the Gifford Pinchot–Theodore Roosevelt school of thought: what remained of the public domain was to be set aside in perpetuity—homesteading would have to be ended once and for all. The Taylor Grazing Act of 1934 contributed hugely to that goal by declaring the bulk of unappropriated grasslands—80 million acres—closed to further settlement; those lands henceforth were to be kept as a grazing resource, managed by local livestock growers organized in districts and supervised by the Department of the Interior.[9]

Gray's second stage of conservation, the submarginal purchase scheme, proposed to add to the public domain selected private lands that ought to be taken out of production because they were either unprofitable or badly abused. The target set in 1934 was 75 million acres, amounting to almost 8 per cent of the total farm area. Most of this submarginal land could be found on the steep hillsides of Appalachia, in the cutover forests around the Great Lakes, and on the Western plains. New York State had begun such a retrenchment program while F.D.R. was its governor, and now the scheme was to be applied nationally, on the assumption that it was sometimes easier to buy problem areas and remove the people living there to better ground than to try to regulate and rehabilitate lands under private ownership.[10]

Submarginal purchase, officially known as the Land Utilization Project, was Lewis Gray's major responsibility through the decade, and his most acclaimed achievement. BAE economist Howard Tolley called it "a turning point in agricultural policy." Its first appropriation came in February 1934, from the Federal Emergency Relief Administration; after 1937, under the Farm Tenant Act's Title III, agents were allowed to buy more land. By 1947, when submarginal purchase ended, a total of $47.5 million had been spent. For that sum Gray's office had acquired not 75 million, but only 11.3 million acres, covering an expanse equal to Massachusetts and Vermont, two-thirds of it located in the plains and in the Southwest. It was, after all, a smallish increment to the public domain, although out of the acquired lands came Shenandoah National Park, enlarged Indian reserva-

Homestead near Elkhart, Kansas, abandoned in 1935. It was purchased by the Land Utilization Project and revegetated; now it is part of the Cimarron National Grassland. (*National Archives*)

tions, and new wildlife preserves. There was also a series of National Grasslands, scattered from the Texas-Oklahoma panhandles north to Montana. Although the project could have spent much more public money and come nearer to achieving its goals, for the first time it gave the federal government a tool, a reason, and a base for embarking on agricultural land-use planning. That was what Tolley undoubtedly had had in mind when he had called it a "turning point."[11]

Despite his constant advocacy of submarginal purchase, Lewis Gray was never misled into thinking it would be enough. Agricultural conservation also had to be extended over the remaining billion acres of private farm and forest land, both by inducing individual farmers to voluntarily respect the interests of society as a whole and by protecting that interest "where a recalcitrant individual owner fails to do so." This was the third stage of Gray's conservation—the most radical, the most diffuse, and the most difficult to put into practice. He had no desire to set up himself or anyone else as a land-use czar enforcing an anti-expansionist philosophy; he preferred to have local communities run their own lives as much as possible and, with government advice and gentle prodding, evolve their own environmental equilibrium. When he was once again back in the Bureau of Agricultural Economics, he and his colleagues there promoted an idea John Wesley Powell would have heartily endorsed: a decentralized system of county planning committees, made up largely of ordinary farm folk. They would decide how and where to restrain commercial agriculture and coordinate, at the local level, all of the alphabet agencies' programs for rural welfare. By the end of the decade two-thirds of the nation's counties had BAE-style planning committees. But after 1941, when Henry Wallace, who had enthusiastically backed these experiments in social democracy, left the Department of Agriculture, the committees disappeared. They had been destroyed by hostility from groups like the Farm Bureau and land-grant extension agents, who wanted more power for themselves and more freedom for business farming. And with the county committees went the main mechanism for achieving a European type of countermovement to defend the American environment.[12]

Grassroots collective planning was Gray's last—and unrealized—hope for evolving a compromise between socialism and capitalism in agriculture. Following its defeat there was no public organ anywhere to take the broad social view in conservation and to exercise coordinated control over individual land practices. Without such an organ, whether for the nation in general or the counties in particular, the new agricultural conservation lay scattered across the political landscape—too weak to challenge commercial farming's hegemony, too confused to contain the nation's expansionary forces, too undirected to persuade Americans that they had to have an abiding awareness of limits.

One of the most revealing expressions of New Deal conservation was *The Future of the Great Plains,* a 194-page report submitted to President Roosevelt in December 1936. It was intended to be a model for regional land-use planning as well as a blueprint for restoring environmental stability to one of the nation's worst problem areas. But from the beginning of its preparation there were powerful constraints on what the model could be expected to do. In the first place, it was put together by a committee of eight members and their staffs, including the Bureau of Reclamation, the Works Progress Administration, the Soil Conservation Service, and the National Resources Committee, each of which had a different outlook. Although Lewis Gray was the principal author of the report, it inevitably had to be a consensus effort, and thus it could not be bold or innovative. A second constraint was President Roosevelt's instructions to the committee, which made it clear they were to blame the Dust Bowl simply on inappropriate institutions and practices "brought from the humid part of the country"—immediately closing off broader economic analysis. Finally, the committee, understandably, sought the region's quick acceptance of their recommendations; therefore they had to avoid all mention of resettlement outside of the plains or radical changes in land use.[13] The result of those constraints was a document that was only the barest shadow of new conservation thinking and, philosophically, a muddle.

The idea of such a report began as a worry in the mind of Rexford Tugwell in late 1935. Fearing that the black blizzards of the previous spring would reappear within a few months, he appointed two groups—one based in Washington, the other on the plains—to investigate "fundamental causes and remedies." To Roosevelt he wrote: "They will, of course, report that arable farming ought not to be carried on over a large part of the area" and that federal assistance ought to be withheld from those who persisted in plowing in that area.[14] The regional group (actually, there were at first two of them, called Regional Advisory Committees on Land-Use Practices in the Southern/Northern Great Plains, later merged as the Great Plains Council) began a series of meetings that over the next few years seldom got down to Tugwell's "fundamentals"; they talked at length about seed loans, freight rates, and coordinating their bureaucracy.[15] Meanwhile, the Washington group did next to nothing, and the next summer F.D.R. appointed in its place the Great Plains Drought Area Committee, led by the Philadelphia engineer Morris Cooke, who was head of the Rural Electrification Administration, and including Rexford Tugwell. On 15 August 1936 this new committee began a two-week tour of the plains, traveling from Amarillo, Texas, northward to Rapid City, South Dakota. The short preliminary report made after the tour went further than the regional groups ever got; the basic cause of the area's distress, it argued, was "an attempt to impose upon the region a system of agriculture to which the Plains are not adapted—to bring into a semi-arid region methods which, on the whole, are suitable only for a humid region."[16] It was now almost autumn, and the 1936 dirt storms had come and gone. There were as yet no fundamental remedies being applied, but there was at last the beginning of an official argument that pointed to something besides drought, and there was a conservation program to elaborate upon.

Roosevelt appointed a second Great Plains Committee on 17 September, with Morris Cooke serving again as chairman and most of the other members staying on. Tugwell did not; he was replaced by Lewis Gray. The committee was to prepare a fuller report, which was to be ready by the end of the year. Gray had been frequently sitting in for Tugwell since July and early on had submitted to Cooke a "Memorandum regarding [a] proposed longtime program for the Great Plains." This initiative immediately lifted the committee's discussions to socio-

The Great Plains Committee meeting with farmers in Scott City, Kansas, August 1936. Rexford Tugwell is standing; Chairman Morris Cooke is the second man on his right. (*Franklin D. Roosevelt Library*)

economic rather than merely technical issues. In mid-October a tentative outline for the final report came from Gray and E. H. Wiecking of the Resettlement Administration, and other agencies were invited to make objections or add their pet ideas. The product of that process, although it was a pastiche of recommendations, followed the October outline closely, beginning with the physical characteristics of the area, then setting forth the pathological conditions that had appeared, and ending with a "program of readjustment and development."[17]

The Future of the Great Plains opened its recommendations for reform boldly enough. Land destruction, it argued, was basically the result of "attitudes of mind"—by some means they had to be changed. All of the attitudes identified were those found at the heart of the expansionary, free-enterprise culture. First on the committee's (or Gray's) list was the domination-of-nature ethic, which, it was objected, reduced the land to nothing more than raw material for man to take advantage of and to exploit for his own ends. That natural resources were inexhaustible was a corollary view, a self-deception preventing environmental adaptation and restraint. Other destructive values of the plainsmen were more social than ecological: that what is good for the individual is good for everybody, that an owner may do with his property what he likes, that markets will grow indefinitely, that "the factory farm is generally desirable"—leading, in this last case, according to the report, to irresponsible non-resident ownership, speculative commercialism, and land-abusing tenantry among the less successful operators.[18] These attitudes were unmistakably associated with capitalism's evolution on the plains. The remedy, it would seem, therefore, would have to involve a pronounced shift away from that economic order to what Lewis Gray had elsewhere called his "intermediate ground." Whether the shift had first to occur in the attitudes themselves or in the institutions with which they were intertwined was not spelled out and was perhaps immaterial. What really mattered was that, if one followed the report's own causal reasoning, there had to be far-reaching changes made in the Dust Bowl economy— an end to factory farming, for example, and tight controls over agricultural investment, profit-making, and land ownership—if the destruction were to be avoided in the future and people there were to have a permanent home.

That conclusion, however, was not at all the one arrived at in the report. The destructive attitudes, strange to say, were enumerated and then implausibly explained as "humid-land" notions that had been carried too far west.[19] Conquering the land, industrial farming, aggressive self-assertion—the Great Plains Committee supposed that these worked well enough in the East, but were unsuited to a drier environment. What the committee tried to do, whether out of political timidity or the confusion of groupthink is hard to say, was to fall back on the sixty-year-old analysis of John Wesley Powell—to base their remedies on his geographical distinctions, to talk as he had done about institutional adjustments to climate. Powell's ideas, to be sure, still offered valuable lessons about the need for cooperative settlement and environmental realism in the West. But Powell had failed to come to grips with the American economic forces of his own day that had determined, more than did the experience of little rainfall, how the West was won. Now the committee, although faced with a more nationally integrated society than ever, also evaded the basic problem. Their solutions, while useful enough, were narrowly conceived and often merely exhortatory. Among the institutional changes they recommended were larger farm units, submarginal purchase, cooperative grazing associations and soil conservation districts, farm loans conditioned on approved land practices, county zoning to protect the most erodible lands, consolidation of local governments into more efficient units, property tax relief in drought years, conservation training in school curricula, and a permanent Dust Bowl agency to promote those policies.[20] No fundamental reform of attitudes could be expected from such solutions. They did not begin to touch the commercial mode of farming. Nor did they deal at all with the extra-regional factors involved: the hucksters, investors, grain purchasers, machinery salesmen—indeed, the entire tangled web of American business. The Great Plains Committee, although it was aware that new engineering works, new agronomic practices, or new county tax laws would be inadequate without basic changes in attitudes and institutions, was not prepared to go far enough to meet its own announced ends. To do that it would have had to treat the plains as an extension of, not an exception to, the rest of America.

The Dust Bowl presented by far the best opportunity the land-use planners had to make their case for production limits as concrete and persuasive as possible and to relate regional problems to national issues. Dirt storms and exodusters had made much of the nation aware of serious maladjustments there. The wheat glut raised questions about the expansionary drive of American agriculture that had created those conditions. A few federal planners such as Lewis Gray and Rexford Tugwell had examined alternative land-use attitudes and policies in western Europe and had talked bravely of a new ecological and economic order in the United States—a nation in equilibrium with nature, in retreat from the capitalist ethos. But for the Dust Bowl, as elsewhere, the new conservation amounted to much less than that in the end. Neither the BAE's county planning committees nor regional groups like the Great Plains Committee were able to go very far toward reconstruction. What was needed, in light of the centralized nature of the economy, was a broad-gauged alternative to commercial farming—at the very least, a more clearly defined "intermediate ground." Anything short of that was too piecemeal, too halfhearted, to be truly effective. Nor could a county or a region devise a new land-use order alone, in a vacuum of federal leadership.

That such a national alternative did not come to be was due partly to the fact that men like Gray and Tugwell in Washington did not give enough attention to the broader issues, nor did they talk boldly enough about the dimensions of change. They were, perforce, problem-solvers, often bogged down in the immediate issues of Depression America. Perhaps they could not have gone further than they did toward substantial economic reconstruction without more political support. And, for all its concern, the nation, like the plains, was not yet ready to hear about or support fundamental environmental reform. The gospel of more was still the American religion. Its believers included not only the genuinely poor, who fell short even of the European peasants' standard of living, but also the middle class, which had not given up the ideal of a world without consumer limits. For most citizens, as judged by their subsequent behavior, the 1930s brought only a momentary disenchantment with their maximizing creed, and that soon gave way to a determination to see their old creed revived as soon as possible. Expanding production rather than facing limits thus remained the major function of the Great Plains. The region, despite the storms, was still expected and encouraged to do its part in the nation's race to get ahead.

Learning

NEW DEAL CONSERVATION came dressed in the dark suits and eyeglasses of academic experts. It was nothing if not rational, unsentimental, and technically proficient. Among its proponents in Washington, who were typically from social-science fields, especially land or agricultural economics, scientific intelligence was where conservation must begin. Their own approach to protecting the land was to create new institutions for America that would represent society's interest: public planning was their main hope, application of those plans in a free-market economy was their unresolved difficulty. But all the while they understood that there was a second kind of expertise they needed—that of the new science of ecology.

The Dust Bowl tragedy helped bring ecology to their attention. They found it in a like-minded emphasis on accepting limits to economic expansion, although in ecology's case the limits were those inherent in nature—the capacity of the earth and its network of life to sustain man. The land-use planning advocates, quick to appreciate whatever support they could get toward a disciplined agriculture, brought in the ecologists as counselors to the nation. It would have been a splendid union if it had worked, for the planners needed to know more about nature, the ecologists about society. Unfortunately, the ecologists, once introduced to the public limelight, tended to go their own way. They were eager to tutor Americans in the idea of ecological land use, but generally they ignored the economic reforms needed to achieve it. The nation therefore ended up not with a coordinated program of conservation in which experts from different disciplines worked together for common ends, but with many discrete sets of recommendations. Perhaps that is where reliance on scientic experts inevitably must lead.

Chapter Thirteen

from Nature

Ironically, ecology was so broad in its intentions that several observers called it "scientific natural history." It professed to be a great exception to this age of narrowing specialization; its purpose was nothing less than to explain the interrelations of all plants and all animals in their environments. As early as the 1890s, however, ecology had begun to aspire beyond its natural history origins, and within the thirty years that followed it acquired all the paraphernalia of a modern science: graduate programs, unreadable journals, professional societies, and ruling doctrines.

One of the leading centers in the United States for the new discipline was the University of Nebraska, where Charles Bessey, the botanist, trained a number of converts, most notably, Frederic Clements. It was Clements who gave early American ecologists, including those of the 1930s, their explanation of the way nature works—the succession-climax model. The vegetation in every broad climatic zone, Clements demonstrated, evolves from a pioneering stage, when new plants rush in to settle the bare soil, to a climax, or mature, stage, at which point a stable, self-replicating community has emerged. With this last step of development the composite of plants and animals are put in as perfect a balance with their environment as nature can devise. Such a community can go on reproducing itself forever— unless the climate changes or new organisms invade it. More recent ecologists, who usually prefer to speak in the language of physics, call this climax a "steady state," suggesting again that organic nature always struggles toward creating an enduring equilibrium. That insight, old and familiar although it may have been, was what the new science had mainly to offer the dirty thirties.[1]

Was the Dust Bowl in such an equilibrium? Absurd question—the entire nation and much of the world knew it was not. It was the very negation of an ecological climax, for the forces of life had to fight for the barest toehold against the elements. Soil churning upward in dense black clouds or falling around a baby's face on a pillow made that fact obvious. But there were other evidences of disturbance that scientists were the first to understand and explain: the hordes of grasshoppers and Mormon crickets that swept over the hot, baked landscape, devouring what little remained of crops; the rabbits that came from every corner to nibble on isolated green fields, where they were shot or clubbed to death by frenzied farmers; the spread of weeds such as Russian thistles and sunflowers in the absence of the climax sod; the increasing numbers of Hessian flies, cutworms, wireworms, and cattle parasites. Nature's entire system of checks and balances had been destroyed on the plains, wrote a Kansas entomologist, and now the insects and rodents were multiplying toward man's ruin. The most important popular ecological work of the decade, *Deserts on the March,* published in 1935 by University of Oklahoma scientist Paul Sears (also once a Bessey student at Nebraska), predicted a similar outcome. Excessive plowing as well as overgrazing had turned the plains into a spreading wasteland, threatening civilization itself, he warned:

> The white man in a few centuries, mostly in one, reversed the slow work of nature that had been going on for millennia. Thus have come deserts, so long checked and held in restraint, to break their bonds. At every step the girdle of green about the inland deserts has been forced to give way and the desert itself literally allowed to expand. . . . If man destroys the balance and equilibrium demanded by nature, he must take the consequences.[2]

The defense of civilization against nature's revenge required the counsel of ecologists, it was held, for they alone could lay claim to an expert understanding of what environmental equilibrium meant. Frederic Clements was one of the first to make the case for what he called "ecological synthesis" in land management. Farmers, ranchers, foresters, engineers, subdividers—none of them fully understood that their actions in one place could ripple out over the entire surface of the nature of the world. Nor were any of these professionals trained to skillfully manipulate the process of natural succession, deflecting or arresting it as they chose, managing the organic order for man's well-being. With the Dust Bowl's advent, Clements argued, there was more need than ever for scientific leadership on the plains. Support for this involvement came from Paul Sears, who recommended that individual counties hire ecologists as permanent land advisers. In Great Britain, he noted, such scientists were being consulted as the Empire developed its untapped resources; the United States, in contrast, although its ecologists stood at the international forefront of their discipline, had not yet made much use of their intelligence.[3] An agricultural dean in North Dakota, H. L. Walster, then put the case for ecological conservation in the productivity terms his peers well understood:

> Our approach to some of the fundamental problems in production in the Great Plains has been, from [the] beginning of settlement, that of a rather blind faith in machinery, and with little or no faith in biological science. This is well illustrated by the early adherence to the fallacious notion that "rain follows the plow" and the continuing fallacious notion that we can be saved by some new tillage implement. Improved tillage implements are helpful but they are not the complete answer. The answer to the problems of the Great Plains lies in a more complete ecological approach. More people must come to understand human ecology, plant ecology, and animal ecology. When we understand the Great Plains "ekos," the environment about its people, its plants, its animals, we shall be able to deal with the Great Plains intelligently.[4]

For all of these champions the emerging science was to be, first, an instructor in the laws of nature and, second, a servant of man, showing him how to exploit the land without destroying it, how to create, where necessary, a new system of checks and balances.

Probably not one farmer in a thousand, it must be said, would ever come to recognize the names of Clements, Sears, or the dozens of other academic ecologists of the decade. Even the science of the experiment stations was often suspect to the man on a tractor, who was an innovator when it paid, but was seldom a patient listener to his armchair, college-based advisers.[5] Government officials, on the other hand, were more easily impressed by expertise, and it was they who gave the ecologists growing public recognition. Clements, for one, soon had all the audience among that group he could want. He had early left Nebraska and in the 1930s was a research associate at the Carnegie Institution's Coastal Laboratory at Santa Barbara, California. He had also spent much time in Arizona, introducing federal soil technicians and other students to drylands ecology. When M. L. Wilson wrote to the Carnegie Institution's president in 1939 to arrange a meeting of key scientists with the USDA research staff, he singled out one name for emphasis: "I think particularly of Dr. Frederick [*sic*] Clements, whose ecological work is very highly valued and is forming a scientific basis for a number of administrative judgments with reference to land use at the present time." Closer to the Dust Bowl scene was Paul Sears, who was asked to be the chairman of a committee to draft a soil conservation district law for Oklahoma and get it through the state legislature. "I was present," he recalls, "when an avalanche of frustrated farmers descended on Gov-

Paul B. Sears, ecologist and botanist, with a clump of big bluestem grass in Oklahoma about 1935. (*Paul B. Sears*)

ernor Marland in Oklahoma City. Things were getting no better when a newspaper friend whispered something to His Eminence [*sic*] who immediately named me to head a committee."[6] Thrust abruptly and unceremoniously as he was into a public role, Sears, like other ecologists, proved to have something valuable to say. If his views were not heard clearly out in the panhandle, they were getting the attention of policy-makers in the state capital.

Granted, then, that the sodbusters and cattlemen had been blind to nature's order in the grassland, that ecologists were demonstrating the ramifying consequences of that blindness to a growing audience, the task now remaining was to undo the mischief. The choices of action were deceptively simple. "Nature has established a balance in the Great Plains," observed the Great Plains Committee, "by what in human terms would be called the method of trial and error. The white man has disturbed this balance; he must restore it or devise a new one of his own."[7] The first of those choices, full restoration of the pre-settlement climax, was never taken seriously by anyone. Who would now "dance the buffalo back," as the Indians in their last days of defeat had wanted to do? Who would move all the farmers away, and to where? Did anyone even fully know what the climax stage had been like where it had vanished? Partial, imperfect restorations here and there—that could be imagined. But over most of the Dust Bowl the strategy had to be the devising of a new, man-made equilibrium with all the qualities of the one nature had so laboriously made: an "anthropogenic" climax, as ecologists called it, a steady state that was dominated and managed by man, with his own welfare taken for granted as its *raison d'être*.

Over the decade there were enough suggestions made by scientists to comprise, if one brought them together, a program for farming by ecological principles. To scholars, predictably, the first step in that conservation program had to be a much improved understanding of the grasslands in their native condition—more research, in other words. In 1929 the Ecological Society of America set up a Committee for the Study of the Ecology of the Grasslands; during the thirties it became a joint venture with the National Research Council, under the direction of one of Clements's close associates, Victor Shelford of the University of Illinois. The committee looked into the impact of grazing, the control of insect pests, and the decline in soil micro-organisms due to plowing. If for no other reason than to provide a laboratory for this research, it was proposed that substantial remnants of the grassland climax be preserved. "A thorough study of Nature's crops and Nature's way of making the most of a sometimes adverse environment is of scientific importance," wrote John Weaver and Evan Flory of Nebraska. Preserving relics for that study—leaving stretches of land wild and untouched—"furnishes a basis for measuring the degree of departure of cultural environments from the one approved by Nature as best adapted to the climate and soil."[8]

Outside of these research areas, the land, unavoidably, would be put to man's use. On the looser soils that use must be strictly limited to grazing, the ecologists believed, and the grasses must be maintained—or restored where they had been plowed under. Elsewhere, on the tighter lands, the monoculture of wheat ought not to be permitted. Creating a man-made climax required following nature's way, which was to work toward sustaining as much variety as possible in an area. Complexity of plant life was the best guarantee of stability: it was that simple and commonsensical. Each farm, in order to function as a well-balanced, organic unit, ought to be species-diversified; it ought to support a carefully interrelated set of crops and animals, just as the grasslands had always done. Millions of acres growing nothing but wheat, however, was, for all its profitability and ease of management, an invitation to disaster—to insect and disease outbreaks, soil depletion, and wind erosion. It was economically shortsighted to place so much reliance on a single crop, and it was ecologically unworkable.[9]

To carry out any of these recommendations would require a substantial increase in public ownership and public regulation on the plains, whether federal or
local, and a 180-degree turnaround in the drift toward the specialized factory farm,
non-residency, and market speculation. But there were even more radical ideas
hinted at in the ecological writings of the period, although the implications were
not always clearly understood or pursued by the scientists themselves. "Attainment
by the people of equilibrium with the environment," argued Herbert Hanson of
North Dakota in his presidential address to the Ecological Society of America,
rests ultimately on achieving a stable human order—on reaching something like
a climax stage in social development. What that notion suggested was that, like a
grama and buffalo grass association, man's communities had to move from their
pioneering phase toward a steady state: recycling to the soil what they took out,
simplifying their demands on the land to what it could bear, and depending as
little as possible upon external inputs, except for the sun, on which every part of
nature must rely: in other words, each community should live much more as an
economic world to itself. At that climax stage, close cooperation and interdepend-
ence, rather than the prevailing individualism and communal disintegration, would
be essential to hold the social order in dynamic equilibrium. "The ecological ideal,"
wrote Frederic Clements, is one of "wholeness, of organs working in unison within
a great organism."[10]

By that point ecology's program for the plains, which attempted to draw
from the laws of nature a direction for man to go, had become explicitly ethical,
if not metaphysical. More than a decision about which crops to plant was indicated;
there were, according to several scientists, moral changes to be made, too, not only
in human relations, but in man's attitude toward nature. Clements's "organic" consciousness vaguely summed up this moral outlook, but the idea was more fully
developed by others. Easily the most influential of these men was Aldo Leopold, a
game biologist at the University of Wisconsin, who published a landmark essay,
"The Conservation Ethic," in 1933. The Great Plains Committee (Gray again?)
was so impressed by that writing that it quoted a portion of it in its final report,
including these words: "Civilization is not . . . the enslavement of a stable and
constant earth. It is a state of *mutual interdependent cooperation* between human
animals, other animals, plants, and the soils, which may be disrupted at any moment by the failure of any of them."[11] Leopold's ecology-based ethic did not altogether reject the old ideal of dominion over nature, but it did lay a new responsibility upon man to respect other organisms' right to life, to protect the integrity
and stability of natural communities, and to discipline the human economy more
carefully toward those ends.

Here, then, were the leading land-use recommendations made by ecologists in the 1930s, most of them directly concocted for the Dust Bowl, others, like Leopold's conservation ethic, applied to the situation. When culled from many writings in this fashion, it amounted to an impressive and comprehensive set of ideas. But having reviewed this program, it is necessary for us to ask, as in the case of the Great Plains Committee report, whether America's economic culture—the ethos that had so far shaped farming on the plains—was compatible with its intentions. Could a policy of crop diversification, a climax social order, or a new land ethic develop or survive alongside the basic economic values and institutions that had already done so much damage? Ecologists seldom asked that question; as they moved beyond the scientific problems of the region toward the problems of moral and social reconstruction, they were less concerned about making their analysis a thorough and penetrating one.

At least one observer, however, charged that the thrust of the ecologists' ideas was decidedly threatening to a laissez-faire, business-based system of plains agriculture. University of Kansas historian James Malin, although he himself was a student of ecological biology, in the 1950s began a sustained attatck on that science and its conservation program of the Dust Bowl days—first, on the grounds that its theories of equilibrium and climax made the grasslands a too idealized world and the white man a too disruptive presence; and, more important, on the grounds that its land-use ideas would do away with freedom of enterprise and technological progress in the region. All of the conservationists, he insisted, had exaggerated the severity of the dust storms and their effect on the land's productivity. They had tried, through such distortions, to put unacceptable limits on human exploitation of nature, to diminish man's dominion over the earth. They had little confidence in American ingenuity, which would always find the resources needed for future economic expansion. But above all it was the ecologists whom Malin criticized; he was sure that their recommendations would have reduced the plains to a regimented welfare state in which the individual landowner would no longer be given the liberty, or the encouragement, to maximize his profit. "Scientism, along with statism," he wrote, "have become major social myths that threaten freedom."[12] Malin's charges, though prompted by his own intense ideological biases, at least raised the still neglected question: what were the implications of ecology not only for southern plains farming, but also for the larger American economic culture controlling that use of the land?

Once upon a time it had been assumed that ecology and capitalism were mutually supportive sets of ideas. Professor Malin wanted that time back—to hear science again reinforce the economic doctrines taught by Adam Smith in *The Wealth of Nations*. Every plant or animal organism greedily pursues its own gain, the old thinking had gone, while an "unseen hand" always makes sure there is a harmonious meshing of interests. Well, was not nature in fact like that still—a perfect model for capitalist man to emulate, not some fragile thing he was stepping on? The scientist's nature had long been like that, all right, but no longer was it so. Ecologists had eventually come to understand and emphasize the cooperative as well as competitive qualities of organisms. Their perception of nature had changed, as Clements's vision of organic unity in the plant climax illustrated. But perhaps the more important change had come in capitalism through the development of its ethos of unlimited economic growth. No eighteenth-century ideal of social equilibrium or harmony, such as that projected by Adam Smith, could survive that fierce, aggrandizing energy for long. Nor could the ideal of ecological balance/climax/steady state as elaborated in the twentieth century. Capitalism proved to be a profound disrupter, not a stabilizer, of both those ideals of order. As Karl Marx and Friedrich Engels remarked:

> Constant revolutionizing of production, uninterrupted disturbance of all social [add "ecological"] conditions, everlasting uncertainty and agitation distinguish the bourgeois epoch from all earlier ones.[13]

In contrast to this anarchy of capitalism, the evidence of natural scientists suggested that organic nature, although never fixed or static, worked toward perfecting an equilibrium for every climatic region, indeed, for every hillside and every pool of water on the earth. Capitalism, though celebrated by Adam Smith as a "natural" order, had turned out to be, especially in its most recent phase, when it was armed with powerful technology and corporate organization, a malignant growth—a disease born in but now eating away at the body of the earth. This economic critique was what Malin feared was implied in the ecology taught by Clements and Sears.

Malin's fears that something would come of this implication were unwarranted, however. There were almost no ecologists in the 1930s who tried to express the incompatibility between the economy of nature as described by modern science and that of capitalism as practiced in the United States. A notable exception was Carl Sauer, the University of California geographer. Perhaps because he alone had one foot in the social sciences and the other in the biological—the term "human ecologist" would fit him well—he was especially sensitive to the varying impacts of different cultures on the land. Like others in the decade, he reviewed the long history of abusive practices in the Old World, "from Cape Verde to Mongolia," and he could tell many horror stories from that history. But it was modern man, more particularly, modern western man, and more particularly yet, modern western man in the New World, who had far outdistanced his predecessors in sheer destructiveness. "The United States," Sauer noted, "heads the list of exploited and dissipated land wealth. Physically, Latin America is in much better shape than our own country." Commercial agriculture had most often been the source of this abuse—exterminating species and their habitats, recklessly wasting the soil. The "causative element is economic," he maintained, and no amount of engineering brilliance could compensate for that hard-driving, exploitative force of the American economy.

> We are too much impressed by the large achievement of applied science. It suits our thinking to rely on a continuing adequacy on the part of the technician to meet our demands for production of goods. Our ideology is that of an indefinitely expanding universe, for we are the children of frontiersmen. We are prone to think of an ever ampler world created for our benefit, by anthropocentric habits of thinking.

Sauer capsulized the economic institutions created by these attitudes in his phrase "the whole occidental commercial system"—and it was beginning, he added, to look like "a house of cards."[14]

Sauer's indictment was, unfortunately, not complete or nicely defined, nor was it accompanied by even the vaguest of economic alternatives. Among most other ecologists, however, there was not even this much attention paid to the fundamental cultural origins of land abuse. Moreover, what small interest could be found was typically expressed in terms never really threatening to the economic system, whether as represented in agriculture or anywhere else. The fact was that, by and large, the ecologists, having made farsighted suggestions for reconstructing the Dust Bowl, were not ready to examine in detail the cultural obstacles to those recommendations, nor were they convinced that it was necessary to do so.

The only other natural scientist to take up the social and economic implications of ecology was Paul Sears, who throughout his long and active career has been an unusually wide-ranging thinker on the subject. "Science," he was ready to grant in 1935, "has the power to illuminate, but not to solve, the deeper problems of mankind." But when he moved beyond science to consider cultural issues, Sears clearly felt himself on shakier ground and stepped along with considerable caution. For him the remedy for the desolated plains lay in a reformed, cleansed private enterprise, not radical initiatives. To be sure, he was compelled to put the entire nation as well as the plains in a most unfavorable light. Peasant farmers in Germany or Flanders, he pointed out, showed a much greater sense of husbandry than did the modern American business farmer or his frontier predecessor; even the Chinese, Indians, and Egyptians, all of whom had failed to some extent to preserve the soil's fertility, were not so ruthlessly destructive. But to

Sears, hope for American improvement lay in a more responsible, self-disciplined freedom—in giving the old economic ideas another chance. "Is it not possible that the trouble has not been with private ownership as such, but with the fact that it has not seriously and consistently been the rule in this country?" A public domain open to exploiters had led to the worst land abuses on the continent, he believed, momentarily ignoring the dust storms, which had taken place on private property. Although he admitted that in "the more stable socialistic countries of Europe" communal ownership had not been at all disastrous, it would mean in the United States the government's taking over the "white elephants" that private citizens had ruined or not wanted—more "unwise and indulgent paternalism," he feared. A better solution, in his view, was simply to teach ecological principles to the new generation and to encourage "the efficient stewardship of private property" by state tax policies that penalized bad farm practices. That stance was as far as he would go toward a critique and reform of the economy in its relations with nature.[15]

Sears again considered the social roots of environmental problems in his 1937 work, *This Is Our World,* but without altering his position. There he described the basic causes of ecological damage as the "technological culture mechanism," by which he meant a "system of *manufacture-advertising-credit-consumption-adjustment* (which are surely better described as the ingredients of capitalism than of technology). But he was still not ready to call for major changes in any or all of the system's elements. The reason for his reticence was given a few pages on— he had been, he admitted, "born and raised in the tradition of conservatism."[16] As much as he could admire homegrown socialists like Norman Thomas or socialist land protection abroad, he would not endorse them. Those rival economic ideas, no matter how pacific their methods, posed a danger of disorder and violence that, in the end, was a more serious worry than the "lustful march" for wealth and heedless approach to farming of traditional American entrepreneurs. His suspicion of outside ideologies he once put in a casual metaphor: "Weeds, like red-eyed anarchists, are the symptoms, not the real cause, of a disturbed order." The image was doubly revealing, first for what it said about radicalism, and second for what it said about ecology. The scientist's concern for preserving balance, equilibrium, and stability in nature was directly linked to a fear of foreign political ideas and abrupt cultural changes. Put another way, the conservation of nature implied in this instance the conservation of the social status quo—or at least improving its ability to endure and keep out invaders—weeds such as communists or fascists. "Our only defense," Sears argued, "is to set our house in order, if we think it worth saving."[17] That it was in fact worth saving was never really doubted, although no ecological merits for it were set forth, either. This connection between conserving the land and defending the economic order was, of course, not at all a necessary one, certainly not a tenable one. It was more a matter of temperament than reasoning, perhaps; the ecological conservationist's instincts ran more toward preserving things than changing them, even where logic, as in the case of the Dust Bowl, led another way—toward choosing between incompatibles.

Many years later the same writer introduced a phrase that has become for many people a synonym for ecology—"the subversive subject."[18] Sears had in mind primarily the elevation of his science to a more respected place in university curricula, not subverting the economic underpinnings of American life. So it was among ecologists in the thirties: there was little in their explicit advice that was truly subversive in this latter sense. They brought their expertise to problems like the Dust Bowl, made important suggestions about farming that required fundamental cultural changes, then backed off from the job. Plains agriculture, they told the laymen, violated the laws of nature—but their strategy was merely to point out the laws to people and then assume things would be all right. Or to suggest remedies that would have a chance of being accepted in Washington, Austin, or Boise City. But ecological equilibrium in the region was not to be realized so easily, so rationally. There were too many social forces working against the counsels of science, too many feelings and values working even within the scientists' own minds to counter their professional warnings, working to compromise their position. No doubt the science of ecology added much that was useful to the New Deal prescription for agricultural conservation. But in the final analysis the ecologists were doomed to futility and self-deception as long as they supposed that man's use of the land was controlled by disinterested reason alone or that recommendations served up with scientific credentials would necessarily be adopted. Very little of the ecological conservation program was ever put into general practice on the southern plains. The experts spake, and the world went plunging on as before. Evidently, something more than science was needed—to wit, the recognition that the economic culture of the American people could not be safely ignored if an ecological balance on the plains was really wanted.

Make Two Blades

IN 1936, eight miles north of Dalhart, Texas, on Andy James's farm, the once level land was growing a crop of sand dunes. As late as 1930 there had been native grasses here, but in the next year the sod was broken and wheat was sown. Now on a single field 57 dunes could be counted, the largest of them looming in a great crescent 880 yards long, 30 yards wide, and 26 feet high. Around and between the dunes lay a bare floor of rocklike earth, left exposed when the top ten or twelve inches of loose soil had blown away. Then Charles Whitfield of the Soil Conservation Service (Ph.D., University of Arizona) undertook the job of making this hummocky, windblasted field produce vegetation again. In Arizona he had studied, under Frederic Clements, the processes of ecological succession, which Whitfield was sure could be used to bring even the Dalhart dunes under control.

First he broke the hardpan surface with listers and chisels; then he planted a stabilizing crop of kaffir and Sudan grass, those drought-defying immigrants from Africa, along with black amber cane and broom maize. On the leeward side of the dunes he disked repeatedly, and along their top edges he dragged an eight-foot pole, trying to loosen the sandy soil so the wind could spread the dunes back over the land. Within three months, more than half the dunes had disappeared, and those remaining had shrunk considerably. The stalks of new plants caught the drift, spreading it out like the teeth of a comb. By the summer of 1937 Whitfield was proudly exhibiting roasting ears from the field at the Amarillo Tri-State Fair. New sandlove grass and little bluestem were taking hold under the protective stubble. What many feared had become an irreversible man-made desert was greening up.[1]

# of Grass Grow

Whitfield's achievement—heroic is not too strong a word to describe it—may have owed something to his training in ecological dynamics, but the purpose he had in mind was distinctly and traditionally agronomic: he was not interested in the preservation of nature nor in the evolution of an equilibrium state, but in the successful growing of a crop that could be harvested and sold. Proper farm management—the right tools, the right crops—was all the southern plains really needed to become productive again, so his triumph suggested. Journalist Ben Hibbs came away from the Dalhart project confident that "our blunder was not in breaking the sod but in the farming methods we used afterwards. The scientific men are developing methods that will do the job."[2] There was no reason to waste time on devising major institutional reforms or teaching people a new set of ethics. The remedy would come from action in the fields—from experimenting with the duckfoot cultivator or dwarf maize or contour plowing. This was the message of a third group of New Deal conservationists, the agronomists: salvation through technique, they promised, recovery through scientific manipulation of the land. Although their program could have been a supplement to the others, in fact it became more of a competitor, and a successful one, at that. Their reforms were all in method, while their motives conformed to those of commercial agriculture. And that formula was guaranteed to have an impact—an acceptability—that those of the other conservationists could not match.

Conservation agronomy was, according to its proponents, simply good business-like farming. An operator who used the best technical advice available would get the highest return from the land, not in a single boom year, perhaps,

Sand dunes in Dallam County, Texas, 1936. This land was covered by blue grama grass before 1930, cultivated for three years, then abandoned. The stakes indicated the rate of movement. (*Western History Collection, University of Oklahoma Library*)

but over several years of steady, thoughtful management. The Dust Bowl was proof that technique was lacking; remedy the plainsmen's incompetence, and their agricultural factory would be saved, rationalized, and set going again. Greater output and greater profitability, the aims that had fueled the tractors in the great plow-up, would be the reward as before, but not at the risk of destroying the landed capital, as farmer Andy James had almost done. Conservation for the agronomist, therefore, meant a renewed commitment to making the land pay off. It was, as one government group has more recently defined it, "an investment (1) in maintaining productive potential, (2) in decreasing the productivity deterioration or (3) in enhancing the productivity potential." No wonder, then, that the editor of *Business Week* could call himself a conservationist; why, any progressive industrial leader could see the wisdom in this "scientific agriculture" and support its endeavors to put the plains back to work, earn a better dividend, produce more efficiently.[3] These were social aims thoroughly compatible, so it seemed, with enlightened capitalism.

The well-heeled network of county extension services had, since its establishment in 1914, been dinning the agronomist's message into the heads of rural Americans. But in the 1930s a rival bureaucracy, the Soil Conservation Service, appeared on the scene and, again with generous public funds, began to preach on the same text. The main evangelist of the SCS was Hugh Hammond Bennett

("Big Hugh," or "the Chief"), the son of a North Carolina cotton planter, and a Chapel Hill graduate in soils and agronomy. He had joined the Department of Agriculture in the first decade of the twentieth century, when Progressive conservation was all the rage. The fear that America was running out of the raw materials of prosperity was confirmed by his own knowledge of Southern poverty and soil exhaustion. But as yet few Americans, even among conservationists, paid much attention to dirt. In 1909 the Bureau of Soils, much to Bennett's consternation, announced: "The soil is the one indestructible, immutable asset that the nation possesses. It is the one resource that cannot be exhausted; that cannot be used up." For the next five decades, until he died in 1960, Hugh Bennett worked to correct that misconception.[4]

During the thirties Bennett became one of Washington's most listened-to conservationists, playing for the soil the alarmist role Gifford Pinchot had once played for the forests. In 1933 he became the first director of the Soil Erosion Service, a temporary agency then located in the Department of the Interior. But that was only a beginning of the Bennett empire. Two years later, as he was on his way to testify before a Congressional committee on the need for a permanent status, he learned that a great dust storm, which had originated in New Mexico, had almost reached the nation's capital. Stalling and dawdling, he managed to keep the committee in session until a copper gloom had settled over the city and blotted out the light. "This, gentlemen," he announced with an impresario's flourish, "is what I have been talking about!" Congress quickly passed legislation establishing the Soil Conservation Service under the USDA umbrella and with Bennett as head— the first government office of its kind in world history, and a model other nations came to imitate. Without the Dust Bowl's potential for theater there most likely would not have been such a large commitment of money and federal personnel to protect the soil. Wind erosion, however, accounted for only part of America's soil losses; by 1934, 262 million acres—an area 2.5 times the size of the Dust Bowl— had been severely damaged or destroyed by erosion, for the most part by water run-off. It was now Bennett's responsibility to reverse both kinds of soil destruction where possible and to prevent the wasting away of land still farmable.[5]

Although the soil saviors worked alongside Rexford Tugwell and Lewis Gray and had their support in giving technical assistance to farmers, there were differences of outlook that a New Deal spirit of common cause could not always smooth over. The conservationism of the land-use planners held that America had more productive capacity than it needed or than was good for the land, and that public power ought to restrain the agricultural economy; the SCS-agronomist group, on the other hand, was dedicated to helping private citizens manage their soils for greater productivity. This difference became more and more pronounced after 1935, so that federal conservationists were openly working at cross-purposes. Bennett,

Hugh Hammond Bennett visiting the irrigated alfalfa field of the Tucker brothers in northwest Cimarron County, Oklahoma. (*Oklahoma Historical Society*)

unlike some of his underlings, went on maintaining that sizable portions of the Great Plains ought to be put back into grass, even arguing the point with state-college agriculturists, who were vociferously opposed to making any land off-limits to the plow and put their trust in better farming techniques. But all the same, he was a "developer" too, a believer in the gospel of more, and increasingly he spoke against the matured economy notion and in defense of the old commitment to produce. In 1943, with wartime opinion firmly on his side, he wrote:

> Probably the greatest single barrier to rapid nation-wide adoption of the [soil conservation] system is an erroneous idea still held by too many agriculturists, both in and out of Government, Federal and State, that we as a nation have about reached our food production limits. They appear to have become preoccupied with problems of handling food after it is produced and to have failed to recognize that under conservation treatment, soil generally will yield much more than it ever has in the past. As a nation we need to renew our acquaintance with the land and reaffirm our faith in its continuity of productiveness—when properly treated. If we are bold in our thinking, courageous in accepting new ideas, and willing to work *with* instead of *against* our land, we shall find in conservation farming an avenue to the greatest food production the world has ever known—not only for the war, but for the peace that is to follow.

There was a wide, hungry world out there, Bennett added a few years later, waiting for American know-how and American plenty. "By increasing the per-acre, per-farm, and per-nation supply of food and fiber, conservation technology can provide the basis for an improved standard of living and simultaneously reduce the hunger and discontent among peoples which so frequently leads to discord, dictatorships, and war."[6]

Conservation is land technology—so the agronomists and soil engineers believed, with all the idealistic fervor of Point Four missionaries introducing hybrid rice and water pumps to backward peasants. In this case, however, the recipients of aid were living at home, and they usually showed little of the traditional peasant's reluctance to take up new-fangled ideas. The agronomic conservation of the New Deal came to them as a free technical assistance program, with all the skillful blandishments once limited to machinery salesmen. Most important, it told Dust Bowl folks precisely what they wanted to hear—that their predicament could be explained and solved by technique alone. With that assumption began what Hugh Bennett hoped would be a revolution on the plains. It would certainly be the only kind that plainsmen had much faith in.

"Remember the stories about the Old West, of hair-raising incidents in which the government's soldiers came galloping in barely in time to save the day? That same government sent troopers to the dust bowl." So a Texas newspaperman recalled the arrival in August 1934 of Howard H. Finnell to take charge of the soil conservation work on the southern plains—the new Region VI office, it was called, Operation Dust Bowl, with its headquarters in Amarillo. One year earlier Hugh Bennett had sent H. V. Geib of the Texas Erosion Station at Temple over to the panhandle on a scouting mission. Geib had recommended a plan of deep listing and terracing that would have cost the government $3 million a year, and he put in Finnell's name as the man to carry it through. For eleven years Finnell had been director of the agricultural experiment station on the Panhandle A & M campus in Goodwell, Oklahoma. A no-nonsense man with a toothbrush mustache and a scientist's passion for details, Finnell was widely known over the wind erosion area as an advocate of engineering works to save the soil. Now with a job offer and a long-term leave of absence from the station, he headed for Texas. He took with him a handful of Goodwell graduates looking for work, and later picked up Charles Whitfield. Finnell's first annual budget was a mere $60,000, but by 1942, when Region VI was abolished (it was dispersed into other regional divisions), he was spending almost $11 million. In the early years most of the money went for demonstration projects, beginning with the Dalhart dunes and eventually totaling 26 such devastated areas, covering 956,000 acres—all private land managed under five-year contracts by the SCS technicians. The infantry of this dirt-saving army were young men in the Civilian Conservation Corps, with no other employment

Fire drill in a Civilian Conservation Corps camp in Oklahoma. (*Oklahoma Histori-cal Society*)

open to them and needy families depending on their paychecks; there were as many as 25 camps of them under Finnell's command.[7]

Emergency listing against the wind was, from the outset, regarded in the Region VI office as nothing more than a stopgap measure; permanent changes in farming techniques, based on careful experimentation, would have to be made. But when the dust storms began to howl there were only the crudest data on soils and their distribution—wholly inadequate for detailed planning. Consequently, the SCS began to draw maps and take aerial photographs of every county in the Dust Bowl and to classify their soil types and subtypes, sometimes coloring them in with brilliant reds and greens and burnt oranges, transforming the plains map into an abstract expressionist masterpiece. They also mapped the extent and kinds of erosion, giving approved treatment procedures for each corner of a field so that the farmer would not have to fumble toward his own cures: on very heavy clay soils of Type III, use Practices 2, 6, and 15. The most comprehensive of their early erosion maps was prepared by Arthur Joel as part of the National Resources Board's Reconnaissance Erosion Survey. Joel traipsed over twenty counties. He calculated that 80 per cent of the cultivated land in them was affected by serious erosion, and 90 per cent of the idle land, but only 20 per cent of the pastures. The worst damaged counties were, in order of severity, Morton (78.4 per cent of its total area seriously eroded), Stevens, and Stanton in Kansas; Baca in Colorado; Dallam and Sherman in Texas—all extensively plowed. If nothing else, the maps made it clearer than ever that a cover of vegetation on the land was infinitely more effective than listing, and getting such a cover was the only technique with reason behind it.[8]

For Arthur Joel the erosion menace required draconian measures. Almost one-half of the land in his twenty counties was cultivated or idle; 52 per cent of it, or 4.2 million acres, he urged, must be put back into grasses if the problem was not to become unsolvable by the next generation. But the Amarillo office trimmed that figure down to a more "realistic" 6 or 7 million acres for the entire Dust Bowl area of 100 counties—about one in five plowed acres. Even then they were never fully to have their way. It was, to tell the truth, difficult to get the old native grass to creep back over the bare soil. For natural vegetation to take place, forty or fifty years of protection from the plow and hoof might be needed. Man could help the process along by sowing grass seed (although no one knew how to harvest the low-lying buffalo grass economically) or by first planting a protective "nursery" crop of sorghum. Exotic imports were another possibility: weeping love grass from Africa was tried, and botanists traveled to the Gobi Desert, the Kalahari, and the Atacama for even more outlandish panaceas. In the end they came back to the native species, but they still had no sure, speedy way to make the grass reappear. Above all, they needed the cooperation of the southern plains farmer—and when a hundred acres of grass would give only a fraction of the potential income that that farmer would get from wheat, they could not get his help. The Soil Conservation and Domestic Allotment Act of 1936 paid operators to take some of their land out of "soil depleting" crops such as wheat and put it into the "soil conserving" grasses or legumes. But that was a mere two-year program, and eventually impractical in the face of rising grain prices. Only when the government purchased the land did the SCS make much progress toward permanent regrassing, and that was not a popular solution either, at least not for long.[9]

Save the plains for the plow, then. Put every acre to its "most economical use" and figure out how to minimize the risks. Having paid lip service to the superior holding power of the grass, Finnell's troops adopted this alternative strategy, which was more suited to their clientele's wishes and to their own agronomic biases. A vegetative cover, they conveniently discovered, might just as well be a cash crop as grass; wheat, for instance, could, with good rainfall, tie down the soil as well as anything nature provided (of course, the problem was what to do when the wheat died in drought, which it did, and quickly). Where the ground was light and sandy, one could plant wheat in strips, alternating with rows of sorghum that could check the wind when the wheat failed. If the soil was bone-dry down a foot or two at planting time, the farmer might let it lie fallow or put in another, emergency crop instead. Fallowing, or resting, a field every other year was a well-established way to improve wheat fields. He also ought to keep as much "trash" or vegetable matter as possible in the dirt and on the surface to break the wind's velocity and retain moisture; burning stubble after harvest was a fool's way. This policy of "residue management," Finnell repeated to everyone he met, would make dryland farming a financial success. But clean farming that robbed the dirt of all plant material, plowing in straight rows that ran parallel to the winds, drilling wheat when there was no chance of its taking root—these were all bad practices, he explained, that invited ruin. They could be stopped and cropping rationalized, so there would be no reason to give up. The plains farmer could still be a gambler, but he ought to be a calculating one, never betting on a full house when the cards in his hand added up to nothing more than a pair of deuces.[10]

The tight, or compact, lands posed special challenges to the technician's ingenuity. Their dark loam and clay texture held rainwater better than the sand did, but took it up more slowly too. When those fields were bare, and there was a heavy downpour, the water ran off them as if they were coated with wax. Out of twenty inches of precipitation in a year, perhaps a mere three and a half would survive runoff and evaporation to soak down where the wheat roots grew. That was enough to produce a respectable crop, but it was a bare minimum, and in droughty years there was not even that much. Water conservation was the problem the Region VI office worked on more than any other—trying to increase the water take-up and storage rate at the subsoil level, using the earth itself as a kind of reservoir. Admittedly, a sturdy stand of native grass was a terrific sponge, thirty times more effective in stopping runoff than young wheat was. But technology could even things out. "The complete conservation of rainfall on wheat land," Finnell explained, "requires contour tillage supported by terraces." Plowing along wriggly contour lines that followed the lay of the land was standard SCS practice in the humid states to prevent dirt from washing away, but in the semiarid country it was also valuable: it slowed down drainage and increased absorption. Terracing, the second major tool in water conservation, was needed in conjunction with contour plowing wherever the slope was 2 per cent or more. Terraces on the plains were nothing like those emerald-green platforms built for rice cultivation in the Philippine mountains; they were simply ridges of earth thrown up on the contour every hundred feet or so to dam the runoff, forcing the water to travel back and forth across the field until, as B. W. McGinnis, Finnell's lieutenant, said, "it gets disgusted and quits."[11] Both techniques were promoted primarily for use in wheat fields, although Finnell and others demonstrated that cattle pastures would profit from a similar treatment—a few contour furrows through the grass could put 25

Contour furrows across a Texas pasture. (*Panhandle-Plains Historical Museum*)

per cent more rain and snow into the soil. Wherever they were used, these were both engineering solutions, requiring trained surveyors, special machines, and CCC labor, and marking the land with new evidences of man's manipulation. In principle, they were not so very different from building dams and irrigation works along rivers, which chambers of commerce on the plains tirelessly demanded; but contouring and terracing interfered less with nature, cost far less, gave better returns on investment, and helped more people. If wheat had to be raised in the Dust Bowl, this system of water conservation made sense—which undoubtedly was why the dam boosters found it unappealing.[12]

Potentially, the most important innovation the SCS offered the plains, however, was not technical, but political. Soil and agronomy specialists though they were, Hugh Bennett and Howard Finnell perceived that new farming methods would be more acceptable if they came not from federal experts, but from community groups run by those affected. Since everyone else was trying to organize farmer committees in the Bowl, the SCS came up with their own—the soil conservation district—and it is the only New Deal grassroots organization that has survived. Its function was to see that the new techniques were implemented beyond the demonstration areas by reassuring the suspicious and policing the mavericks. In May 1936 the SCS published a standard soil conservation district law, which, if passed by the states, would allow local people to set up, through petition and referendum, their own district, with self-determined boundaries, and to make binding regulations for a five-year period. By 1939 all of the southern plains states had passed such laws—but there were few districts established in Region VI. The Regional Advisory Committee reported in that year that no districts had been formed anywhere in Texas, none in the Oklahoma panhandle (one had been voted down in Cimarron's northwest corner), none in southwest Kansas (Haskell County in 1937 had voted 151 to 70 for a district, falling short of the 75 per cent majority of residents needed under state law; in six other counties referenda also failed). Only New Mexico and Colorado showed much success. By the summer of 1940, however, farmers had begun to come around; by then the Amarillo office could boast 37 districts covering 19 million acres, or one-fifth of the Dust Bowl.[13] These soil conservation districts, identified by neatly painted green and white signs along the roads, were widely hailed as a significant advance over the old days of self-reliant, slovenly, seat-of-the-pants farming. In fact, they were a limited and illusory evidence of progress toward Great Plains reform—not true land-use planning groups, but only mechanisms to promote the agronomists' tools, methods, and narrow view of the land.

Planting shelterbelts of trees was another agronomist solution, although it was one the Soil Conservation Service had little to do with in the beginning. The idea was to manipulate the climate, stop the winds, and save the soil. A row of trees around a house, everyone knew, cut the wind's velocity and cooled the air in summer. Expand the row around the farm, across the plains, and the dust would cease to blow, crops would have a better chance. The Russians had planted shelterbelts to that end in the Ukraine during the 1880s—not solid blocks, as in a forest plantation, but strips lining the fields. President Roosevelt, himself an ardent tree planter on his New York estate, was sure that the same remedy would work in the West; nothing, in fact, appealed more to him as a solution for the Dust Bowl. Trees would humanize the harsh, inhospitable plains. They would turn its drabness into a garden of shade and greenery, and no one would ever want to leave; farmers would put down their roots alongside the hawthorn and mulberry. Critics hooted and raged: the idea was as silly as pouring plaster of Paris on listed ridges or spraying banana oil on the dust. Congress repeatedly refused to go along, complaining of the high cost. Geographers such as Ellsworth Huntington and ecologists such as Frederic Clements argued that it was going against nature to plant trees in a semi-arid climate—it was an Easterner's folly. But Roosevelt persisted against all those criticisms, until in the end he could say that, if he had not been altogether right, he had not been completely wrong, either. Trees did get planted, 220 million of them on 30,000 farms, and a high percentage have survived to this day, bringing many of the benefits they were supposed to. But hardly any of them were planted in the Dust Bowl.[14]

Given $500,000,000 to spend on Great Plains drought relief in 1934, Roosevelt siphoned off a small part of it for the Forest Service to gear up for a shelterbelt program. Paul Roberts was appointed project director, and he immedi-

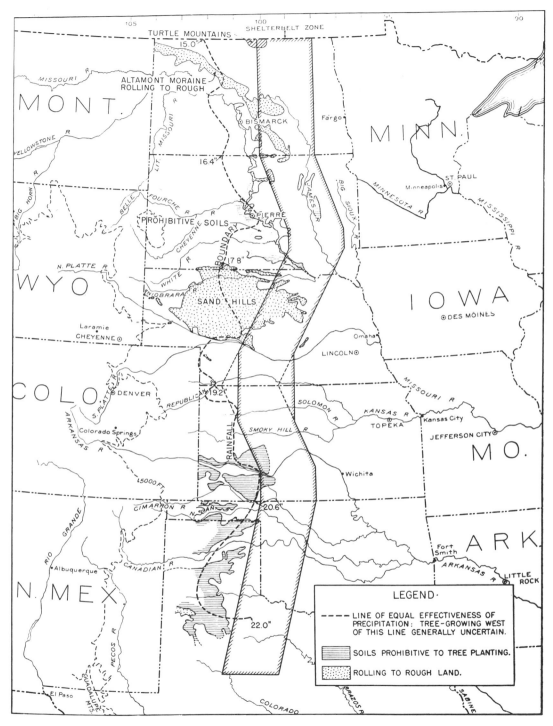

Shelterbelt Zone. (*From U.S. Forest Service.* The Possibilities of Shelterbelt Planting in the Plains Region)

ately moved to Lincoln, Nebraska, to organize nurseries, hire trained help, and most important, decide where to put the trees. By March 1935 the foresters had settled on a shelterbelt zone and had their first saplings in the ground. Trees were to be planted where they had a chance to grow, in a narrow, 100-mile zone running from Childress, Texas, to the Canadian border—essentially along the 99th meridian, the transition line between the tallgrass prairie and the shortgrass plains. "West of this line," wrote Raphael Zon of the Forest Service's scientific staff,

> extensive planting of shelterbelts is considered hazardous, because of the low rainfall, difficulty of establishment, short life, poor survival and adverse soil conditions. . . . Such a land should best be converted to grass and a simpler form of use, such as grazing.

It was useless to expect, then, as the public did, that the trees would stop the dust storms—they were too far to the east for that. Instead, their purpose was to keep the desert from creeping into the farmland on the rim of the Bowl. But despite the conviction of the Prairie States Forestry Project personnel in Lincoln that it was a worthy objective, there was no way to get an appropriation through Congress for their support; through the rest of the decade they limped along as a WPA appendage, trying to do a professional job with relief laborers. In 1942 they stopped planting trees, and the shelterbelts, many of them as tall as a man by then, were turned over to the Soil Conservation Service for it to manage.[15]

The first belt was planted near Mangum, in the southwestern corner of Oklahoma, although more trees were planted in Nebraska than in any other state. The typical belt was a strip eight rods wide, one-half mile long, and containing ten to twenty rows of trees. Down at Childress a typical belt was fifteen rows across: two of cottonwoods at the center, flanked by honeylocust, osage orange, hackberry, ash, ailanthus, walnut, soapberry, and desert willow—forming, at maturity, an upside-down "V." Around the St. John vicinity of Kansas fast-growing Chinese elms were planted with cottonwoods and honeylocusts, and more rarely, catalpa, apricot, tamarix, and cedar. It was the responsibility of the farmer on whose land they were placed to fence them in against rabbits and keep the weeds down. In return, his fields got protection: winds below twenty miles per hour were reduced by more than half over distances from four to eight times the height of the trees. With belts growing a mile, better yet, a half-mile, apart there was far less evaporation of precious moisture, improved refuge for winter-weary cattle; and, as in the English hedgerows, the trees were filled with birdsong from spring to midsummer. All this for a little over $20 per acre in labor and materials, which was five to ten times the cost of High Plains land. Fourteen million dollars spent on the shelterbelts—a pittance, of course, in the New Deal budget, but it was as much

Young shelterbelt on the plains. (*Franklin D. Roosevelt Library*)

as the federal government spent on all its submarginal land purchases in the region. Viewed as a contribution to the plains' ecological recovery, it was of little utility; the money might have been better used to buy more abused lands, revegetate them, and set them aside as scientific or wilderness reserves. But, on the other hand, the project gave many men work, gave farmers a practical amenity, and gave the agronomist another tool to make Western agriculture more secure.[16]

"Production, of course, is and must at all times be the first consideration of any program of land use management." The words were those of an obscure SCS fieldman at a Denver conference. But they were also the official agronomic creed, undoubtedly drawn up for public consumption, and strongly held as a personal article of faith by soil and crop technicians setting up residence on the southern plains. Their bulletins and speeches were filled with data showing the economic returns from conservation. Two blades of grass—or, more likely, wheat—were soon to grow in the Dust Bowl where only one, or none, had grown before. Fields surrounded by shelterbelts would produce 50 per cent more fodder. Fallowed ground would give twice as many bushels of wheat as unfallowed. Terraces would improve annual earnings from wheat by $2.00 an acre and increase sorghum yields 262 pounds per acre. Spring vegetation on the furrowed range would sprout faster and thicker and support more cows. Howard Finnell, adding up the benefits of increased production derived from SCS programs in Region VI, put the total at $37,737,000 from 1935 to 1942. The cost to the taxpayer, he admitted, had been even higher— $43,327,000. But the benefits, although they were slow to appear, were, by the last year of the Amarillo office's work, 50 per cent higher than the expenditures (never mind that there were two different pockets involved—the taxpayer's and the farmer's—and that the movement was from the former to the latter). "A private industry operating on such a rate of return on its investment," Finnell concluded, "would be criticized for profiteering." One day, when the region's resources were all exploited "to their highest productive efficiency commensurate with permanent maintenance," the added net profits would amount to a cool $98 million a year. That was making the land produce on a scale undreamed of in the days of the wheat kings.[17]

Dust Bowl farmers could almost hear the coins jingling in their jeans, and they signed up for terracing and the rest with an enthusiasm they had once reserved for tractors and combines. This was a government venture that especially made sense to them, and only a mossback would stay out. In the first 8 years, 22 million acres on the southern plains were given SCS treatment. Agronomic conservation thus came in a rush to the region, breathing new life into the old, unquenchable, go-ahead spirit of the plains farmer. Agronomists promised him anew the tomorrow world of infinite abundance, when all the land would be contoured to the horizon, every drop of water captured and used, straight even rows of trees planted wherever they would grow—a landscape of engineering and efficiency. It was a rare man who could stare out of his windows at sand dunes and empty barns and wholly resist the vision; he had long ago learned to live by dreams of wealth and conquest. As one "canny" resident expansively pointed out to a reporter:

> Listen. If this country could produce the trainloads of products that it did before we knew anything about how to farm this land, before we had put this great program into effect, what will it be capable of in the future? Its future is just opening up. It is just being tamed. There will be as much difference between this country in the past, productive as it was, and what it will be in the future as there is between a wild flea-bitten longhorn and a modern purebred white-face steer. Then we will really go places. Our future is all before us.[18]

That attitude, it must be said, was not quite universal. Although New Dealers may have believed, as Alastair Cooke put it, that the common man was one who could "take up contour plowing late in life," the SCS program appealed in particular to the young, the well-to-do, the educated, and the progressive entrepreneurs who had led the way to factory farming in the 1920s. Agronomists and soils experts repaid those farmers' confidence with solicitation; they had little patience with the poor, dull-witted, unambitious farmers who were slow to innovate. Eventually, they hoped, their clients would all be efficient businessmen, quick to understand and take up the new production methods that would make more money for them. Big Hugh Bennett made it clear whom the vision of abundance through conservation technology was meant to help: "Farming will become an expert profession; the inexpert and inept will be forced off the land."[19]

The agronomists, like the ecologists, were optimists about the power of reason to rule over human affairs on the plains. They were even more confident than the scientists were of their ability to work with commercial farming. Conservation and business can pull in the same harness, they were sure, and that team in fact did seem remarkably well matched in the late 1930s. But the commercial farmer needed blinkers if he was to stay in the SCS furrow. At the first sight of better profits elsewhere, he was all for pulling away, snorting and straining and dragging the agronomist after him. Already the farmer had veered off wildly: although in 1935 Finnell's office had recommended a 30 per cent cut in wheat acreage in 72 southern plains counties, the reality achieved 5 years later was only 16 per cent—a fact carefully ignored in all the progress reports.[20] But it was during World War II and the later forties that the farmer really stampeded. What those years proved beyond any doubt was that the old economic culture could still pull stronger than any conservation ideal, and the agronomist, though increasingly nervous about where he was going and sometimes jerking back in panic, was yoked to a runaway.

Munich, Pearl Harbor, Dunkirk—and then rain. War and Providence had conspired to bring an end to the hard times of the dirty thirties. The land had begun to come back in 1941, and grain had begun to ripen as it had not done for years. Even where its top five or six inches had blown away, the deep and mineral-rich soil usually had the power to produce good crops on what remained. Soon it was 1918-19 all over again. But now there were more machines, there were water-saving techniques, and there were government advisers available to make the boom bigger and better. The 1942 wheat harvest was larger than it had been in the over-flowing year of 1931, and it came from a smaller acreage. More bumper crops followed in 1943 and 1944, keeping pace with soaring demand. By 1945 the wheat area in 69 southern plains counties had expanded by 2.5 million acres, and lands that had been reclaimed at federal expense—their dunes removed and their hardpan surface broken up for sorghum or grass—were being replowed at a faster rate than they had been in the late twenties. Within two more seasons the Great Plains farmers were producing 958 million bushels of wheat, more than twice what they had gleaned in 1939, and they were getting good money for it, including government price supports. Everywhere, suddenly, the suitcase farmers reappeared, smelling a chance to make a killing, buying land in 5000- and 10,000-acre parcels, and hiring laborers to till and harvest it. Corporations were formed to do the same thing; one in southeastern Colorado farmed 28,000 acres in 1946 and made $1 million on its crop.[21]

Once brought back to prosperity, the plains farmers began growing restless under conservation leadership: terraces, more and more operators complained, were too costly, and it was hard to pull the new 42-foot plows on them; shelterbelts were taking up too much land that might raise a cash crop; soil conservation district rules were too restrictive; the government was too cautious about selling or leasing back the submarginal lands on which a thin stand of grass had so laboriously been established. "The voice of two-dollar wheat is far more persuasive than scientific facts on wind, rain, sun and soil," observed a *Saturday Evening Post* writer. Big-scale progressive farmers, he noted, who had been among the most eager converts to the SCS program, now led a revolt against advice and interference: they were "belligerently positive about their ability to take care of their land, no matter what happens." By 1947 the new surge of commercial farming was so reckless, and the anti-conservation mood so strong, that Secretary of Agriculture Clinton Anderson, a former Senator from New Mexico, had to speak out sharply: "What we are doing in the western Great Plains today is nothing short of soil murder and financial suicide."[22]

If production was the first principle of land use, as the agronomists and soil technicians had said, then they should have been bursting with pride. But instead they found themselves on the defensive, their productivity sermons turned against them—and they began to worry. It was proving harder and harder to demonstrate to a rambunctious region the cost-effectiveness of conservation technology; the old strategy of encouraging a return to full production and emphasizing dollar earnings from the land was exploding in the technicians' faces. Howard Finnell, back on the A & M campus after 1942, watched the expansion of the forties with considerable anxiety. In the fall of 1946 he estimated that four million acres of grassland had been recently plowed: some of the grass was virgin sod, the rest new vegetation on fields that had been abandoned in the thirties. Worse yet, the new crop lands had intermediate and low-grade soils for the most part. In the ten years before 1936 only 23 per cent of the sod broken was on Classes IV to VIII land—all unsafe categories for cropping; from that portion came most of the dirt in the air. But in the ten years after 1936 the percentage was 47.5. Increasingly, Finnell, the onetime prophet of abundance, became a Jeremiah of the plains:

> We are heading into the same conditions that gave us the old Dust Bowl. The next Dust Bowl will be bigger and better. . . . Frankly, we haven't stemmed the tide. We have been overrun by the plow-up. Soil conservation districts, organized by farmers to promote good land use, haven't had the backbone to stand up to the money pressure behind the plow-up.[23]

No agronomist, including Finnell, was willing to admit that conservation technology may have contributed to, rather than corrected, the mentality behind the new expansion—that they themselves might have obscured the need for more basic economic reforms in their urgent promotion of technical assistance. But by the mid-1940s they were beginning to claim that this turn of events was not quite what they had meant when they had said that productivity shall be increased and the land should be made to yield a good profit.

With each new harvest the lessons of the dirty thirties seemed to be more and more forgotten. Newspapers carried one story after another celebrating the Dust Bowl's recovery, with photographs of plump melons, truckloads of grain, and cattle belly-deep in bluestem. In 1947, Haskell County, according to an astonished Kansas City reporter, reaped five million bushels of wheat, worth $3333 for each inhabitant. New gas royalties added $750,000 to its total income. There were now four millionaires in the county, and a half-dozen residences worth $100,000 each—all paid for with wheat. More of the farmers' earnings went into new kitchen appliances, automobiles, farm machinery, land, mail-order clothes, and even airplanes than ever before. That same year, when Kansas State College agronomist R. I. Throckmorton, who had scoffed at the doomsayers a decade earlier, warned that ten million acres on the southern plains were again in serious danger of wind erosion, there were guffaws from all quarters. A prominent wheat farmer retorted: "It is time western Kansas began talking back to the dust bowl prophets." His home town, Liberal, once in the heart of the Bowl, now had a growing population and a housing shortage; its good crop land was selling for $60 an acre. Farther west, in Springfield, Colorado, a sidewalk farmer said that he and his neighbors now had the tools and techniques to control the soil—that there was absolutely no chance of another disaster.[24] The New Deal had given them a few good cards, they had drawn a few more, now it was time to go for the jackpot. No kibitzers looking over their shoulders, clucking their tongues and wagging their heads ominously, were wanted around the table.

Drought returned to the southern plains in the summer of 1952, and it brought what Clinton Anderson, Howard Finnell, and Professor Throckmorton had feared would happen: another round of savage dusters, the "filthy fifties." This drought was less drawn out than that of the thirties—it ended early in 1957. But while it lasted it was often more severe; September 1956 was the driest month ever recorded in the region.[25] In 1952 there ten major dust storms that rolled across naked fields, up from only one in 1945. Then, in the next few years, things got bad in the old, familiar way. Fred Maxwell and his wife hurried home to Kansas from a Florida vacation in March 1954 to find their driveway filled with tumbleweeds, their new wheat blown out, their living room carpet covered with an inch of topsoil. Basketball games that month were interrupted by dirt on the court. Street lights came on at midday, as they had in 1935. A man blinded by blowing sand smashed himself and his car on a bridge abutment. Cattle choked to death in drifted-over draws. Tourists found themselves stranded on lonely high-

ways, and businesses had to close their doors. That same March a black blizzard
darkened the skies from Amarillo all the way to the Canadian border. Winds blew
at 80 miles per hour, dust mounted to 20,000 feet, and schoolchildren raced for
home at noon, with handkerchiefs pressed tightly against their faces. In Washington, President Eisenhower and Secretary of Agriculture Ezra Taft Benson met to
consider what emergency aid they might send, while farmers hauled out their
listers and chisels to stop their farms from going. "Nature has set the stage for a
real disaster, if the rains fail to appear," wrote *U.S. News and World Report.*[26]
More to the point was what man had again done to the grassland. Fortunately, in
any case, the rains did return for a while—then it was drought again, then rain.
Had the dry spell lasted longer than it did, a full-scale replay of the thirties collapse and exodus might have taken place. Even so, the land took a dreadful pum-
meling: from 1954 to 1957 there were twice as many acres in the Great Plains
damaged annually by wind erosion as there were from 1934 to 1937.[27]

So much for salvation by technique. The Dust Bowl was dead, long live the
Dust Bowl. By then it should have been clear to everyone that the persistent problem of the plains was not *au fond* incompetence or ignorance, but motivation. "We
know all these things," admitted a farmer back in 1936. "We have learned them
from experience. We know how to farm better than we do farm. We simply take
chances, winning in good season, and losing when it falls to rain, or if the wind
blows out our crops." "It's not in our blood to play a safe game," said another.[28]
From the point of view of capitalistic farming, that thinking was less irrational
than it might otherwise appear—especially when there was a government willing to
clean up the results and absorb the social costs. It was a classic manifestation of
business-like rationality, which teaches that you cannot make more money without
taking more risks. Conservation, by this way of calculating, was acceptable so long
as it paid a higher return than did risk, so long as it enhanced rather than diminished all-out crop production. For a short while it did pay, then it did not—and
there went the revegetated pastures, the cumbersome terraces, the confining rules
and regulations. Only when looked at from the perspective of the land, the less
successful operators, the next generation, or the taxpaying public did the economic
rationalism of plains agriculture seem lunatic. And no amount of mere technical
advice could make a different kind of reasoning prevail. By 1954 Howard Finnell
had come to see that fact at last, and he spoke with bitterness and disillusion.

> The people of the region are now talking about conservation legislation.
> They have done that before. Several states passed conservation laws and
> tested them successfully in the courts, but, when the pressure of natural
> emergency eased, so did the public conscience: the laws were repealed and
> land exploitation was resumed with the vicious result we see today. It is not

law, nor incentive payments, nor more scientific information that we need. It is the will to conservation.[29]

It had taken twenty years for the former SCS official to reach that conclusion. Even then he had not come around to believing that the obstacles to conservation were deeply embedded in the economic culture of the region—that commercial agriculture might not be the way toward harmony with the land. He was not yet ready to say that changing the bases of that culture might be necessary. But he was no longer sure that technology was the answer or the profitability of conservation a convincing argument.

Agricultural conservation of the New Deal era was, on balance, a failure in the Great Plains. Neither the federal land-use planners nor the ecologists made a lasting impact on the region. The agronomists and soil technicians, although they were more successful in getting their version of conservation translated into action, were ultimately ineffectual, too. Give them credit for this: the region would not have come back so spectacularly without their assistance. Farmers did learn from these advisers a few tips that stayed with them, making them more of an "expert profession," as Hugh Bennett had hoped. But all the same, the agronomists' success in reforming the plains was, to put it in the best light, partial, and, to put it in the most critical light, self-defeating. Nothing Finnell and his fellow conservationists said in the thirties could have encouraged plainsmen to think of the land as something more than a commodity—a "resource"—for their enrichment. They offered farmers a technological panacea for ecological destructiveness, when the root issue was motivation and values—a deeply entrenched economic ethos. The return of dust-bowl conditions in the 1950s demonstrated, or should have demonstrated, the inability of a technical assistance program by itself to reform the old ethos. And that program was, in the end, by far the major legacy of New Deal conservation.

Were the plains, then, in much the same position they occupied in the tear-em-up twenties? By many indices they were not. America in general had changed significantly as a consequence of the Depression and dust storms, and the West, though less affected than other regions, had changed, too. There were new countervailing powers throughout the country that were supposed to restrain and direct the free-enterprise economy. The government was irrevocably committed to farm subsidies and marketplace intervention. Social chances had slightly improved for the poorer class of tenants and owners. It was unlikely that the plains residents would again suffer such hardship as they had gone through in the 1930s. Conservation, too, had made a few gains. National opinion was more educated in ecological principles and more ready to criticize farmers who violated them. Some of the most marginal lands were back in the public domain. Shelterbelts and contour plowing, residue management and fallowing, were more widely understood and practiced than ever before, although they all could be neglected in a new rush to the elevators. But, as post-thirties history revealed, each of those changes lay on the periphery; none of them touched the core of Great Plains agriculture—its devotion to unlimited expansion and its attendant sense of autonomy from nature. Subsequent events revealed that those environmental attitudes were not much affected by the years of turmoil and tempest, boom and bust, experts and exodusters. Conservation as a cultural reform had come to be accepted only where and insofar as it had helped the plains culture reach its traditional expansionary aims. If that was not failure, then success had a strangely dusty smell about it.

EPILOGUE:
ON A THIN EDGE

"Man strides over the earth, and
deserts follow in his footsteps."
Ancient proverb

MEN HAVE NOW been farming and ranching on the southern plains for a century. That is a very short time by world standards; in contrast, along the Nile and the Yangtze rivers agriculture has been practiced for more than forty centuries. Their soils are as rich and fertile now as they were in the beginning, while on the plains depletion is widespread, although that is concealed by chemical additives and plant breeding that keep yields high.[1] The Old World ways of working the earth, however, are disappearing. They require too much labor that might better be employed, so modern man thinks, in making automobiles and apartment houses or teaching school and treating diseases. All over the world agriculture has been undergoing a more radical set of changes than it has at any time since its invention some 8000 years ago. In the future, many authorities predict, it will look increasingly like the American model: a highly mechanized system of cropping plants and animals, making the earth a vast food factory, controlled by a very small number of multinational corporations and their employees. But before a full commitment to that version of the future is made, the rural dwellers of the world should know about and question more closely the historical as well as the present-day use of land in America. Would the spreading of this agriculture to Brazil or

Nigeria or Indonesia produce a new era of progress and plenty—or would it lead instead to a dark, bitter age of dust bowls? The southern plains today have a few reassuring answers to give, but they also have many fresh warnings that ought not to be ignored.

On the hopeful side, one should consider a successful couple like George and Irene McDaniels. It is hard to visit their home in the Oklahoma panhandle and not come away impressed by American farming. Their way of life shows the plains at their best. Drive north out of Texhoma on a late summer afternoon, cross the Beaver River where the cottonwoods throw long shadows over the cracked mud bottom, and rattle across a cattle guard onto the McDaniels's land. Fields of milo and native grass rustle in the wind. Chunky young Herefords skitter from the road like a team of fullbacks in white socks. Dogs come out to sniff and bark. The house, sheltered by a grove of trees, sits cool and quiet and modern, offering incredible luxury by world standards—or by those of America's dirty thirties—although it is nothing more than can be found in any contemporary American suburb. The Mc-Daniels are an unaffected and openhanded pair, satisfied with what they have achieved, philosophical about the hard days of the past, quietly enjoying the fruits of forty years' labor. They have approached the land more cautiously than most: George has always put his cows first, his wheat a distant second. When he was graduated in 1935 from Oklahoma A & M in Stillwater, he worked out of Clayton, New Mexico, purchasing submarginal land for the federal government; what he saw then of reckless farming he has not forgotten. In good years, when his neighbors have "their tails hanging over the fences," George keeps his herds and ambitions under shrewd control. He is a commercial farmer-rancher, although more diversified and more careful than most, and he is undeniably interested in making some money. But he tries hard to be a responsible trustee of the land, all the same.[2]

Every culture presents a spectrum of possibilities, narrow or wide, but also a median about which clusters the majority of people. The McDaniels are not near that median; they admit that their neighbors do many things differently, including taking more risks, forgetting when they do so the lessons of the past. Even farm families like the McDaniels, however, are having economic troubles these days, and it is not clear how long they or their neighbors can survive or what the next generation may expect to inherit. The McDaniels's machinery repair bills alone amount to $16,000 a year, and recently the market prices of crops and cattle, due to the latest surge of overproduction, have not been high enough to meet their enormous operating costs. Their barnyard has long been replaced by an elaborate machine shed, and there is enough equipment standing about to make a respectable-sized Allis-Chalmers sales lot: two $60,000 combines, a couple of tractors costing up to $30,000 each, and rows and rows of haybalers, wheat drills, disk plows, spring-tooth harrows, bulldozers, augers, and grain trucks. The total investment in such an assortment of machinery may amount to several hundred thousand dollars; add in the cost of 1300 acres (an average-sized farm in the panhandle), and few young people can get a start in this business any more. It is another of capitalism's shrinking realms. Then again, it takes fossil-fuel energy to run these machines—more, in fact, than the farmer produces in food energy, creating a net loss that only a gasoline-cheap era could have found sensible or economic. Although burdened with these escalating technological expenses, plains farmers in 1977 sold a bushel of wheat for no more than they did twenty years before. Hence, all through the region they are talking once more of depression and strike and higher government price supports. They live, of course, on a scale exceeding the wildest dreams of Dust Bowl days, but they are all, good and bad operators alike, up to their eyebrows in debt and as fearful of going under as any hardscrabble case of the 1930s. Poverty is a relative condition, and after decades of rising affluence the people of the plains are feeling as poor and pinched as ever. They also have reason to worry all over again about the land.[3]

In 1974 severe drought returned to the panhandle, and, indeed, to the entire West, all the way to the redwood coast. The regional climate pattern is now well-established and fairly predictable, some scientists say; every twenty years we may expect this part of the nation to suffer from a major drought, as in the 1890s, 1910s, 1930s, 1950s, 1970s, and someday, the 1990s.[4] But in 1974, the average plainsman was no better prepared than before. Like an old movie rerunning on the late show, the dirt began to blow, much of it coming from four million acres of former grassland in the Great Plains, some of it unplowed since the thirties, now lying bare. It had been torn up and seeded to grain following the massive Russian wheat purchase of 1972, when the per bushel price shot up to almost $6.00 and Secretary of Agriculture Earl Butz urged farmers to plant "fence row to fence row." By February 1976 the Soil Conservation Service estimated that over ten million acres from the Dakotas to Texas were open to serious erosion and that more than one million acres had already been damaged. Grain elevators in Texhoma were coated with red dust. Roadblocks were set up on Colorado's Interstate 70 to prevent travelers from driving into a nightmare, and motels and bars filled up with stranded motorists. In the following spring one of George McDaniels's neighbors lost 2600 acres of wheat to the wind, and another had seven cattle choke to death on dust. Farmers wore ski masks while driving their tractors, and still they would cough for a week after a blow. With their bigger machines they could deep plow their fields more quickly than they had been able to in earlier crises, getting clods on the surface to check the wind. But, as before, it was the fortuitous return of rain in the late summer of 1977 that really brought Dust Bowl III to an end. The drought lasted less than half as long as it had in the 1930s and was far less searing than it had been in the 1950s. But once more nature had warned the plainsmen not to take their successes for granted. It is still nature that gives, and nature that takes away, especially when the land has been pushed beyond its safe limits.[5]

The plains today can show a few wise farmers, such as George McDaniels, who have learned how to live, and live well, on this volatile land. It can boast of a high standard of living that now and then is also gracious, intelligent, and humane—a genuine, not always spurious, advance over the two-holer past. Its wheat has fed not only this nation, but Frenchmen struggling back from the ravages of World War II, Arabs wanting something in exchange for oil, Russians facing crop failures, Bengalis holding out empty bowls. But on the other side of the ledger there are the old economic uncertainities of business farming, the old squeeze play that leaves the land in fewer and fewer hands. And there are the most recent dust storms, familiar evidence of ecological maladaptation. Once more they have indicted the aggressive, expansionary, exploitative energies of an agriculture founded on capitalist values and methods. As always, the indictment is ignored; the storms have become an unpleasant but necessary part of doing business on the plains—an unavoidable side effect that society and nature must endure for somebody's profit. Next time they could well be more dangerous than anything yet encountered. That possibility, however, is not yet real enough to disturb the region's plans. This, then, is the agriculture that America offers to the world: producing an incredible bounty in good seasons, using staggering quantities of machines and fossil fuels to do so, exuding confidence in man's technological mastery over the earth, running along the thin edge of disaster.

During the past two decades the southern plains have had a new reason to feel supremely sure that the Dust Bowl era was over and would never return: deep-well irrigation. As one USDA official announced in the early 1970s, "We have achieved a climate-free agriculture on the plains." The Great American Desert would at long last blossom like the rose, and nothing in nature's cycles could wither that bloom. Irrigation was begun in the region at Garden City, Kansas, in 1879, when developers dug ditches to carry water from the Arkansas River to their crops. Plains rivers have never been a reliable source of water, however, and today, with a reservoir and irrigation canals upstream in Colorado, the river at Garden City is a dry, brushy wash. Water for crops in this area and throughout the High Plains now generally comes from reservoirs deep within the ground, especially from the Ogallala aquifer, which in some places lies at a depth of six hundred feet or more—a sand, gravel, clay, and caliche layer holding water that has seeped down over centuries at the rate of a quarter-inch or a half-inch a year. A simple windmill could not generate enough energy to raise this water, but powerful new centrifugal pumps, along with the experience of drought, encouraged farmers in the 1930s to invest thousands of dollars to tap the aquifer, at first in the most southerly portion of the Bowl around Lubbock and Plainview, Texas, where water-bearing strata are not so deep. Then, in the late fifties and the sixties, following another drought, underground water became the newest bonanza resource, to be exploited as quickly as possible lest someone else get there first. Five and a half million acres of Texas cotton, sorghum, sugar beets, alfalfa, wheat, and corn were being watered in 1969 by "underground rain," as Donald Green has aptly called it, and he added that plains farmers chose "a superabundance for a few years" rather than a reasonable abundance for many years.[6] They thus created a patchy greenbelt that could stop some of the dust they stirred up elsewhere. By the 1970s, however, many wells had gone dry and others had a rapidly falling water table. There was by no means enough recharge from the surface to balance the withdrawals being made. Early enthusiasts had maintained that the water supply was inexhaustible, but now, after a few years of heavy use, the end of it, and the end of "climate-free agriculture," is within sight: it will be virtually all gone, says Jack Alexander of the Panhandle Experiment Station in Goodwell, Oklahoma, in twenty years.[7] Dust may not blow out of irrigated land—but what are you going to do when the well runs dry?

No plains community has been more profoundly affected by the irrigation boom than has Haskell County, Kansas. Although Haskell has very little surface water, it sits over one of the thickest sections of the Ogallala. In 1939 the first deep well was drilled—Warren Moore and Wallace Schmidt each claim priority— and today there are 864 wells in the county. Most of them are used for gravity systems, in which the water goes by aluminum pipe from the well to the field, pours into ditches, then, where it does not soak into the soil, runs at a slight downhill grade to a tailwater recovery pit. If the land is not as perfectly flat as a tilted pool-table, engineers knock of its "knobs" and fill in the shallows, charging $500 an acre (and this is land that once sold for $2.00 or $3.00). The other major irrigation system, which is used on hilly, sandy terrain, is a giant sprinkler, which pivots around the well in a circle, rolling over the irregularities on huge rubber tires. Both systems are astronomically expensive to install and operate. It may cost anywhere from $50 to $100 per acre to irrigate a crop with ditches; sprinklers cost even more, and are more wasteful.[8] Today, during much of the year, the massive pumps work in Haskell, burning costly fuel from near-by natural gas wells and emitting a steady, deafening roar.

The plains once offered a great soothing peace to the harried mind. Now they are filled, obliterated, shattered by the noise and clatter of industrial America, drowning the song of the meadowlark and the rush of the wind.

The economic returns from irrigated farming, at least for a few, have been extraordinarily enriching. Recently this Dust Bowl county has consistently ranked as one of the wealthiest in per capita income in the United States, thanks to the affluence of the agribusiness farmers here. In 1976, when the stock market took a nose dive, Haskell raised $7 million worth of wheat on 95,000 acres, down from $17.3 million three years earlier. It sold a $4.5 million sorghum crop, too. But corn produced the greatest agricultural earnings, $27.4 million on 108,000 acres, all irrigated. Haskell County is now the largest producer of corn in the state of Kansas. It is also one of the largest producers of feedlot cattle, selling some $25 million worth a year. There are commonly more than a hundred thousand animals standing about on manure piles in nine such factory-feeding operations; on the site of the first county seat, for instance, now sprawls Santa Fe Feeders, an entire city of beef and flies and concrete troughs ringed with ensilage mountains. To make the Haskell agro-industrial empire keep on producing, fertilizer is essential: not the manure from feedlots, however, but anhydrous ammonia manufactured from natural gas. Along the highway, fertilizer dealers display scores of gleaming white tanks arrayed like capsules on a druggist's shelf—vitamin pills for an undernourished land. Today, Kansas farmers spend almost twice as much on artificial fertilizers as they do on property taxes. The returns from such investments, for those who have the capital, have been substantial in most years. During the recent downturn, however, five farmers in the county went under in a single year: they were no longer able to compete with agribusiness. There are now about 370 farms left, compared with the 423 that were in operation at the end of the 1930s.[9] But that first number, 370, is deceptively high, for in fact Haskell farming is carried out more and more by a few millionaire operators. One day, and it will be soon if the present crunch continues for long, they will have it all—oil and gas wells, feedlots, rendering plants, grain elevators, fertilizer stations, alfalfa mills, machinery dealerships, airplane hangars, and the land itself.

"Those that left never gained by it; those that stayed, gained." Helen Meairs, now a widow, is talking about the thirties generation in this county. She sits small and a bit severe on her sofa as Charlie Pride sings "Did You Think To Pray?" on the cassette tapedeck. Her two sons are among the new Haskell men of wealth, rich enough to lose $1 million in cattle speculation and still come out solvent. She has considerable money herself, which she spends on trips to Singapore and Zurich.

"There's no place in the world where you can make more than right here," she says, "unless you go into government or into fraud."

But what happens when the irrigation water runs out?

"I don't think that in our time it can. And if it does we'll get more from someplace else. The Lord never intended for us to do without water."

What then will you do for fuel?

"There's plenty of oil and gas here and will be for a long while yet."

Can the Dust Bowl come back as it was in the 1930s?

Circular or center-pivot irrigation fields, watered by giant sprinklers and deep wells. (*U.S. Department of Agriculture*)

"No sir, there's no way that could happen. We've got the machinery to stop it, and we know how to farm better."

Are you happier today than you were in the Depression years?

"Well, that was the most happiest time of my life. We had the children, you know, and each other. Of course I don't believe in the 'good old days.' We've got things really nice around here today."[10]

Along the wide, almost empty streets of Sublette weeds grow in the pavement cracks. An elegant German sedan purrs by, carrying a lady to Garden City to a hairdressing appointment. In the country Mennonites argue over whether CB radios and microwave ovens are too worldly. In the old Colusa area a television station has become the most visible feature in the landscape, even dwarfing the county's elevators. The mass production–mass consumption economy holds this community in its grip as firmly as ever. When and if that economy fails, Haskell will be left with precious little of its own. Its culture—which is to say, its agriculture—is, to an extent unmatched in other rural places of the world, summed up and defined by the technology it buys with the land's products. And therein lies its social and ecological vulnerability; commercial farming has given this community neither an identity of its own nor a nurturing relationship with the source of its wealth. Nowhere is there much sense of living in the presence of nature: of working with and being a part of an organic order that is complex, mysterious, awesome, and alive. The land of Haskell is by and large as sterile and uninteresting as a shopping center's parking lot—almost every acre totally, rigidly, managed for maximum output. Under this regimen the soil has become a dead, inert, brown flatness. A few wild creatures, one gathers from their smashed remains on the roads, live here, but they are unseen and forgotten. It is an environment that comes from and leads back to alienation—not a place that can stir much love or concern in the human heart. Can any genuine, fulfilling culture take root and flourish and endure in such a setting? Will there be a community here not only forty years from now, but forty centuries? Or will it have become a graveyard of industrial farming?

Wheat is king in the Great Plains still, and, as the water wells dry up, it is likely to recover lost territory. Rising international demand for the crop will reinforce this hegemony. Among the cereals, only rice is as widely and heavily consumed in the world—20 per cent of mankind's food energy comes from wheat. The United States produces two billion bushels of this grain a year, two-thirds of which is above our domestic needs and is sold abroad or stored at great expense. We have an abundance to sell. But that surplus is unlikely to last. Most of the world is in a nip-and-tuck race to keep up with demand, now succeeding, now falling behind and calling for help. Therefore, America will play, as it has in the past, the role of international grain supplier, much as the Middle East plays supplier for the oil-hungry. Almost half of all wheat exports in the world now comes from our farms. But each year that outside demand will get bigger, until even the American breadbasket will no longer be able to provide enough. By the end of this century, the United Nations predicts, there will be twice as many people on earth as there are now; simply to feed them at present dietary levels, which are at best meager, will require *four times* the current production of North America. Even that will not be sufficient, however, for the rest of the world wants to eat as well as the rich nations do. Today the average American or Canadian annually consumes as much grain—2000 pounds—as five Pakistanis do, most of the difference going to feed cattle and to put meat on the table. Bringing all of the future human population up to American dietary standards would require four times the current grain production of the entire world, or over five billion tons per year. Measured against its own needs, American wheat output is grossly excessive. But measured against potential world demand, that same output looks dismally low. Even now it is not enough to pay for the oil, the coffee, the Sonys, and the European vacations we want, and also to satisfy the hunger of the world's poor. The pressures on Great Plains land thus must continue to mount.[11]

If farmers and ranchers on the plains are persuaded by rising demand abroad and by USDA officialdom and acquisitive values at home to expand their operations further, the region may be in the most serious ecological trouble it has ever seen. Three times in the twentieth century the grasslands have been assaulted and pushed back to make room for wheat. Following each expansion a dust bowl has occurred as soon as the drought cycle has come around again. Nature, it should be clear, has limits; they are neither inflexible nor are they constant, but they do exist. Whenever the dust begins to blow we are being told what those limits are. American agriculture, however, persists in believing that it can ignore ecological truths, that it can live and plow and prosper without restraint. Already we have forgotten the débacle and the discipline of the 1930s. If we believe that we can repeat all the old mistakes of overexpansion and escape the consequences, we are heading, as surely as we were in the roaring twenties, for Dust Bowl IV. It will not come in precisely the same way as earlier ones, nor will it hurt in all the same spots, for the past never exactly repeats itself. But that new ecological disasters can be created by man on the plains, and on a scale greater than anything experienced before, is a conclusion that historians and scientists must emphatically agree upon. The Great Plains cannot be pushed and pushed to feed that world's growing appetite for wheat without collapsing at last into a sterile desert.

Is there an alternative to that fate? Luckily, there are two, though neither of them is easy, fully accepted, or sufficient in itself. The harder, yet more essential response is to moderate our demands on this limited planet: to learn to discipline our numbers and our wants before nature does it for us. That will require searching reappraisal of the cultures by which we live, not least so of capitalism. The second response is to help less fortunate nations improve their ability to raise their own wheat—making them more self-sufficient in ways that are ecologically sensitive. Even though that strategy could mean, and ought to mean, the loss of many of our overseas markets, it is by far the most effective way to increase production—a ton of fertilizer will do far more good in the Punjab than in Texas. In fact, Americans have been promoting agricultural expansion in the poorer countries for some time now. But we have usually given our help in the full confidence that our own agriculture and our economic system were the ideals for others to follow. Earl Heady, a prominent professor of agricultural economics at Iowa State University and a frequent consultant to other nations' leaders, has expressed this thinking as well as anyone:

> Agricultural economists and other agricultural specialists in the U.S. have been probing the world of developing countries over the past two decades

to find the key to successful agricultural development. They need not have
traveled so far; the secrets of successful agricultural development are best
found in the past history of the U.S. Over the past 200 years the U.S. has
had the best, the most logical and the most successful program of agricultural development anywhere in the world. Other countries would do well
to copy it.[12]

To be charitable, perhaps he was writing with a George McDaniels in mind, or
perhaps he was remembering the Food for Peace we have distributed around the
globe. He was emphatically not recalling, however, the Dust Bowl of the southern
plains—nor the cattle kingdom bust of the 1880s, nor the improvident mining of
underground water today, nor the grinding expenses of fertilizer and gasoline and
combines, nor the faces of defeated exodusters, nor the hard, wracking, wheezing
cough of an old man whose lungs were full of dirt. American farming has some
things to boast of, but much more to regret and remedy. Its expansion to other nations has already begun to create a new chain of environmental disasters that ought
to make us at least think twice about our evangelism.

In 1968, a drought set in across the Sahel, the border country south of the
Sahara Desert. For six years the people and the land struggled to survive, and often
failed; as many as 250,000 men, women, and children may have died of hunger,
and seven million more became international beggars, living on handouts from
other nations. In Mali, one of the six Sahelian states, the per capita national product before the drought was less than $100, making it, at least by that standard, one
of the dozen poorest nations on earth. More than 90 per cent of its cattle, sheep,
and goats had perished by 1974. Each year of the drought the desert advanced
southward, the vegetation and livestock died, and destitute Tuaregs and Bedouins
were forced into refugee camps around Timbuktu and Lake Chad, their lives and
cultures irreparably torn apart. Dust storms blew from the heart of this blighted
landscape well out into the Atlantic Ocean, even as far as Bermuda. But there have
long been severe droughts in the area; why was this one so much more destructive
and more calamitous than any other?

Nicholas Wade, writing in *Science,* explains what really was to blame for
the Sahelian dust bowl: "Over-population, deterioration of the climatic conditions
and, above all, the impact of the western economic and social system."[13] Taking
French and American advice to heart, these nations had greatly expanded their livestock numbers to earn foreign exchange, until there were twice as many animals to
support as there had been forty years before. Nomadic tribesmen, who for centuries had moved lightly across the land with their herds, were restricted by new
political boundaries, taxed, and forced to earn cash; gradually they stripped away

Sahelian dust bowl, June 1973. (*Food and Agriculture Organization, United Nations*)

the grass and trees on which their way of life depended, leaving the dirt exposed to the hot winds. Sedentary farmers moved northward into the same marginal areas, plowed up the soil, and planted peanuts, cotton, and vegetables to sell to western Europe. One-third of Niger's export earnings from such agricultural practices was spent on cars, gasoline, tobacco, and liquor by an urban elite. Even during the worst of the drought some export crops, controlled in most cases by a small handful of entrepreneurs, including at least one California agribusiness corporation, were being shipped abroad—while the people starved because they lacked enough arable land to grow food.[14] The consequence of all this "agricultural development" was that a highly successful human ecology that had proved its value in drought after drought was abruptly undermined, and a "natural catastrophe" followed. No one can predict when the land will recover enough to support the remaining population—or whether there is sufficient will to start over again.

The devastation of the Sahel prompted the United Nations to call a special conference on "desertification." It met in Nairobi in August and September of 1977. Because of man's mismanagement, it was reported at that meeting, fertile, productive land is being denuded and destroyed at a rate of fourteen million acres a year. While world population and food needs increase, arable land is shrinking. By the end of the century one-third of it may be gone. The Nairobi conference recommended, much as the Soil Conservation Service had in the 1930s, a program of shelterbelts, livestock management, new cultivation methods, drought insurance, and water conservation.[15] It carefully avoided discussing most of the social and economic forces that are the primary explanation for the new deserts on the march. Population is clearly one of those forces, pressuring nations to occupy their marginal lands. Others are the ancient class structures that have allowed a few people to monopolize the best land while the poor masses must crowd onto thin soils that deteriorate quickly under much use. Then there is the spread of western commercial farming through investment, foreign aid, and colonialist influence. Taken together, these explain why the world is facing a future of dust bowls.

Droughts will come and go on the earth—that much is certain. We may see many more of them in the future if world climate, as some observers argue, is moving into a new, volatile, unpredictable phase, either warming up or cooling off.[16] There have been 200-year droughts in the past; for all we know there may be one in the near future. In any event, man's ability to deal with drought is largely determined by his culture and social system as they influence farming. He may adapt himself and his institutions to the foreseeable limits of the environment, working cooperatively with other organisms to survive, or he may act as though he were autonomous and invulnerable. The first strategy is sometimes less productive in a short-term, quantitative sense, but it is what the oldest farming cultures of the world have always done and it is by that they have endured; they could teach many lessons to ecologically heedless modernizers in agriculture. American farming, on the other hand, has filled up our granaries again and again—but at a high social and environmental cost. To follow such a culture substantially unreformed into the future would be the most foolhardy risk we have taken yet in this country. To export it lock stock and barrel would be unconscionable.

As the world's population moves increasingly onto marginal land—and already more than half a billion people live in deserts or semiarid places—and as unfavorable shifts in climate appear likely, even in temperate zones, the need for ecologically adaptive cultures becomes all the more crucial. Capitalism cannot fill that need; all its drives and motives tend to push the other way, toward overrunning a fragile earth. Man, therefore, needs another kind of farming by which he can satisfy his needs without making a wasteland. It would be fitting if we should find this new agriculture emerging someday soon in the old Dust Bowl.

NOTES

Notes to Introduction

1. George Borgstrom, *World Food Resources* (New York: Intext Educational Publishers, 1973), p. 203.
2. K. William Kapp, *The Social Costs of Private Enterprise* (Cambridge: Harvard University Press, 1950), remains an important exception. So is Joseph Petulla, *American Environmental History* (San Francisco: Boyd & Fraser, 1977).
3. Although Alexis de Tocqueville noted in the 1840s that the American farmer was temperamentally close to the industrialist, business farming did not become a full-blown phenomenon until the 20th century. See Paul Johnstone, "Old Ideals and New Ideas in Farm Life," USDA, *Farmers in a Changing World* (Washington, D.C., 1940), pp. 111-70.
4. Khrushchev, quoted in Erik Eckholm, *Losing Ground: Environmental Stress and World Food Prospects* (New York: Praeger, 1976), p. 56. On the virgin lands, see also V. A. Kovda, "Land Use Development in the Arid Regions of the Russian Plain, the Caucasus and Central Asia," in L. Dudley Stamp (ed.), *A History of Land Use in Arid Regions* (Paris: UNESCO, 1961), pp. 175-218.

Notes to Chapter One

1. *Fifteenth Census of the United States: 1930. Unemployment* (Washington, D.C., 1931), 1:8-9. William Leuchtenburg, *Franklin D. Roosevelt and the New Deal, 1933-1940* (New York: Harper & Row, Torchbooks, 1963), p. 19. Dixon Wecter, *The Age of the Great Depression, 1929-1941* (New York: Macmillan, 1948), p. 123.
2. John Hoyt, *Drought of 1930-34,* U.S. Geological Survey, Water Supply Paper 680 (Washington, D.C., 1936), p. 6. Ivan Tannehill, *Drought: Its Causes and Effects*

(Princeton: Princeton University Press, 1947), p. 83. Harley Van Cleve, "Some of the Biological Effects of Drought," *Scientific Monthly,* 33 (Oct. 1931), 301-6.

3. John Hoyt, *Drought of 1930-34,* pp. 8-9, 66; Hoyt, *Drought of 1936,* U.S. Geological Survey, Water Supply Paper 820 (Washington, D.C., 1938), pp. 1, 7, 27. *Newsweek,* 15 Aug. 1936, pp. 17-18. "The Effect of Drought on Prairie Trees," *Science,* 8 Mar. 1935, Supp. p. 7. Joseph Kincer, "The Drought of 1934," *Scientific Monthly,* 39 (July 1934), 95-96.

4. *Newsweek,* 19 May, pp. 5-6; 4 Aug., pp. 6-7; 18 Aug. 1934, pp. 5-6, 4 July, p. 10, 11 July, p. 13, 18 July, pp. 7-11, 25 July 1936, p. 72. M.L.G., "The Drought and Its Effect on Agricultural Crops," *Scientific Monthly,* 39 (Sept. 1934), 288. Martha Bruère, "Lifting the Drought," *Survey Graphic,* 23 (Nov. 1934), 544-47.

5. P. H. Stephens, "Why the Dust Bowl?" *Journal of Farm Economics,* 19 (Aug. 1937), 750-55. F. W. Albertson and J. E. Weaver, "History of the Native Vegetation of Western Kansas during Seven Years of Continuous Drought," *Ecological Monographs,* 12 (Jan. 1942), 26, 31. S. D. Flora, "Is the Climate of Kansas Changing?" Kansas State Board of Agriculture, *31st Annual Report* (Topeka, 1938), pp. 30-33. Willis Ray Gregg, "Meteorological Aspects of the 1936 Drought," *Scientific Monthly,* 43 (Aug. 1936), 190.

6. Eric Miller, "The Dust Fall of November 12-13, 1933," *Monthly Weather Review* 62 (Jan. 1934), 14-15. W. A. Mattice, "Dust Storms, November 1933 to May 1934," *ibid.* 63 (Feb. 1935), 53-55. Charles Kellogg, "Soil Blowing and Dust Storms," USDA Miscellaneous Publication 221 (Washington, D.C., 1935).

7. W. O. Robinson, "The 'Brown' Snowfall in New Hampshire and Vermont," *Science,* 19 June 1936, pp. 596-97.

8. B. Ashton Keith, "A Suggested Classification of Great Plains Dust Storms," *Kansas Academy of Science Transactions,* 47 (Sept. 1944), 96-109.

9. Soil Conservation Service, "Some Information about Dust Storms and Wind Erosion in the Great Plains" (Washington, D.C., 1953), p. 9. H. F. Choun, "Duststorms in the Southwestern Plains Area," *Monthly Weather Review,* 64 (June 1936), 195-99.

10. *Kansas City Times,* 22 Feb. 1935; *Dodge City Globe,* 16 Mar. 1935; *Topeka Capital,* 17, 19 Mar. 1935; *Amarillo Sunday News-Globe,* 17, 26 Mar. 1935; *Kansas City Star,* 20-24 Mar. 1935. Smith Center Centennial Committee, *History of Smith Centre, Kansas, 1871-1971* (n.p., 1971), pp. 14-15.

11. *Kansas City Star,* 21 Mar. 1935; *Kansas City Times,* 20 Mar. 1935; *Topeka Journal,* 20, 23 Mar. 1935.

12. *Newsweek,* 30 Mar. 1935, pp. 5-6. For early April storms, see *Garden City Telegram,* 10 Apr. 1935; *Amarillo Globe,* 11 Apr. 1935; *Kansas City Star,* Apr. 11, 1935. According to J. S. Ploughe, there were 19 days of dust between March 15 and April 15. ("Out of the Dust," *Christian Century,* 22 May 1935, pp. 691-92.)

13. John and Louise Garretson to author, taped interview, 9 Sept. 1977. Ed and Ada Phillips to author, taped interview, 21 Sept. For other dust-storm experiences see Stanley Vestal, *Short Grass Country* (New York: Duell, Sloan & Pearce, 1941), pp. 196ff.; and Vestal papers, Western History Collection, University of Oklahoma, Norman.

14. Helen Wells to author, taped interview, 10 Sept. 1977.

15. Raymond Ellsaesser to author, taped interview, 8 Sept. 1977.

16. Lawrence Svobida, *An Empire of Dust* (Caldwell, Id.: Caxton, 1940), p. 97.

17. *Kansas City Star,* 27, 30 Apr.; 1, 2 May 1935. "Effect of Dust Storms: Replies of County Health Officers," Mar. 1935, National Archives Record Group (RG) 114.

18. Earle Brown, Selma Gottlieb, and Ross Laybourn, "Dust Storms and Their Possible Effects on Health," *U.S. Public Health Reports,* 50 (4 Oct. 1938), 1369-83. See also *Dallas Morning News,* 14 Apr. 1935, for another study of dust composition.

19. Warren Moore to author, taped interview, 9 Sept. 1977.

20. Margaret Bourke-White, "Dust Changes America," *The Nation,* 22 May 1935, pp. 597-98. *Kansas City Star,* 30 Apr. 1935. Caroline Henderson, "Spring in the Dust Bowl," *Atlantic Monthly,* 159 (June 1937), 715. Marilyn Coffey, "Dust Storms of the 1930s," *Natural History,* 87 (Feb. 1978), 80-81.

21. *Kansas City Star,* 22 Apr. 1935. "Effects of Dust Storms: Chambers of Commerce Reports," Mar. 1935, National Archives RG 114.

22. Avis Carlson, "Dust," *New Republic,* 1 May 1935, p. 333. Ira Wolfert, *An Epidemic of Genius* (New York: Simon & Schuster, 1960), pp. 61-62.

23. *Dodge City Globe,* 18 Mar. 1935. Charles Peterson, "Drama in the Dustbowl," *Kansas Magazine* (1952), 94-97. For samples of Dust Bowl humor, see Vance Johnson, *Heaven's Tableland: The Dust Bowl Story* (New York: Farrar, Straus, 1947), p. 194.

Notes to Chapter Two

1. Thomas Saarinen, *Perception of Drought Hazard on the Great Plains,* Department of Geography Research Paper 106 (Chicago: University of Chicago Press, 1966), p. 132.

2. Robert Geiger, *Washington Evening Star,* 15-17 Apr. 1935. Geiger's priority was established by Fred Floyd, A History of the Dust Bowl, (Ph.D. thesis, University of Oklahoma, 1950), Chap. 1. An earlier effort to locate the origin of the phrase "Dust Bowl" is discussed in David Nail, *One Short Sleep Past: A Profile of Amarillo in the Thirties* (Canyon, Tex.: Staked Plains Press, 1973), p. 124. William Gilpin's major work was *The Central Gold Region* (Philadelphia: Sower, Barnes & Co.; St. Louis: E. K. Woodward, 1860).

3. Tom Gill to Robert Geiger, 14 Apr. 1941, along with "Blow Area Map," National Archives RG 114. An earlier map is in H. H. Finnell Correspondence, *ibid.* Roy Kimmel, "A United Front To Reclaim the Dust Bowl," *New York Times Magazine,* 14 Apr. 1938, pp. 10-11, 20.

4. George Taton to author, taped interview, 11 Sept. 1977. *Dalhart Texan,* 5 July 1937. Hugh H. Bennett, "The Vague, Roaming 'Dust Bowl,'" *New York Times Magazine,* 26 July 1936, pp. 1-2, 17.

5. Soil Conservation Service, "Some Information about Dust Storms and Wind Erosion in the Great Plains" (Washington, D.C., 1953), p. 10. H. H. Finnell, "Southern Great Plains Region," Oct. 1940, National Archives RG 114. Kimmel, "A United Front," p. 11.

6. George Greenfield, *New York Times,* 8 Mar. 1937. Walter Davenport, "Land Where Our Children Die," *Collier's,* 18 Sept. 1937, pp. 11-13, 73-77. *Dalhart Texan,* 24 Mar. 1936.

7. Albert Law, *Dalhart Texan,* 17 June 1933. Mrs. M. A. Turner, Moore County, Tex., "Effects of Dust Storms: Chambers of Commerce Reports," Mar. 1935, National Archives RG 114.

8. Albert Law, *Dalhart Texan,* 24 Mar. 1936. John McCarthy, *Amarillo Globe-Times,* 13 Sept. 1937.

9. Hogue to author, 2 Mar. 1978. Ironically, Hogue's "Drouth Survivors" was burned after all—in an accidental fire in Paris at the Jeu de Paume Museum, which had purchased it. See also *Life,* 21 June 1937, pp. 60-61. Drought, incidentally, is always spelled "drouth" on the plains.

10. *Kansas City Star,* 12, 13 May 1935. Ida Watkins, *ibid.* 7 June 1936. *Dodge City Globe,* 12 May 1935. Robert Geiger, *Amarillo Sunday News-Globe,* 15 Mar. 1936. Ward West, "Hope Springs Green in the Dust Bowl," *New York Times Magazine,* 16 July 1939, pp. 7, 21.

11. Robert Martin, "Duststorms of 1938 in the United States," *Monthly Weather Review,* 67 (Jan. 1939), 12-15; Martin, "Duststorms of 1939," *ibid.* (Dec.), 446-51. *Daily Oklahoman* (Oklahoma City), 19 Mar. 1939.

12. Dorothea Lange and Paul Taylor, *An American Exodus* (New Haven: Yale University Press, 1969), p. 70. Vance Johnson, *Heaven's Tableland: The Dust Bowl Story* (New York: Farrar, Straus, 1947), pp. 173-76. "Effect of Dust Storms: County Agents' Reports," Mar.-Apr. 1935, National Archives RG 114.

13. Francis Cronin and Howard Beers, *Areas of Intense Drought Distress, 1930-1936,* WPA Research Bulletin, Series V, no. 1 (Washington, D.C., 1937). Charles Loomis, "The Human Ecology of the Great Plains," *Oklahoma Academy of Science Proceedings,* 17 (1937), 21. Johnson, *Heaven's Tableland,* pp. 190-91. Lange and Taylor, *American Exodus,* p. 82. Howard Ottoson *et al., Land and People in the Northern Transition Area* (Lincoln: University of Nebraska Press, 1966), p. 73.

14. Paul Kellogg, "Drought and the Red Cross," *Survey,* 15 Feb. 1931, pp. 535-38, 72-76. See also Pete Daniel, *Deep'n As It Come: The 1927 Mississippi River Flood* (New York: Oxford University Press, 1977), pp. 10-11, 84-95.

15. Bureau of the Census, *Vote Cast in Presidential and Congressional Elections, 1928-1944* (Washington, D.C., 1946).

16. The record of F.D.R.'s first 100 days is summed up in Arthur Schlesinger, Jr., *The Coming of the New Deal* (Boston: Houghton Mifflin, Sentry ed., 1965), pp. 1-23.

17. Mary Gallagher of Amarillo to F.D.R., 15 Mar. 1934, National Archives RG 114.

18. All these suggestions are from letters in the National Archives RG 114. See also Dr. Preston Pratt, *Kansas City Star,* 11 May 1935; and Harlan Miller, "Dust Rides the Winds Out of the West," *New York Times Magazine,* 11 Mar. 1935, pp. 11, 14.

19. H. H. Finnell Correspondence, National Archives RG 114. For an actual rain-making experiment, see R. Douglas Hurt, "The Dust Bowl," *American West,* 14 (July-Aug. 1977), 26.

20. Samuel Rosenman (ed.), *The Public Papers and Addresses of Franklin D. Roosevelt,* (13 vols., New York: Random House, 1938), Vol. III, pp. 293-97. See also Michael Schuyler, "Federal Drought Relief Activities in Kansas, 1934," *Kansas Historical Quarterly,* 42 (Winter 1976), 403-24.

21. Memorandum, C. W. Warburton to Henry Wallace, 22 Dec. 1937, National Archives RG 16.

22. George Wehrwein, "Wind Erosion Legislation in Texas and Kansas," *Journal of Land and Public Utility Economics,* 12 (Aug. 1936), 312-13.

23. This program was called the "Kansas Plan," after Governor Landon, on the advice of state agriculturists, presented the idea to F.D.R. (*Kansas City Star,* 29 Mar. 1935.) Kansas received the first federal grant for listing—$250,000 paid out at 10 cents an acre. See also Edgar Nixon (ed.), *Franklin D. Roosevelt and Conservation, 1911-1945* (2 vols., New York: Arno Press, 1972), 1:367-68; and Donald McCoy, *Landon of Kansas* (Lincoln: University of Nebraska Press, 1966), p. 325.

24. The itineraries and correspondence for this trip are in Official File 200, F.D.R. Library, Hyde Park, N.Y. See also Nixon (ed.), *Roosevelt and Conservation,* 1: 559-67, for the follow-up conferences in Des Moines, Iowa; and Michael Schuyler, "Drought and Politics, 1936: Kansas as a Test Case," *Great Plains Journal,* 14 (Fall 1975), 3-27.

25. Nixon (ed.), *Roosevelt and Conservation,* 2:247-49. *Amarillo Daily News,* 12 July 1935.

26. Telegram, Emergency Dust Bowl Committee, Liberal, Kansas, to Governor Walter Huxman, 23 Apr. 1937, Huxman Papers, Kansas State Historical Society, Topeka. Letter, H. A. Kinney to Huxman, 29 April 1937, *ibid.* Telegram, Liberal committee to F.D.R., 22 April 1937, National Archives RG 114. Letter, Fred Sykes to H. H. Finnell, 23 Apr. *ibid.*

27. *Boise City* (Ok.) *News* (hereafter cited as *BCN*), 2 Nov. 1933.

28. *Dalhart Texan,* 29 Apr. 1935. *Amarillo Daily News,* 27 May 1936. Evon Vogt, *Modern Homesteaders* (Cambridge: Harvard University Press, 1955), p. 66.

Notes to Chapter Three

1. Archibald MacLeish, *Land of the Free* (New York: Harcourt, Brace, 1938), pp. 49, 50, 77, 80, 83, 84.

2. Stryker, quoted in Alfred Stefferud (ed.), *After a Hundred Years: The Yearbook of Agriculture* (Washington, D.C., 1962), p. 513. Lewis Hine perhaps best distilled the intentions of the documentary photographers of this period: "I wanted to show the things that had to be corrected. I wanted to show the things that had to be appreciated." Quoted in William Stott, *Documentary Expression in Thirties America* (New York: Oxford University Press, 1973), p. 21.

3. Among outstanding collaborations were Erskine Caldwell and Margaret Bourke-White, *You Have Seen Their Faces* (1937); Richard Wright and Edwin Roskam, *12 Million Black Voices* (1941); and James Agee and Walker Evans, *Let Us Now Praise Famous Men* (1941).

4. This disillusion was anticipated by such 1920s writers as T. S. Eliot and F. Scott Fitzgerald; see Leo Marx, *The Machine in the Garden* (New York: Oxford University Press, 1964), Epilogue. See also Richard Pells, *Radical Visions and American Dreams* (New York: Harper & Row, 1973), for the mood of intellectuals in the Depression years.

5. Ralph Borsodi's books include *This Ugly Civilization* (1929) and *Flight from the City* (1933); see also his "Plan for Rural Life," in Baker Brownell et al., *Agriculture in Modern Life* (New York: Harper & Bros., 1939), pp. 187-211. The Nash-

ville Agrarians were also the "Twelve Southerners" who wrote *I'll Take My Stand* (1930).

6. Cited by Charles Hearn, *The American Dream in the Great Depression* (Westport, Conn.: Greenwood Press, 1977), pp. 63-64. See also "The Agrarian Dream as Delusion," pp. 84-92.

7. Edmund Brunner and Irving Lorge, *Rural Trends in Depression Years* (New York: Columbia University Press, 1937), pp. 4-7. "Farm Population and Migration to and from Farms," *Monthly Labor Review*, 41 (Aug. 1935), 358-59.

8. *Interstate Migration*, U.S. House Report 369, 77th Congress (Washington, D.C., 1941), pp. 320-21. William Weber Johnson, *Kelly Blue* (Lincoln: University of Nebraska Press, 1960), p. 176.

9. *Amarillo Times*, 25 June 1940. Roy Roberts, "Population Changes in the Great Plains," *Rural Sociology*, 7 (Mar. 1942), 40-48. Olaf Larson, "Farm Population Mobility in the Southern Great Plains," *Social Forces*, 18 (May 1940), 514-20. Conrad Taeuber and Charles Hoffman, "Recent Migration from the Drought Areas," *Land Policy Circular* (Sept. 1937), 16-20. Earl Bell, "About the People," *Land Policy Review*, 3 (Oct. 1940), 18. Two personalized accounts of being dusted out are Lawrence Svobida's autobiographical *An Empire of Dust* (Caldwell, Id.: Caxton, 1940) and Lois Hudson's novel, *The Bones of Plenty* (Boston: Atlantic Monthly Press, 1962).

10. *Sixteenth Census of the U.S., 1940: Population, Internal Migration, 1935 to 1940* (Washington, D.C., 1946), pp. 176-77. Evon Vogt, *Modern Homesteaders* (Cambridge: Harvard University Press, 1955). Neil Lane, "The Dust Farmer Goes West," *Land Policy Review*, 1 (May-June 1938), 21-25. *Rocky Ford* (Colo.) *Tribune*, 1 May 1936.

11. Charles Hoffman, "Drought and Depression Migration into Oregon, 1930 to 1936," *Monthly Labor Review* 46 (Jan. 1938), 27-35. David McEntire, "Migrants and Resettlement in the Pacific Coast States," *Land Policy Review*, 1 (July-Aug. 1938), 1-7. Willard Troxell and W. Paul O'Day, "The Migrants: III. The Migration to the Pacific Northwest, 1930-1938," *ibid.* 3 (Jan.-Feb. 1940), 32-43.

12. *Interstate Migration*, pp. 305-8, 324-25. Dorothea Lange and Paul Taylor, *An American Exodus* (New Haven: Yale University Press, 1969), p. 110.

13. Paul Taylor and Tom Vasey, "Drought Refugee and Labor Migration to California, June-December 1935," *Monthly Labor Review*, 42 (Feb. 1936), 312-18. Edward Rowell, "Drought Refugees and Labor Migration to California in 1936," *ibid.* 43 (Dec. 1936), 1355-63. John Webb and Malcolm Brown, *Migrant Families*, WPA Research Monograph 18 (Washington, D.C., 1938), pp. xxiii-xxix, 7, 137. Lange and Taylor, *American Exodus*, p. 110.

14. Walter Stein, *California and the Dust Bowl Migration* (Westport, Conn.: Greenwood Press, 1973), Chap. 2.

15. "Migratory Labor: A Social Problem," *Fortune*, 19 (Apr. 1939), 90-92.

16. H. L. Mencken, "The Dole for Bogus Farmers," *American Mercury*, 39 (Dec. 1936), 404.

17. Martin Shockley, "The Reception of *The Grapes of Wrath* in Oklahoma," *American Literature*, 15 (Jan. 1944), 351-61. W. Richard Fossey, " 'Talkin' Dust Bowl Blues': A Study of Oklahoma's Cultural Identity during the Great Depression," *Chronicles of Oklahoma*, 55 (Spring 1977), 31-33. Warren French (ed.), *A Com-*

panion to The Grapes of Wrath (New York: Viking, 1963), pp. 106, 116, 167. MS on Steinbeck, Box 130, W. S. Campbell Papers, Western History Collection, University of Oklahoma, Norman. *Tulsa Daily World,* 2 Sept. 1945.

18. John Steinbeck, *Their Blood Is Strong* (San Francisco: Simon Lubin Society, 1938), pp. 4, 33. In the same year these articles were being written, Steinbeck published *In Dubious Battle* (1936), the novel that followed the career of a radical labor organizer in California's apple country from initiation to violent death.

19. "Migratory Labor: A Social Problem," pp. 90, 114.

20. John Steinbeck, *Their Blood Is Strong,* p. 31. Lange and Taylor, *American Exodus,* p. 112.

21. The Tolan Committee's findings have been called "the most comprehensive body of historical material on migrant problems in the United States" (Stein, *Dust Bowl Migration,* p. 214). See also Fossey, "Dust Bowl Blues," pp. 20-21. Unfortunately, this material came on the eve of World War II—too late to stir the public to action. Many of the Okies solved their own problems by going to work in armaments plants, and the growers went back to hiring imported Mexican labor.

22. John Steinbeck, *The Grapes of Wrath* (New York: Viking, Compass ed., 1939), p. 65.

23. Lange and Taylor, *American Exodus,* p. 68. Paul Taylor, "Again the Covered Wagon," *Survey Graphic,* 24 (July 1935), 348-51, 368; Taylor, "What Shall We Do with Them?" address before the Commonwealth Club of San Francisco, 15 Apr. 1938; Taylor, "Power Farming and Labor Displacement: Southwestern Oklahoma and Mississippi Delta," *Monthly Labor Review,* 46 (Apr. 1938), 852; Taylor, "Good-by to the Homestead Farm: The Machines Advance in the Corn Belt," *Harper's,* 182 (May 1941), 589-99.

24. See Eugene Genovese, *The Political Economy of Slavery* (New York: Pantheon, 1965), pp. 85-105; and Lewis C. Gray, *History of Agriculture in the Southern States to 1860,* (2 vols. Washington, D.C.: Carnegie Institution, 1933), 1:301-11. The former discusses soil exhaustion but denies that the South had a capitalist system, while the latter—more convincing—argues that antebellum slavery had its capitalist elements, too.

25. Carey McWilliams, *Ill Fares the Land* (Boston: Little, Brown, 1942), pp. 187, 192, 195.

26. Angus McDonald, "Erosion and Its Control in Oklahoma Territory," USDA Miscellaneous Publication 301 (Washington, D.C., 1938). Hugh Bennett, "Land Impoverishment by Soil Erosion," Kansas Board of Agriculture, *27th Biennial Report* (Topeka, 1931), pp. 177-87. Edward Hyams, *Soil and Civilization* (London: Thames and Hudson, 1952), Chap. 10. According to McWilliams, 6.5 million people lived on farms needing erosion treatment in Oklahoma, Texas, and Arkansas (McWilliams, *Ill Fares the Land,* p. 199).

27. Guy Logsdon, "The Dust Bowl and the Migrant," *American Scene.* 12 (1971). Logsdon observes that the population of the 7 northwestern counties of Oklahoma, all in the dust area, dropped by 12,808 over the decade. That number, of course, does not include all those who left these counties; high birth rates and some in-migration concealed the true size of the population loss. On the other hand, many of those who left did not move out of the state. It is clear, therefore, that the Dust Bowl counties contributed only a small percentage of the out-migrants. But Oklahoma was less affected in area by the dust storms than Kansas and Texas were.

28. See Woody Guthrie's autobiography, *Bound for Glory* (New York: Dutton, 1943).
    More reliable for dates, however, are Henrietta Yurchenco, *A Mighty Hard Road:
    The Woody Guthrie Story* (New York: McGraw-Hill, 1970); Harry Menig,
    "Woody Guthrie: The Oklahoma Years, 1912-1929," *Chronicles of Oklahoma,* 53
    (Summer 1975), 239-65; and Frederick Turner, " 'Just What the Hell Has Gone
    Wrong Here Anyhow?': Woody Guthrie and the American Dream," *American
    Heritage,* 28 (Oct. 1977), 34-40. As for the songs themselves, there are *Hard-
    Hitting Songs for Hard-Hit People* (New York: Oak Publications, 1967), and
    "Dust Bowl Ballads," RCA Victor Vintage Series.
29. Larson, "Farm Population Mobility," p. 517. Robert MacMillan, "Farm Families in
    the Dust Bowl," *Land Policy Review,* 1 (Sept.-Oct. 1938), 14-17. See *Report of
    the President's Committee on Farm Tenancy* (Washington, D.C., 1937), pp. 89,
    96, 100, for demographic data and plains tenure.
30. Steinbeck, *Grapes of Wrath,* pp. 44, 49, 158. According to Peter Lisca, "the human
    erosion pictured in the book is as much the result of a separation from the land as
    it is of poverty." Lisca, *The Wide World of John Steinbeck* (New Brunswick:
    Rutgers University Press, 1958), p. 153.

Notes to Chapter Four

1. [Archibald MacLeish], "The Grasslands," *Fortune,* 12 (Nov. 1935), 59.
2. William Baker, "A History of Cimarron County," *Chronicles of Oklahoma,* 31
   (Autumn 1953), 255-57. *BCN,* 13 June 1935.
3. John Brophy, "Synopsis of Geology of the Great Plains," in Carle Zimmerman
   and Seth Russell (eds.), *Symposium on the Great Plains of North America* (Fargo,
   N.D., North Dakota Institute for Regional Studies, 1967), pp. 32-34. J. C. Frye,
   "The High Plains Surface in Kansas," *Kansas Academy of Science Transactions,*
   49 (1946), 71-86. Nevin Fenneman, *The Physiography of the Western United
   States* (New York: McGraw-Hill, 1931), pp. 11-14, 25, 88.
4. M. M. Leighton, "Geology of Soil Drifting on the Great Plains," *Scientific
   Monthly,* 47 (July 1938), 29-32. "Dust Storms Can Build Up as Well as Tear
   Down," *Scientific American,* 165 (Dec. 1941), 340. *Topeka Capital,* 1 Oct. 1939.
5. Curtis Marbut, "Soils of the Great Plains," *Annals of the Association of American
   Geographers,* 13 (Mar. 1923), 41-66. USDA, *Soils and Men* (Washington, D.C.,
   1938), pp. 1075-92.
6. C. Warren Thornthwaite, "Climate and Settlement in the Great Plains," USDA,
   Climate and Man (Washington, D.C., 1941), pp. 178-83; and Thornthwaite, "The
   Great Plains," in Carter Goodrich *et al., Migration and Economic Opportunity*
   (Philadelphia: University of Pennsylvania Press, 1936), pp. 205, 217-27. Joseph
   Kincer, "The Climate of the Great Plains as a Factor in Their Utilization," *Annals
   AAG,* 13 (Mar. 1923), 67-80.
7. Paul Sears, *Lands Beyond the Forest* (Englewood Cliffs, N.J.: Prentice-Hall,
   1969), pp. 60-65.
8. Johnson, "The High Plains and Their Utilization," U.S. Geological Survey, *22nd
   Annual Report, 1900-1901, Part IV, Hydrography* (Washington, D.C., 1902), pp.

637-38. John James Ingalls, "In Praise of Blue Grass," reprinted in USDA, *Grass* (Washington, D.C., 1948), p. 7.

9. H. L. Shantz, "The Natural Vegetation of the Great Plains Region," *Annals AAG*, 13 (Mar. 1923), 81-107. John Weaver, *North American Prairie* (Lincoln, Neb.: Johnsen, 1954); and John Weaver with F. W. Albertson, *Grasslands of the Great Plains* (Lincoln, Neb.: Johnsen, 1956). James Malin, *The Grassland of North America* (Lawrence, Kans.: n.p., 1961), pp. 62-81.

10. Ernest Thompson Seton, *Life Histories of Northen Animals* (2 vols., New York: Scribner's, 1909), I:259. Cf. Frank Roe, *North American Buffalo,* 2nd ed. (Toronto: University of Toronto Press, 1970), pp. 489-520.

11. Durward Allen, *The Life of Prairie and Plains* (New York: McGraw-Hill, 1967), pp. 80-83. See also Victor Shelford, *The Ecology of North America* (Urbana: University of Illinois Press, 1963), pp. 344-47.

12. Paul Martin, George Quimby, and Donald Collier, *Indians before Columbus* (Chicago: University of Chicago Press, 1947), pp. 83-85. See also Paul Martin and H. E. Wright, Jr. (eds.), *Pleistocene Extinctions* (New Haven: Yale University Press, 1967), pp. 89-102, 179-89.

13. Waldo Wedel, "Environment and Native Subsistence Economies in the Central Great Plains," *Smithsonian Miscellaneous Collections,* 101 (1941), 27; Wedel, "Culture Sequence in the Central Great Plains," *ibid.* 100 (1940), 291-352; and Wedel, "Some Aspects of Human Ecology in the Central Plains," *American Anthropology,* 55 (Oct. 1953), 499-514. See also William Van Royen, "Prehistoric Droughts in the Central Great Plains," *Geographical Review,* 27 (Oct. 1937): 637-50. That there was soil blowing before the white man came is also argued by James Malin, "Dust Storms, 1850-1900," *Kansas Historical Quarterly,* 14 (May 1946), 129-44; (Aug.), 265-96; (Nov.), 391-413.

14. Andrew Douglass, "Tree Growth and Climatic Cycles," *Scientific Monthly,* 37 (Dec. 1933), 481-95; and Douglass, "The Secret of the Southwest Solved," *National Geographic,* 56 (Dec. 1929), 737-70.

15. H. E. Weakly, "A Tree-Ring Record of Precipitation in Western Nebraska," *Journal of Forestry,* 41 (Nov. 1943), 816-19.

16. George Winship, "The Coronado Expedition, 1540-1542," U.S. Bureau of American Ethnology, *14th Annual Report, 1892-93* (Washington, D.C., 1896), Pt. I, pp. 329-637.

17. Standard accounts are Robert Lowie, *Indians of the Plains* (New York: McGraw-Hill, 1954); and Clark Wissler, *North American Indians of the Plains* (New York: American Museum of Natural History, 1912).

18. Mildred Mayhall, *The Kiowas* (Norman: University of Oklahoma Press, 1962), p. 93. See also Peter Farb, *Man's Rise to Civilization* (New York: Dutton, 1968), pp. 112-32, for a more exaggerated account of the horse's impact.

19. See e.g. Carl Sauer, "Grassland Climax," in *Agricultural Origins and Dispersals,* 2nd ed. (Cambridge: Massachusetts. Institute of Technology Press, 1969), pp. 15-18. Waldo Wedel refutes him in "The Central North American Grassland: Man-Made or Natural?" *Studies in Human Ecology* (Washington, D.C., Pan-American Union, 1957), pp. 39-69.

20. Jerrold Levy demonstrates that these Indians were in an equilibrium state with their natural resources: their population in the 19th century had stabilized at

about 10,000, or 1 person per 31 sq. mi. Levy, "Ecology of the South Plains," in Viola Garfield (ed.), *Patterns of Land Utilization and Other Papers* (Seattle: University of Washington Press, 1961), pp. 18-23. That this stability has also been the case with most "primitive" societies is argued by Richard Wilkinson in *Poverty and Progress: An Ecological Model of Economic Development* (London: Methuen, 1973), Chap. 3.

21. N. Scott Momaday, "A First American Views His Land," *National Geographic,* 150 (July 1976), 18.

22. Walter Prescott Webb, *The Great Plains* (Boston: Ginn, 1931), p. 44. See also T. R. Fehrenbach, *Comanches: The Destruction of a People* (New York: Knopf, 1974).

23. David Dary, *The Buffalo Book* (Chicago: Swallow, 1974), pp. 127-29. A buffalo hunter armed with a Sharps rifle could kill 200 head a day; Thomas Nixon set the all-time record: 120 in 40 minutes.

24. Stuart Chase, *Rich Land, Poor Land* (New York: McGraw-Hill, 1936), p. 117.

Notes to Chapter Five

1. Donald Jackson (ed.), *The Journals of Zebulon Montgomery Pike* (2 vols., Norman: University of Oklahoma Press, 1966), 2:28. For the subsequent history of the Great American Desert idea, see Walter Prescott Webb, "The West and the Desert," *Montana,* 8 (Winter 1958), 2-12; Martyn J. Bowden, "The Great American Desert in the American Mind," in David Lowenthal and Martyn J. Bowden (eds.), *Geographies of the Mind* (New York: Oxford University Press, 1976), pp. 119-47; and Terry Alford, "West as a Desert in American Thought Prior to Long's 1819-1820 Expedition," *Journal of the West,* 8 (Oct. 1969), 515-25.

2. Martyn J. Bowden, "The Great American Desert and the American Frontier, 1800-82," in Tamara Hareven (ed.), *Anonymous Americans* (Englewood Cliffs, N.J.: Prentice-Hall, 1971), pp. 48-79; Bowden, "Desert Wheat Belt, Plains Corn Belt," in Brian Blouet and Merlin Lawson (eds.), *Images of the Plains* (Lincoln: University of Nebraska Press, 1975), pp. 189-202.

3. Henry Nash Smith, "Rain Follows the Plow," *Huntington Library Quarterly,* 10 (Feb. 1947), 187-88. See also David Emmons, *Garden in the Grasslands* (Lincoln: University of Nebraska Press, 1971), pp. 128-61.

4. The following are useful on the southern plains cattle kingdom: Edward Everett Dale, *The Range Cattle Industry* (Norman: University of Oklahoma Press, 1960); J. Evetts Haley, *The XIT Ranch of Texas and the Early Days of the Llano Estacado* (Chicago: Lakeside, 1929); and Frederick Rathjen, *The Texas Panhandle Frontier* (Austin: University of Texas Press, 1973), pp. 228-49.

5. U.S. Forest Service, *The Western Range,* Senate Document 199, 74th Cong. (Washington, D.C., 1936), pp. 51-52, 119-33.

6. John Ise, "Pioneer Life in Western Kansas," in Norman Himes (ed.), *Economics, Sociology and the Modern World* (Cambridge, Harvard University Press, 1935), p. 131. Ise, *Sod and Stubble* (Lincoln: University of Nebraska Press, 1936), is an excellent family history account. See also his edited collection of letters, *Sod House Days* (New York: Columbia University Press, 1937); and Carl Coke Rister, *Southern Plainsmen* (Norman: University of Oklahoma Press, 1938), pp. 148-59.

7. James Malin, *Winter Wheat in the Golden Belt of Kansas* (Lawrence: University of Kansas Press, 1944), p. 127. See also Malin, "The Turnover of Farm Population in Kansas," *Kansas Historical Quarterly,* 4 (Nov. 1935), 339-72. Edward Higbee, *The American Oasis* (New York: Knopf, 1957), p. 126. Conrad Taeuber and Carl Taylor, *The People of the Drought States,* WPA Research Bulletin, Series V, no. 2 (Washington, D.C., 1937), p. 15. Fred Shannon, *The Farmer's Last Frontier* (New York: Farrar and Rinehart, 1945), pp. 215-20.

8. Robert Dunbar, "Agricultural Adjustments in Eastern Colorado in the Eighteen-Nineties," *Agricultural History,* 18 (Jan. 1944), 41-52. Vance Johnson, *Heaven's Tableland* (New York: Farrar, Straus, 1947), pp. 60-63.

9. See the latest reprint of Powell's book, Wallace Stegner (ed.), *Report on the Lands of the Arid Region of the United States* (Cambridge: Harvard University Press, 1962), esp. pp. 15-16, 31-32. Where irrigation could be practiced, Powell recommended 80-acre homesteads organized in colonies like the Western mining districts. For the hostile public reaction to his proposals, see Wallace Stegner, *Beyond the Hundredth Meridian* (Boston: Houghton Mifflin, 1954), p. 209-38; Henry Nash Smith, *Virgin Land* (Cambridge: Harvard University Press, 1950), p. 196-200; and Walter Prescott Webb, *The Great Plains* (Boston: Ginn, 1931), pp. 419-22.

10. Stegner (ed.), Powell, *Report on the Lands of the Arid Region,* p. xv.

11. Gilbert Fite, "Plains Farming: A Century of Change," *Agricultural History,* 51 (Jan. 1977), 254.

12. Mary W. M. Hargreaves, *Dry Farming in the Northern Great Plains, 1900-1925* (Cambridge: Harvard University Press, 1957), pp. 21, 85-95.

13. Paul Gates, "Homesteading in the High Plains," *Agricultural History,* 51 (Jan. 1977), 125. Garry Nall, "Panhandle Farming in the 'Golden Era' of American Agriculture," *Panhandle-Plains Historical Review,* 46 (1973), 76. Johnson, *Heaven's Tableland,* pp. 71-81. USDA, *The Dust Bowl,* Editorial Reference Series No. 7 (Washington, D.C., 1940), pp. 37-38. A splendid personal account of this period in eastern Colorado is Hal Borland, *High, Wide and Lonesome* (Philadelphia: Lippincott, 1956).

14. A. B. Genung, "Agriculture in the World War Period," USDA, *Farmers in a Changing World* (Washington, D.C., 1940), p. 278. Johnson, *Heaven's Tableland,* pp. 109-11.

15. A. B. Genung, "Agriculture," pp. 280-84. Lloyd Jorgenson, "Agricultural Expansion into the Semiarid Lands of the West North Central States during the First World War," *Agricultural History,* 23 (Jan. 1949), 30-40. *Kansas City Star,* 19 Apr. 1935.

16. WPA National Research Project A-10, "Changes in Technology and Labor Requirements in Crop Production: Wheat and Oats" (Washington, D.C., 1939), pp. v-vi, 37, 51-52, 178. Reynold Wik, "Henry Ford's Tractors and American Agriculture," *Agricultural History,* 38 (Apr. 1964), 81. R. S. Kifer, B. H. Hurt, and Albert Thornbrough, "The Influence of Technical Progress on Agricultural Production," *Farmers in a Changing World,* pp. 509-32. Wayne Rasmussen, "The Impact of Technological Change on American Agriculture, 1862-1962," *Journal of Economic History,* 22 (Dec. 1962), 578-91.

17. Morrow May, "The Man on the Tractor," *Harper's,* 177 (Nov. 1938), 624.

18. WPA, "Changes in Technology and Labor Requirements," pp. 21-23.

19. *Ibid.* pp. 28-32. L. A. Reynoldson, "Combine Harvester in the Great Plains," *USDA Yearbook, 1926* (Washington, D.C., 1927), pp. 232-34. The passing of the itinerant harvest crew is noted by Henry Allen, "The New Harvest Hand," *American Review of Reviews,* 76 (Sept. 1927), 279-80.

20. Garry Nall, "Specialization and Expansion: Panhandle Farming in the 1920's," *Panhandle-Plains Historical Review,* 47 (1974), 64-66. USDA, *The Dust Bowl,* pp. 33-34, 36. W. E. Grimes, "Some Phases of the Hard Winter Wheat Grower's Problem in Readjustment," *Journal of Farm Economics,* 17 (Apr. 1925), 195-219.

21. Johnson, *Heaven's Tableland,* pp. 136-37. *Topeka Capital,* 3 Aug. 1926. *Panhandle Herald* (Guymon, Ok.), 13 Dec. 1928. Nall, "Specialization and Expansion," pp. 66-67. The largest operator of all was located in Montana: see Hiram Drache, "Thomas D. Campbell—The Plower of the Plains," *Agricultural History,* 51 (Jan. 1977), 78-91. Campbell's ambition was to be a "manufacturer of wheat"; he farmed, with House of Morgan backing, over 100,000 acres.

22. Leslie Hewes, in *The Suitcase Farming Frontier* (Lincoln: University of Nebraska Press, 1973), is a well-informed apologist for these mobile entrepreneurs. "TRB" was not so impressed: see *New Republic,* 9 June 1937, p. 128.

23. H. B. Urban, transcribed interview, 15 June 1974, Panhandle-Plains Historical Museum, Canyon, Texas. USDA, *The Dust Bowl,* p. 44. Clifford Hope, "Kansas in the 1930's," *Kansas Historical Quarterly,* 36 (Spring 1970), 2-3. Johnson, *Heaven's Tableland,* p. 146.

24. Lorentz, quoted in Robert Snyder, *Pare Lorentz and the Documentary Film* (Norman: University of Oklahoma Press, 1968), p. 31. For Hollywood antagonism to the film, see *Time,* 25 May 1936, pp. 47-48. For plains reactions, see *Amarillo Daily News,* 1 June 1936. There John McCarty thundered: "It is purely a propaganda film. . . . It is bound to do more damage to our credit and our agriculture than it can possibly do good." In Amarillo 1500 persons saw the film at special showings; many of them were more impressed than McCarty was.

25. Thorstein Veblen, *The Theory of Business Enterprise* ([1904], New York: Augustus Kelley, 1965), p. 1. For the capitalist ethos in agriculture, see Louis Hacker, *The Triumph of American Capitalism* (New York: Simon & Schuster, 1940), pp. 17, 430; Thorstein Veblen, *Absentee Ownership and Business Enterprise* (New York: Huebsch, 1923), pp. 129-41; and Avis Carlson, "Dust Blowing," *Harper's,* 171 (July 1935), 154.

Notes to Chapter Six

1. Oliver Baker, "The Agriculture of the Great Plains Region," *Annals of the Association of American Geographers,* 13 (Mar. 1923), 110.

2. "The worst area and the center of this Dust Bowl lies from about 20 miles west of the Oklahoma and New Mexico line to about 10 miles east of the Cimarron and Texas County line and from Boise City, south to Dalhart, Texas." William Baker, "1936 Annual Report [of County Extension Work]," p. 7. This and other annual reports by Baker cited in Part III are on file in the state extension office at the Cimarron County Courthouse.

3. *Census of Agriculture, 1935* (Washington, D.C., 1936), 1:717; and *Sixteenth Census of the U.S.: 1940. Agriculture* (Washington, D.C., 1942), 1: part 5, p. 865.

Unless otherwise identified, all statistics used in Parts III and IV are from these sources. Cimarron's population peak, about 7000, was reached in the boom year of 1931; its decline during the dust years was therefore 50 per cent. By 1970, it had not changed much—there were 4145 inhabitants.

4. Soil Conservation Service, *Soil Survey: Cimarron County, Oklahoma* (Washington, D.C., 1960), p. 8.

5. Charles Brooks Lewis, The Development of Cimarron County (M.A. thesis, University of Oklahoma, 1939), pp. 55-57. *The Boise City News Historical and Anniversary Edition* (Summer 1968), section A, pp. 14-16. Carl Coke Rister, *No Man's Land* (Norman: University of Oklahoma Press, 1948), pp. 12-13, 34. George Rainey, *No Man's Land* (Enid, Ok.: n.p., 1937), pp. 90-115. William Baker, "A History of Cimarron County," *Chronicles of Oklahoma,* 31 (Autumn 1953), 255-67.

6. Bob French to author, taped interview, 20 Sept. 1977. Lewis, Development of Cimarron County, pp. 63, 91-105.

7. Julius Cox to author, 16 Sept. 1977.

8. William Baker, "1936 Annual Report," p. 4; Baker, "Narrative Annual Report of Extension Work, 1937," p. 8; Baker, "Narrative Annual Report of Extension Work, 1938," p. 2. Dorothea Lange and Paul Taylor, *An American Exodus* (New Haven: Yale University Press, 1969), p. 83. The total wheat yield from 1932 to 1939 was only 3 million bushels—half the 1931 crop.

Notes to Chapter Seven

1. Robert Kohler to author, taped interview, 17 Sept. 1977. *The Boise City News Historical and Anniversary Edition* (Summer 1968), section F, p. 6. See also Caroline Henderson, "Letters from the Dust Bowl," *Atlantic Monthly,* 157 (May 1936), 547-48.

2. USDA, "The Beef-Cattle Problem" (Washington, D.C., 1934), p. 3. D. A. Fitzgerald, *Livestock under the AAA* (Washington, D.C.: Brookings Institution, 1935), pp. 11-13.

3. William Baker, "1936 Annual Report," pp. 4-5. U.S. Forest Service, *The Western Range,* Senate Document 199, 74th Cong. (Washington, D.C., 1936), pp. vii, 3, 89, 300.

4. *BCN,* 6 Sept. 1934.

5. *Saturday Evening Post,* 1 June 1935, p. 26. See also Charles Burmeister, "Six Decades of Rugged Individualism: The American National Cattlemen's Association, 1898-1955," *Agricultural History,* 30 (Oct. 1956), 143-50; and James Carey, "William Allen White and Dan C. Casement on Government Regulations," *ibid.* 33 (Jan. 1959), 16-21.

6. USDA, "The Beef-Cattle Problem," p. 7. Fitzgerald, *Livestock,* pp. 192-216. C. Roger Lambert, "Drought Relief for Cattlemen: The Emergency Purchase Program of 1933-35," *Panhandle-Plains Historical Review,* 45 (1972), 34-35. Garry Nall, "Dust Bowl Days: Panhandle Farming in the 1930's," *ibid.* 48 (1975), 50-51.

7. Ross Labrier to author, taped interview, 17 Sept. 1977. Theodore Saloutos, "The New Deal and Farm Policy in the Great Plains," *Agricultural History,* 43 (July 1969), 347. *BCN,* 21 June 1934.

8. C. Roger Lambert, "The Drought Cattle Purchase, 1934-1935: Problems and Complaints," *Agricultual History,* 45 (Apr. 1971), 85-93.

9. John Schlebecker, *Cattle Raising on the Plains, 1900-1961* (Lincoln: University of Nebraska Press, 1963), pp. 119, 139, 152. *Amarillo Sunday News and Globe,* 20 Jan. 1935. *BCN,* 3 Jan. 1935.

10. Schlebecker, *Cattle Raising,* p. 129.

11. Joe Garza to author, taped interview, 19 Sept. 1977.

12. *BCN,* 2 Mar. 1933; 10 Dec. 1936.

Notes to Chapter Eight

1. *Cimarron News,* 10 and 24 Jan., 7 Mar., 25 June 1930.

2. The First State Bank, with offices in Boise City and Keyes, had $1.5 million in deposits in December 1929, only $156,000 four years later. According to its current president, Hallock Johnson, who began working there in 1934, it was never in danger of failing: "It was one of the most conservatively run banks in the State of Oklahoma." Johnson to author, 19 Sept. 1977.

3. *BCN,* 29 June, 13 July, 3 Aug., 7 Sept. 1933. See also James Ware, "The Sooner NRA: New Deal Recovery in Oklahoma," *Chronicles of Oklahoma,* 54 (Fall 1976), 339-51.

4. O. S. Rayner, "A Survey of Cimarron County, Oklahoma," Aug. 1934, Bureau of Agricultural Economics, Surveys of Rural Problem Areas, National Archives RG 83, pp. 43-44.

5. Rayner, "Survey," p. 5. USDA, *The Dust Bowl,* Editorial Reference Series No. 7 (Washington, D.C., 1940), p. 15. Following the 1935 dusters much of the newly plowed land was abandoned and left to blow. That fall only 325,000 acres were worked over and planted—down almost 100,000 acres. William Baker, "1936 Annual Report," p. 2.

6. Rayner, "Survey," pp. 44-97. Despite crop failures and existing debts, between 1929 and 1936 ownership of tractors in Oklahoma's wheat area went up 25 per cent. Paul Taylor, "Power Farming and Labor Displacement," *Monthly Labor Review,* 46 (Apr. 1938), 853.

7. Bob French to author, taped interview, 20 Sept. 1977. Roy Nall to author, taped interview, 19 Sept. 1977.

8. Dwight Sanderson, *Research Memorandum on Rural Life in the Depression* (New York: Social Science Research Council, 1937), p. 5. Great Plains Committee, *The Future of the Great Plains,* House Document 144, 75th Congr. (Washington, D.C., 1937), pp. 53-54.

9. *BCN,* 18 Jan. 1938. *Index to Deeds—Direct,* County Clerk's office, Cimarron County Courthouse.

10. Under FCA guidelines and those of the Frazier-Lemke Act, the three debt adjustment committees in the Oklahoma panhandle, all volunteer groups of farmers, helped 153 families reduce their mortgages and payments and pay overdue taxes.

BCN, 23 Apr. 1934, 22 Apr. 1937. On the FCA's over-all functions, see Arthur Schlesinger, Jr., *The Coming of the New Deal* (Boston: Houghton Mifflin, Sentry ed., 1958), p. 45; and Howard Ottoson *et al., Land and People in the Northern Plains Transition Area* (Lincoln: University of Nebraska Press, 1966), pp. 76-79.

11. Rayner, "Survey," p. 5. Great Plains Committee, *Future of the Great Plains*, p. 55. *BCN*, 31 May 1934. Changes in debt levels and credit policies are described in Regional Agricultural Council for the Southern Great Plains, Report of the 22nd Conference, Oct. 26-28, 1939, National Archives RG 114, pp. 7-18. In Dallam County, Texas, less than 2 per cent of farm mortgages were held by commercial banks in 1938—62 per cent were Federal Land Bank and FLB Commissioner's loans. See R. S. Kifer and H. L. Stewart, *Farming Hazards in the Drought Area*, WPA Research Monograph 16 (Washington, D.C., 1938), p. 191.

12. *BCN*, 2 Aug. 1934, 18 Nov. 1937. *Amarillo Sunday News and Globe,* 5 Dec. 1937.

13. Edwin Henson, "Borrowed Time in the Dust Bowl," *Land Policy Review,* 3 (Oct. 1940): 5. Rayner, "Survey," p. 110. Great Plains Committee, *Future of the Great Plains,* p. 60. For comparison, in some North Dakota counties more than 70 per cent of the farms were tax delinquent in most years; see Northern Great Plains Committee, "Rehabilitation in the Northern Great Plains," 30 July 1938, File 2285, p. 1, F.D.R. Library, Hyde Park, N.Y.

14. Rayner, "Survey," pp. 118-19. *BCN,* 26 Jan., 4 May 1933. Caroline Henderson, "Letters of Two Women Farmers. II," *Atlantic Monthly,* 152 (Sept. 1933), 350, talks about tax revolt in the Eva area, just a few miles east of Cimarron County.

15. *BCN,* 3 Jan. 1935. The county agent's office in 1936 disbursed $910,050 of federal aid to farmers: Baker, "1936 Annual Report." Within two years the total had fallen to $505,000, according to William Baker, "Narrative Annual Report of Extension Work, 1938."

16. Leonard Arrington, "The New Deal in the West: A Preliminary Statistical Inquiry," *Pacific Historical Review,* 38 (Aug. 1969), 312. See also Donald Laird, "The Tail That Wags the Nation," *Review of Reviews,* 92 (Nov. 1935), 45; and USDA, "The Texas-Oklahoma High Plains" (Amarillo, 1941), p. 40. USDA, "Conference Tour Guide to the Southern Great Plains," 26 Aug.-3 Sept. 1939, National Archives RG 114, p. 39.

17. William Weber Johnson, *Kelly Blue* (Lincoln: University of Nebraska Press, 1960), pp. 166-67. *BCN,* 20 July 1933.

18. *BCN,* 5 Mar. 1936.

19. USDA, "Texas-Oklahoma High Plains," pp. 27-28.

20. Dixon Wecter, *The Age of the Great Depression, 1929-41* (New York: Macmillan, 1948), pp. 39-40.

21. D. M. Steel, transcribed interview, 8 Mar. 1971, Panhandle-Plains Historical Museum, Canyon, Texas. The Hendersons of Eva, Oklahoma, had a typical domestic economy based on 9 milk cows, 41 cattle, 100 hens, and 240 chicks. See Caroline Henderson, "Letters of Two Women Farmers. I," *Atlantic Monthly,* 152 (Aug. 1933): 239. See also Jared van Wagenen, Jr., "A Farmer Counts His Blessings," *ibid.* 150 (July 1932), 33-39; and the diversified farming promotion in *BCN.* 11 May 1939.

22. Mr. and Mrs. Roy Godown to author, 20 Sept. 1977.

23. *BCN,* 13 Dec. 1934. Rayner, "Survey," p. 13. "Conference Tour Guide," p. 10.

Presidential Drought Conference, Des Moines, 3 Sept. 1936, File 144, F.D.R. Library, Hyde Park, N.Y. Lack of state cooperation with federal relief agencies, especially in Colorado under Governor Edwin Johnson and in Oklahoma under Governor "Alfalfa Bill" Murray, also hamstrung those programs. See James Patterson, *The New Deal and the States* (Princeton: Princeton University Press, 1969), pp. 54-69; and Donald Whisenhunt, "The Texas Attitude toward Relief, 1929-1933," *Panhandle-Plains Historical Review*, 46 (1973), 94-112.

24. Debs Baker to author, 21 Sept. 1977. *BCN*, 8 Mar. 1934. Arthur Schlesinger, Jr., *The Coming of the New Deal*, pp. 263-96; and Arthur Schlesinger, Jr., *The Politics of Upheaval* (Boston: Houghton Mifflin, Sentry ed., 1960), pp. 343-61.

25. Rayner, "Survey," pp. 13-33, 141-46. Berta Asch and A. R. Mangus, *Farmers on Relief and Rehabilitation*, WPA Research Monograph VIII (Washington, D.C., 1937), pp. 4-5, 26-51. See also Irene Link, *Relief and Rehabilitation in the Drought Area*, WPA Research Bulletin, Series V:3 (Washington, D.C., 1937), pp. 3-4. Nationally, federal relief averaged $30 a month per family in May 1934. Josephine Brown, *Public Relief, 1929-39*, (New York: Holt, 1940), pp. 233-34.

26. *BCN*, 5 Jan., 14 Dec. 1933, 17 May 1934, 16 July, 10 Dec. 1936.

27. Data furnished by Mary Ellsworth, Administrator of the Cimarron County Department of Institutions, Social and Rehabilitative Services, to author, 13 Oct. 1977. *BCN*, 18 July 1930, 16 July 1931, 2 Mar. 1933, 16 July 1936, 14 July 1938. Oklahoma State Planning Board, *Preliminary Report on State Planning* (Oklahoma City, 1936), p. 285.

28. *Cimarron News*, 11 July 1930. *BCN*, 10 Nov. 1932, 5 Nov. 1936, 7 Nov. 1940.

29. *BCN*, 2 May, 27 June 1935; 21 and 28 May 1936.

30. *BCN*, 14 Jan. 1937, 6 Apr. 1939.

31. *BCN*, 9 Feb., 6 July 1939. Baker, "Narrative Annual Report of Extension Work, 1938," p. 33. *Daily Oklahoman* (Oklahoma City), 23 Apr. 1939.

Notes to Chapter Nine

1. Taton to author, taped interview, 11 Sept. 1977.

2. For the origin and development of the land-survey system, see Hildegarde Johnson, *Order on the Land* (New York: Oxford University Press, 1976), Chap. 3.

3. Soil Conservation Service, *Soil Survey: Haskell County, Kansas* (Washington, D.C., 1968), p. 5.

4. The Haskell portion of the Santa Fe Trail was called "the water scrape." See Josiah Gregg, *The Commerce of the Prairies* ([1844], Lincoln: University of Nebraska Press, 1967), p. 59.

5. A. D. Edwards, *Influence of Drought and Depression on a Rural Community: A Case Study in Haskell County, Kansas*, USDA Social Research Report VII (Washington, D.C., 1939), p. 11. George Derby, *Cow Chips to Cadillacs* (Garden City, Kans.: n.p. 1961), reports the early history of the county.

6. Letter from the Clifts's great-grandson, Ron Ott, 26 Apr. 1975, Kansas State Historical Society Archives, Topeka.

7. *Sublette Monitor* (hereafter cited as *SM*), 21 May 1931.

8. WPA Federal Writers Project, *Kansas: A Guide to the Sunflower State* (New York: Viking, 1939), pp. 402, 437.

9. Edwards, *Influence of Drought,* pp. 20, 21, 72. According to the 1970 census, Haskell County had 3672 inhabitants; Sublette, 1908; Satanta, 1161.

10. Earl H. Bell, *Culture of a Contemporary Rural Community: Sublette, Kansas,* Bureau of Agricultural Economics, Rural Life Studies 2 (Washington, D.C., 1942), p. 29.

Notes to Chapter Ten

1. By 1930 Kansas had become the largest wheat-producing state in the nation and fourth largest state in the total volume and value of agricultural products. In cultivation was 90 per cent of its land, a total area exceeded only by that in Texas. Carroll Clark and Roy Roberts, *People of Kansas* (Topeka: Kansas State Planning Board, 1936), pp. 155-56. See also Kansas State Agricultural College, *Types of Farming in Kansas* (Topeka, 1930).

2. *SM,* 16 July 1931. The nationwide glut was all due to putting more land into cultivation; from 1866 to 1936 there was no change in wheat yield per acre.

3. The data in Table I are taken from S. D. Flora, "Climate of Kansas," *Report of the Kansas State Board of Agriculture,* 67 (June 1948), 114; and the *Biennial Reports* of the same board through the 1930s. Table II is derived from *Census of Agriculture, 1935* (Washington, D.C., 1936), 1:355-85; and *Sixteenth Census of the United States: 1940. Agriculture* (Washington, D.C., 1942), 1:part 2; 2:part 1.

4. Earl Bell, *Culture of a Contemporary Rural Community: Sublette, Kansas.* Bureau of Agricultural Economics, Rural Life Studies, 2 (Washington, D.C., 1942), p. 51.

5. *Ibid.* p. 58.

6. *Ibid.* p. 12. A. D. Edwards, *Influence of Drought and Depression on a Rural Community: A Case Study in Haskell County, Kansas,* USDA Social Research Report VII (Washington, D.C., 1939), pp. 50, 85. *SM,* 7 Jan. 1932.

7. *SM,* 26 Jan. 1933, 14 Oct. 1937.

8. Francis Schruben, *Kansas in Turmoil, 1930-36* (Columbia: University of Missouri Press, 1969), pp. 62-63. Wilda Maxine Smith, Reactions of Kansas Farmers to the New Deal Farm Program (Ph.D. thesis, University of Illinois, 1960), pp. 34-35.

9. A critic of this view was Joseph Davis, *On Agricultural Policy, 1926-1938* (Stanford, Calif.: Stanford University Press, 1939), pp. 439-40. See also Theodore Saloutos and John Hicks, *Agricultural Discontent in the Middle West, 1900-1939* (Madison: University of Wisconsin Press, 1951), p. 562.

10. Wilson, "Science and Folklore in Rural Life," in Baker Brownell (ed.), *Agriculture in Modern Life* (New York: Harper & Bros., 1939), p. 265. See also Paul Conkin, *FDR and the Origins of the Welfare State* (New York: Crowell, 1967), esp. p. 23.

11. Griswold, *Farming and Democracy* (New York: Harcourt, Brace, 1948), p. 10. According to Peter Drucker, farm subsidies in Europe were much higher than those in the United States; during the fascist drive for agricultural self-sufficiency in Germany and Italy, 15 to 20 per cent of total national income went to these subsidies, compared to at most 4 per cent in the U.S. "The Industrial Revolution Hits the Farmer," *Harper's,* 179 (Nov. 1939), 592-93.

12. An excellent overview of New Deal agricultural policy is Broadus Mitchell, *Depression Decade* (New York: Rinehart & Co., 1947), pp. 179-227. See also Edward and Frederick Schapsmeier, *Henry A. Wallace of Iowa: The Agrarian Years, 1910-1940* (Ames: Iowa State University Press, 1968).

13. Joseph Davis, *Wheat and the AAA* (Washington, D.C.: Brookings Institution, 1935), is a good review of this program. For some criticism, see Louis Hacker, "Plowing the Farmer Under," *Harper's,* 169 (June 1934), 60-74; Garet Garrett, "The AAA in Its Own Dust Bowl," *Saturday Evening Post,* 2 Mar. 1940, pp. 12-13, 60-63; Alva Johnston, "Wheat, Drought and the New Deal," *ibid.* 13 Apr. 1935, pp. 5-7, 81-83; James Boyle, "The AAA: An Epitaph," *Atlantic Monthly,* 157 (Feb. 1936), 217-25; and Bliss Iseley, "The Case History of Wheat," *ibid.* 165 (May 1940), 632-38.

14. M. L. Robinson, "The Response of Kansas Farmers to the Wheat Adjustment Program," *Journal of Farm Economics,* 19 (Feb. 1937), 359-62. Edwards, *Influence of Drought,* p. 85. *SM,* 21 Sept. 1933.

15. *SM,* 1 Nov. 1934, and 9 Jan. 1936. Smith, Reactions of Kansas Farmers, p. 113. Kansas State Board of Agriculture, *32nd Biennial Report* (Topeka, 1941), p. 357.

16. Smith, Reactions of Kansas Farmers, pp. 61-62. William Zernow, *Kansas: A History of the Jayhawk State* (Norman: University of Oklahoma Press, 1957), p. 275. Kansas Agricultural Experiment Station, "Agricultural Resources of Kansas," *Kansas State College Bulletin,* 21 (15 Oct. 1937), 7.

17. Because of a sharp fall in national production, wheat prices reached 85 cents in 1934, but the drought was chiefly responsible, not the AAA. See Van Perkins, *Crisis in Agricultural Adjustment Administration and the New Deal, 1933* (Berkeley: University of California Press, 1969), pp. 129-30. See also Benjamin Hibbard, "The Drought and the AAA Program," *The Nation,* 139 (4 July 1934), 15. Naturally, the AAA's director, Chester Davis, thought his program deserved more credit. See Davis, "Has the New Deal Helped the Farmer?" *Forum,* 95 (Feb. 1936), 76-79.

18. *Newsweek,* 10 Apr. 1939, pp. 13-14. A major reason for the low composite farm income was the large number of subsistence rural people, living especially in the South. In 1929 almost 1 million farms produced less than $600 worth of products and at the same time had no outside income—a figure that had not improved 10 years later. Oliver Baker, "Our Rural People," in Baker Brownell (ed.), *Agriculture in Modern Life,* p. 62.

19. *SM,* 12 Oct. 1933.

20. Quoted by James Beddow, "Depression and New Deal: Letters from the Plains," *Kansas Historical Quarterly,* 43 (Summer 1977), 144.

21. Edwards, *Influence of Drought,* pp. 88-89. Berta Asch and A. R. Mangus, *Farmers on Relief and Rehabilitation,* WPA Research Monograph VIII (Washington, D.C., 1937), p. 16. *SM,* 13 Dec. 1934, 2 May 1935.

22. The standard account is Sidney Baldwin, *Poverty and Politics: The Rise and Decline of the Farm Security Administration* (Chapel Hill: University of North Carolina Press, 1968).

23. Bell, *Culture of a Contemporary Rural Community,* p. 66.

24. Fred Hammer to Wilson Cowen, 6 May 1940, John McCarty Papers, Amarillo Public Library, Amarillo, Texas.

25. *SM,* 21 May 1936, 24 June 1937, 3 Feb. 1938. M. L. Wilson, "The Department's Program in the Southern Plains," *Land Policy Circular* (Feb. 1938), 20. See also Olaf Larson *et al., Ten Years of Rural Rehabilitation in the United States* (Washington, D.C., 1947); and Clair Bondurant, "A Study of One Hundred Farm Security Administration Grant Families in Ellis County, Kansas, 1939," *Fort Hays State College Studies* (141):37.

26. Kimmel, "Unit Reorganization Program for the Southern Great Plains," *Journal of Farm Economics,* 22 (Feb. 1940), 266. Lionel Holm, "What Is Happening to 'Farms Tailored to Fit'?" *Land Policy Review* (Oct. 1940), 8-13. Also supporting unit diversification were E. A. Starch, "Type of Farming Modification Needed in the Great Plains," *Journal of Farm Economics,* 21 (Feb. 1939), 114-20; and Carl Kraenzel, "New Frontiers of the Great Plains: A Cultural Approach to the Study of Man-Land Problems," *ibid.* 24 (Aug. 1942), 571-88.

27. *SM,* 11 Jan., 15 Feb. 1934. The Farm Bureau's political role is discussed in Grant McConnell, *The Decline of Agrarian Democracy* (New York: Atheneum, 1953); and Christiana Campbell, *The Farm Bureau and the New Deal* (Urbana: University of Illinois Press, 1962).

28. Bell, *Culture,* p. 197.

Notes to Chapter Eleven

1. This argument was developed in considerable detail by Walter Prescott Webb, *The Great Plains* (Boston: Ginn, 1931), and became a constant theme in the decade.

2. Sublette and Satanta were small villages at that, with 1935 populations of 604 and 444, respectively. For a comparative study of such settlements, see Edmund Brunner and Irving Lorge, *Rural Trends in Depression Years* (New York: Columbia University Press, 1937); on demography, see pp. 66-67.

3. A splendid account of the recent decline of an Old World rural community is Ronald Blythe, *Akenfield: Portrait of an English Village* (New York: Pantheon, 1969).

4. Earl Bell, *Culture of a Contemporary Rural Community: Sublette, Kansas.* Bureau of Agricultural Economics, Rural Life Studies, 2 (Washington, D.C., 1942), p. 68.

5. A. D. Edwards, *Influence of Drought and Depression on a Rural Community: A Case Study in Haskell County, Kansas,* USDA Social Research Report VII (Washington, D.C., 1939), p. 80. There were only 57 business establishments left in Haskell by 1936. Nationally, however, small towns and villages saw an increase in their average number of stores. (Brunner and Lorge, *Rural Trends,* pp. 97-102.)

6. Paul Mazur, quoted in Robert and Helen Lynd, *Middletown in Transition* (New York: Harcourt, Brace, & World, Harvest Book, 1965), p. 46. See also Arthur Vidich and Joseph Bensman, *Small Town in a Mass Society* (Princeton: Princeton University Press, 1968), pp. 79-107, 416-17.

7. *SM,* 18, 25 Apr. 1935. Haskell churches were all strongly fundamentalist. (Bell, *Culture,* pp. 86-89.)

8. Bell, *Culture,* p. 77. See also Carl Taylor, "The Wheat Areas," in Taylor *et al., Rural Life in the United States* (New York: Knopf, 1949), p. 396.

9. Helen Meairs to author, taped interview, 8 Sept. 1977.

10. Bell, *Culture*, p. 75. Brunner and Lorge, *Rural Trends*, found an average of 20 social organizations per village, with the biggest growth rates after 1930 among bridge clubs, the biggest declines among fraternal lodges (p. 259).

11. *SM*, 2 Oct. 1930, 19 Feb. 1931.

12. Edwards, *Influence of Drought*, pp. 47-48.

13. Kendall Bailes, "The Mennonites Come to Kansas," *American Heritage*, 10 (Aug. 1959), 30-33, 102-5.

14. See Max Weber, *The Protestant Ethic and the Spirit of Capitalism*, trans. Talcott Parsons (New York: Scribner's, 1930), pp. 44, 144-54.

15. Wallace and Bertha Schmidt to author, taped interview, 9 Sept. 1977.

16. Warren Moore to author, taped interview, 9 Sept. 1977.

17. *SM*, 22 June 1933, 3 Dec. 1936, 18 Mar. 1937, 10 Feb. 1938.

18. Bell, *Culture*, pp. 74-75. *SM*, 30 Mar., 19 Oct. 1933. A minister, however, revisiting a southern plains county seat after 15 years' absence, found "the moral tone . . . definitely down." See Thomas Alfred Tripp, "Dust Bowl Tragedy," *Christian Century*, 57 (24 Jan. 1940), 108-10.

19. On the hinterland and colonial status of the region *vis-à-vis* urban and industrial America, see Carl Kraenzel, *The Great Plains in Transition* (Norman: University of Oklahoma Press, 1955), Chap. 16.

20. *SM*, 2 June 1932.

21. *SM*, 1 June 1939.

Notes to Chapter Twelve

1. Nils Olsen, in *Proceedings of the National Conference on Land Utilization* (Washington, D.C., 1932), p. 7. Overexpansion took place in all the countries evolving toward agribusiness. Canada, for instance, in the 1910-30 period increased its wheat area by 375 per cent, Australia by 350 per cent (p. 11).

2. *Ibid.* p. 29. "Land Utilization and Land Policy," in National Resources Board, *Report on National Planning and Public Works* (Washington, D.C., 1934), pp. 8-25, 108-13.

3. The standard account of the T.R. era is Samuel Hays, *Conservation and the Gospel of Efficiency* (Cambridge: Harvard University Press, 1959). On the 1930s, see Edgar B. Nixon (ed.), *Franklin D. Roosevelt and Conservation, 1911-1945* (2 vols. 1957. F.D.R. Library, Hyde Park, N.Y.); Anna Lou Riesch, Conservation under Franklin D. Roosevelt, (Ph.D. thesis, University of Wisconsin, 1952); Roy Robbins, *Our Landed Heritage*, rev. ed. (Lincoln: University of Nebraska Press, 1976), Chap. 25.

4. Mumford, "In Our Stars," *The Forum and Century*, 88 (Dec. 1932), 338. See also M. L. Wilson, "A Land Use Program for the Federal Government," *Journal of Farm Economics*, 15 (Apr. 1933), esp. 219; and Wilson, "Agricultural Conservation—An Aspect of Land Utilization," *ibid.* 19 (Feb. 1937), 3-12.

5. Putnam Dana McMillan, "Marginal Land and Marginal Thinking," *Saturday Evening Post*, 1 June 1935, p. 89. For an opposing view, see Louis Bernard Schmidt, "The Agricultural Revolution in the Prairies and Great Plains of the United States," *Agricultural History*, 8 (Oct. 1934), 195. On the reclamation debate, see

National Resources Board, p. 194; Mary Hargreaves, "Land-Use Planning in Response to Drought: The Experience of the Thirties," *Agricultural History,* 50 (Oct. 1976), 569-70; and Donald Swain, "The Bureau of Reclamation and the New Deal, 1933-1940," *Pacific Northwest Quarterly,* 61 (July 1970), 137-46.

6. Rexford Tugwell, "The Resettlement Idea," *Agricultural History,* 33 (Oct. 1959), 161. Among his "impractical" ideas were Tugwell's interest in building new greenbelt towns, resettling surplus factory workers on the land, and encouraging subsistence farming. His view of the government's role, however, was decidedly modest—to "supplement" private industry by cleaning up its excesses. See Tugwell, "Our New National Domain," *Scribner's,* 99 (Mar. 1936), 164-68; and Tugwell, "The Place of Government in a National Land Program," *Journal of Farm Economics,* 16 (Jan. 1934); 55-69. See also Bernard Sternsher, *Rexford Tugwell and the New Deal* (New Brunswick: Rutgers University Press, 1964), esp. pp. 212, 219, 221-22.

7. Henry C. Taylor, "L. C. Gray, Agricultural Historian and Land Economist," *Agricultural History,* 26 (Oct. 1952), 165; and Richard Kirkendall, "L. C. Gray and the Supply of Agricultural Land," *ibid.* 37 (Oct. 1963), 205-16.

8. L. C. Gray et al., "The Causes: Traditional Attitudes and Institutions," in USDA, *Soils and Men* (Washington, D.C., 1938), pp. 111-36. Gray, "Land Planning," Public Policy Pamphlet No. 19 (Chicago: University of Chicago Press, 1936), p. 2. See also Gray, "National Policies Affecting Land Use," in *National Policies Affecting Rural Life,* Proceedings of the 16th American Country Life Conference (Chicago: University of Chicago Press, 1934), p. 86; and Gray, "Our Land Policy Today," *Land Policy Review,* 1 (May-June 1938), 3-8.

9. T. H. Watkins and Charles Watson, Jr., *The Lands No One Knows: America and the Public Domain* (San Francisco: Sierra Club Books, 1975), pp. 112-15. Robbins, *Our Landed Heritage,* pp. 421-23.

10. There was no consensus on what "submarginal" meant; for some people, the entire Dust Bowl qualified; for others, none of it did. See Lewis Gray, "Federal Purchase and Administration of Submarginal Land in the Great Plains," *Journal of Farm Economics,* 21 (Feb. 1939), 123-31. In this region the government decided to buy parcels too small to be economically operated rather than simply the worst eroded areas. The average cost was $2.45 per acre in the Baca County, Colorado, project. There were two other southern plains projects—the first located in Dallam County, Texas, Cimarron County, Oklahoma, and Union County, New Mexico; the second in Morton County, Kansas. The total area purchased in all three projects was somewhat less than 500,000 acres. See E. D. G. Roberts, "The Land Utilization Program in the Southern Great Plains," *Science,* 30 Sept. 1938, pp. 289-92.

11. Tolley, quoted in H. H. Wooten, *The Land Utilization Program, 1934 to 1964,* Agricultural Economics Report No. 85 (Washington, D.C., 1965), p. 35. In 1938 the lands purchased on the southern plains were turned over to the Soil Conservation Service for restoration to a grass cover; in 1953 the Forest Service took control, and it manages them today as the Rita Blanca, Cimarron, and Comanche National Grasslands. See Keith Argow, "Our National Grasslands: Dustland to Grassland," *American Forests,* 68 (Jan. 1962), 89.

12. Gray, "Our Land Policy Today," p. 4. Richard Kirkendall, *Social Scientists and Farm Policies in the Age of Roosevelt* (Columbia: University of Missouri Press, 1966), p. 179.

13. F.D.R. to Morris Cooke, 17 Sept. 1936, in Nixon (ed.), *Roosevelt and Conservation*, 1:575. While F.D.R. insisted on maintaining "the largest possible population" on the Great Plains, others called for massive out-migration—beyond even the exoduster movement. See C. Warren Thornthwaite, "The Great Plains," in Carter Goodrich *et al.*, *Migration and Economic Opportunity* (Philadelphia: University of Pennsylvania Press, 1936), pp. 242-45. This author proposed "a practically complete return to a grazing economy," which would have required an estimated population drop of 900,000—40 per cent of the 1930 census. See also Bushrod Allin, "Migration Required for Best Land Use," *Journal of Farm Economics*, 18 (Aug. 1936), 496.

14. Tugwell to F.D.R., 4 Dec. 1935, Nixon (ed.), *Roosevelt and Conservation*, 1:456.

15. Howard Ottoson *et al.*, *Land and People in the Northern Plains Transition Area* (Lincoln: University of Nebraska Press, 1966), pp. 87-89. Reports of the southern plains' Regional Advisory Committee can be found in the National Archives RG 114.

16. "Report of the Great Plains Drought Area Committee," Aug. 1936, p. 5. On Cooke's appointment, see Robert Twombley, *The Life and Times of a Happy Radical* (New York: Harper, 1954), pp. 141-43. See also the committee's tour map and correspondence in Official File 2285, F.D.R. Library, Hyde Park, N.Y.

17. Morris Cooke to Henry Wallace, 24 July 1936, National Archives RG 16. Drafts of the final report and supplementary material are in the Great Plains Committee file, RG 83. Committee members included Cooke, Gray, Harlan Barrows (University of Chicago geographer), Hugh Bennett (Soil Conservation Service), F. C. Harrington (Works Progress Administration), Richard Moore (Corps of Engineers), John Page (Bureau of Reclamation), and Harlow Person (Rural Electrification Administration).

18. Great Plains Committee, *The Future of the Great Plains*, U.S. House Document 144, 75th Cong. (Washington, D.C., 1937), pp. 63-67.

19. *Ibid.* p. 63.

20. *Ibid.* pp. 69-89. "Lines of action" were recommended at federal, state, local, and farmstead levels. Even so, complaints were made that states were being told where to "get off" and that the USDA was hogging the show in Washington. Frederick Delano to Harold Ickes, 13 Jan. 1937, Nixon (ed.), *Roosevelt and Conservation*, 1:611-14.

Notes to Chapter Thirteen

1. Clements's key work was *Plant Succession* (1916). For a discussion of his ideas, see Donald Worster, *Nature's Economy: The Roots of Ecology* (San Francisco: Sierra Club Books, 1977), pp. 205-20, 235-37. See also Richard Overfield, "Charles E. Bessey: The Impact of 'New' Botany on American Agriculture," *Technology and Culture*, 16 (Apr. 1975), 162-81; and Paul Sears, "Frederic Edward Clements,"

Dictionary of American Biography: Supplement Three, 1941-1945 (New York: Scribner's, 1973), pp. 168-70.

2. Paul Sears, *Deserts on the March* ([1935], Norman: University of Oklahoma Press, 1959), p. 67. Roger Smith, "Upsetting the Balance of Nature, with Special Reference to Kansas and the Great Plains," *Science,* 24 June 1932, pp. 649-54. See also Frederick Albertson, "Man's Disorder of Nature's Design in the Great Plains," *Smithsonian Institution Annual Report, 1950* (Washington, D.C.: Smithsonian Institution, 1951), pp. 363-72.

3. F. E. Clements and Ralph Chaney, *Environment and Life in the Great Plains,* Carnegie Institution, Supplemental Publication No. 24, rev. ed. (Washington, D.C., Carnegie Institution, 1937), pp. 47-49, 51. Clements, "Ecology in the Public Service," *Dynamics of Vegetation* (New York: H. W. Wilson, 1949), pp. 266-78. Sears, *Deserts on the March,* p. 162. See also A.G.I., "Arid Farming and Ecology," *Scientific American,* 159 (Nov. 1938), 233.

4. Walster, "Backgrounds of Economic Distress in the Great Plains," in John Hoyt, *Drought of 1936,* U.S. Geological Survey, Water Supply Paper No. 820 (Washington, D.C., 1938), pp. 59-60.

5. The attitude described here had social value when national expansion was desired. "Had the pioneer been an ecologist," wrote Edward Higbee, "he probably would have stayed back East and taught school." *The American Oasis* (New York: Knopf, 1959), p. 125.

6. Wilson to Dr. V. Bush, 14 June 1939, National Archives RG 16. Sears to author, 1 Jan. 1978. See also Sears, "The Black Blizzards," in Daniel Aaron (ed.), *America in Crisis* (New York: Knopf, 1952), pp. 296-97.

7. *The Future of the Great Plains,* U.S. House Document No. 144, 75th Cong. (Washington, D.C., 1937), p. 2.

8. Herbert Hanson and C. T. Vorhies, "Need for Research on Grassland," *Scientific Monthly,* 46 (Mar. 1938), 23-41. John Weaver and Evan Flory, "Stability of Climax Prairie and Some Environmental Changes Resulting from Breaking," *Ecology,* 15 (Oct. 1934), 343.

9. Sears, *Deserts on the March,* p. 127. An ecologist has recently challenged the complexity-stability theory; see Paul Colinvaux, *Why Big Fierce Animals Are Rare* (Princeton: Princeton University Press, 1978), esp. p. 205. His argument, however, is based upon scanty and unpersuasive evidence.

10. Herbert Hanson, "Ecology in Agriculture," *Ecology,* 20 (Apr. 1939), 116. Clements and Chaney, *Environment and Life,* p. 51.

11. *Future of the Great Plains,* pp. 63-64. The original essay was published in *Journal of Forestry,* 31 (Oct. 1933), 634-43. The most thorough account of Leopold's thought is Susan Flader, *Thinking Like a Mountain* (Columbia: University of Missouri Press, 1974).

12. James Malin, *The Grassland of North America* (Lawrence, Kans.: n.p., 1956), pp. 167-68, 335, 406; Malin, "The Grassland of North America: Its Occupance and the Challenge of Continuous Reappraisal," in W. L. Thomas (ed.), *Man's Role in Changing the Face of the Earth* (Chicago: University of Chicago Press, 1956), pp. 351-56. Malin's economic views are expressed in "Mobility and History: Reflections on the Agricultural Policies of the United States in Relation to a Mecha-

nized World," *Agricultural History,* 17 (Oct. 1943), 177-91. See also Worster, *Nature's Economy,* pp. 242-48.

13. Karl Marx and Friedrich Engels, "Manifesto of the Communist Party," in Lewis Feuer (ed.), *Basic Writings on Politics and Philosophy* (Garden City, N.Y.: Doubleday, Anchor, 1959), p. 10.

14. Carl Sauer, "Theme of Plant and Animal Destruction in Economic History," *Journal of Farm Economics,* 20 (Nov. 1938), 765-75.

15. Sears, *Deserts on the March,* pp. 25, 140-56. Sears did support the mildly reformist program of the Great Plains Committee; see Sears, "O, Bury Me Not; Or, The Bison Avenged," *New Republic,* 12 May 1937, p. 10. See also his "Death from the Soil," *American Mercury,* 42 (Dec. 1937), 440-47.

16. Paul Sears, *This Is Our World* ([1937], Norman: University of Oklahoma Press, 1971), pp. 278, 292.

17. Sears, *Deserts on the March,* pp. 92, 146.

18. Paul Sears, "Ecology—A Subversive Subject," *Bioscience,* 14 (July 1964), 11-13.

Notes to Chapter Fourteen

1. Charles Whitfield, "Sand Dunes in the Great Plains," *Soil Conservation,* 2 (Mar. 1937), 208-9. *Amarillo Sunday News and Globe,* 8 Aug. 1934, 13 Dec. 1936. Vance Johnson, *Heaven's Tableland* (New York: Farrar, Straus, 1947), pp. 243-51.

2. Ben Hibbs, "The Dust Bowl Can Be Saved," *Saturday Evening Post,* 18 Dec. 1937, pp. 16-17.

3. John Timmons *et al., Principles of Resource Conservation Policy* (Washington, D.C., National Academy of Sciences, 1961), p. 4. "Creeping Disaster," *Business Week,* 28 July 1934, p. 36. A good summary of conservation agronomy is Graham Jacks and Robert Whyte, *Vanishing Lands: A World Survey of Soil Erosion* (New York: Doubleday, Doran, 1936), Chap. 9. Jacks, who was director of Great Britain's Commonwealth Bureau of Soil Science, put the United States—and the Great Plains in particular—in the forefront of this applied science.

4. Russell Lord, *The Care of the Earth* (New York: Mentor, 1962), p. 190. Hugh Bennett published much in his life, including *Soil Conservation* (1939). The only biography is Wellington Brink, *Big Hugh: The Father of Soil Conservation* (New York: Macmillan, 1951).

5. Peter Farb, "Hugh Bennett: Messiah of the Soil," *American Forests,* 66 (Jan. 1960), 40. National Resources Board, *A Report on National Planning and Public Works* (Washington, D.C., 1934), pp. 170-71. Robert Morgan, *Governing Soil Conservation* (Baltimore: Johns Hopkins University Press, 1966), gives the bureaucratic history of the SCS.

6. Hugh Bennett to R. I. Throckmorton, 16 June 1934, National Archives RG 114. Bennett, "Adjustment of Agriculture to its Environment," *Annals of the Association of American Geographers,* 33 (Dec. 1943), 178-79; Bennett, "Development of Natural Resources: The Coming Technological Revolution on the Land," *Science,* 3 Jan. 1947, p. 3. R. Burnell Held and Marion Clawson, *Soil Conservation in Perspective* (Baltimore: Johns Hopkins University Press, 1965), p. 69.

7. *Amarillo Sunday News-Globe,* 12 Dec. 1937. H. V. Geib to Hugh Bennett, 25 May 1934, National Archives RG 114. Geib, "Report of Wind Erosion Survey in

the Region of the Oklahoma Panhandle and Adjacent Territory," Sept. 1933, *ibid.* USDA, *The Dust Bowl,* Editorial Reference Series No. 7 (Washington, D.C., 1940), p. 26. John Salmond, *The Civilian Conservation Corps, 1933-1942* (Durham, N.C.: Duke University Press, 1967), pp. 124-25.

8. Arthur Joel, "Soil Conservation Reconnaissance Surveys of the Southern Great Plains Wind Erosion Area," USDA Technical Bulletin No. 556 (Washington, D.C., 1937), pp. 33, 45, 47. See also Glenn Rule, "Land Facts on the Southern Plains," USDA Miscellaneous Publications No. 334 (Washington, D.C., 1939).

9. Joel, "Soil Conservation," p. 53. Roy Kimmel, "Planning for the Southern Great Plains," *Soil Conservation,* 5 (Nov. 1939), 120. Roy Hockensmith explained why the Region VI office was against putting much land back into grass: it would someday be "in great demand for crop production, which will be its most economical use." ("The Soil Conservation Program in the Dust Bowl Area," 30 Dec. 1937, National Archives RG 415.)

10. H. H. Finnell, "Prevention and Control of Wind Erosion of High Plains Soils in the Panhandle Area," SCS Region VI Publications, National Archives RG 114. Finnell, "Yardsticks and the Four-Card Draw," *Land Policy Review* (Oct. 1940), 19-23. B. W. McGinnis, "Utilization of Crop Residues to Reduce Wind Erosion," *The Land Today and Tomorrow,* 2 (Apr. 1935), 12. Glenn Rule, "Crops Against the Wind on the Southern Great Plains," *Farmers' Bulletin* No. 1833 (Washington, D.C., 1939), pp. 19-29. E. F. Chilcott, "Preventing Soil Blowing on the Southern Great Plains," *Farmers' Bulletin* No. 1771 (Washington, D.C., 1937), pp. 12-20.

11. H. H. Finnell, "Water Management," n.d., National Archives RG 114; Finnell, "The Moisture-Saving Efficiency of Level Terraces under Semi-Arid Conditions," *Journal of the American Society of Agronomy,* 22 (June 1930), 522-29. McGinnis, "Erosion and Its Control on the Southern Great Plains," SCS Region VI Publications, National Archives RG 114, p. 4.

12. The Water Facilities (Pope-Jones) Act of 1938 provided loans to drill wells, construct small dams and farm ponds, and lay out irrigation systems.

13. "The Report of the 21st Conference of the Regional Advisory Committee," 1-3 Aug. 1939, National Archives RG 114. SCS Region VI, "Annual Report, 1939-1940," *ibid.* See also Charles Hardin, *The Politics of Agriculture: Soil Conservation and the Struggle for Power in Rural America* (Glencoe, Ill.: Free Press, 1952).

14. The controversy was aired in "The Shelterbelt Project," *Journal of Forestry,* 32 (Nov. 1934), 801-12. Recent accounts include Wilmon Droze, *Trees, Prairies, and People* (Denton: Texas Woman's University Press, 1976); and Thomas Wessel, "Roosevelt and the Great Plains Shelterbelt," *Great Plains Journal,* 8 (Spring 1969), 57-74.

15. Raphael Zon, "Shelterbelts—Futile Dream or Workable Plan?" *Science.* 26 Apr. 1935, p. 392. U.S. Forest Service, *Possibilities of Shelterbelt Planting in the Plains Region* (Washington, D.C., 1935), pp. 5, 36.

16. Edgar Nixon (ed.), *Franklin D. Roosevelt and Conservation* (2 vols. 1957, F.D.R. Library, Hyde Park, N.Y.), 1:200-3. State Reports, Fiscal Year 1939, Prairie States Forestry Project, National Archives RG 114. Edwin Henson to Milton Eisenhower, 15 Dec. 1939, *ibid.*

17. Charles Ahlson, Proceedings of the Agronomy and Range Management Conference, Denver, 13-16 Jan. 1937, National Archives RG 114. Finnell, "Conservation Pays

Off in the Plains Country," *Soil Conservation,* 8 (July 1942), 4-5. Hugh Bennett claimed that average per-acre yields on all crops across the country were improved 20 per cent by conservation methods. ("Adjustment of Agriculture to Environment," p. 174.)

18. Francis Flood, "The Dust Bowl Is Being Tamed," *Farmer-Stockman* (Oklahoma City), 1 July 1937.

19. Bennett, "Development of Natural Resources," p. 4. Alastair Cooke, *A Generation on Trial* (New York: Knopf, 1951), p. 28.

20. Hugh Bennett, "The Land and the People," *Scientific Monthly,* 48 (June 1939), 535. Johnson, *Heaven's Tableland,* p. 269.

21. Johnson, *Heaven's Tableland,* pp. 274-75.

22. John Bird, "The Great Plains Hit the Jackpot," *Saturday Evening Post,* 30 Aug. 1947, pp. 16, 90. Clinton Anderson, "Soil Murder on the Plains," *Country Gentleman,* 117 (Sept. 1947), 85.

23. H. H. Finnell, quoted in Bird, "Great Plains," p. 90. Finnell, "Land Use Experience in Southern Great Plains," USDA Circular No. 820 (Washington, D.C., 1940), p. 15; and Finnell, "The Plowup of Western Grasslands and the Resultant Effect upon Great Plains Agriculture," *Southwestern Social Science Quarterly,* 32 (Sept. 1951), 94-100.

24. *Kansas City Star,* 18 July 1948. *Kansas City Times,* 3 Dec. 1947. Bird, "Great Plains," p. 88. See also C. C. Iseley, "Will the Dust Bowl Return?" *Northwestern Miller,* 20 Nov. 1948, pp. 18, 35, 38; and David Coyle, "The Attack on Soil Conservation," *Colorado Quarterly,* 3 (Autumn 1954), 202-14.

25. According to Wayne Palmer's Drought Severity Index (PDSI), there were 57 months of severe or extreme drought in Kansas during the fifties, 99 in the thirties. From 1931-68 extreme drought occurred in 6 per cent of the months, severe drought in 14 per cent. Merle Brown and L. Dean Bark, "Drought in Kansas," Kansas State University, Agricultural Experiment Station Bulletin No. 547 (1971), p. 7.

26. *Topeka Capital,* 2, 6, 7, 20 Mar. 1954. *Kansas City Times,* 12 Mar. 1954. "Is Dust Bowl Coming Back?" *U.S. News and World Report,* 5 Mar. 1954, pp. 35-36. See also Stephen Cole, "Black Death in Kansas," *Esquire,* 34 (Aug. 1950), 67, 107-8.

27. Almost 16 million acres were damaged by wind erosion—impaired in their capacity to grow crops—in 1954-55, 10 million in 1956-57. Carle Zimmerman, "The Future of the Great Plains," in Carle Zimmerman and Seth Russell (eds.), *Symposium on the Great Plains of North America* (Fargo: North Dakota Institute for Regional Studies, 1967), p. 212. High prices, high yields from new varieties, and sorghum saved the region from bankruptcy; Haskell County in 1957 harvested only half as much wheat acreage as it had in 1936, but it got twice as many bushels and 4 times as much money. Its total crop income was $3.5 million in 1957.

28. W. I. Drummond, "Short Grass Country," *Review of Reviews,* 93 (June 1936), 39. Johnson, *Heaven's Tableland,* p. 274.

29. H. H. Finnell, "The Dust Storms of 1954," *Scientific American,* 191 (July 1954), 29. See also Finnell, "The Dust Storms of 1948," *ibid.* 179 (Aug. 1948), 7-11. By 1956 the SCS estimated there were 14 million acres on the plains that ought to be restored to grass, another 10 million that were not profitable for wheat on a long-term basis—and nothing was being done about it (Held and Clawson, *Soil Conservation,* p. 83).

Notes to Epilogue

1. See Franklin King, *Farmers of Forty Centuries* (Emmaus, Pa.: Organic Gardening Press, n.d.).

2. McDaniels to author, taped interview, 12 Sept. 1977.

3. In 1976 the 3 million farms in the U.S. had an average income of $19,100—of which $11,200 came from off-farm jobs. One in 3 farms accounted for 90 per cent of all farm sales, the rest scraped by. USDA, Economic Research Service, *Farm Income Situation* (Feb. 1977).

4. Professor Charles Stockton of the University of Arizona has recently established, with tree-ring data going back to A.D. 1700, a 20.4-year drought cycle in the West. He and Murray Mitchell of the National Oceanic and Atmospheric Administration are carrying out further studies to correlate this cycle with sunspots. Stockton to author, 3 Apr. 1978. See also John Borchert, "The Dust Bowl in the 1970s," *Annals of the Association of American Geographers,* 61 (Mar. 1971), 1-22.

5. *New York Times,* 11 Jan. 1975. *Newsweek,* 23 Feb. 1976, pp. 68, 71; 5 Apr., pp. 71-74. *Time,* 15 Mar. 1976, p. 75. *Denver Post,* 24 Feb. 1977. *U.S. News & World Report,* 4 Apr. 1977, pp. 46-50.

6. Donald Green, *Land of the Underground Rain: Irrigation on the Texas High Plains, 1910-1970* (Austin: University of Texas Press, 1973), pp. 188, 190-238. Richard Pfister, *Water Resources and Irrigation* (Lawrence, Kans.: Bureau of Business Research, 1955). Homer Wells, "Land and Water in the High Plains," *Land Policy Review,* 1 (Jan.-Feb. 1939), 20-24. William Lockeretz, "The Lessons of the Dust Bowl," *American Scientist,* 66 (Sept.-Oct. 1978), 568.

7. Jack Alexander, Superintendent of the Panhandle Experiment Station, Goodwell, Ok., to author, 12 Sept. 1977.

8. Roy Huhn, District Supervisor and Conservationist, Soil Conservation Service, Sublette, Kans., to author, 5 Sept. 1977. See also William Mays, *Sublette Revisited: Stability and Change in a Rural Kansas Community* (New York: Florham Park Press, 1968), pp. 17-21.

9. Kansas State Board of Agriculture, *60th Annual Report and Farm Facts* (Topeka, 1976), pp. 30F, 42F, 56F, 108F. The increasing use of commercial fertilizer farther south is discussed by Garry Nall, Agricultural History of the Texas Panhandle, 1880-1965 (Ph.D. thesis, University of Oklahoma, 1972), pp. 207-8.

10. Helen Meairs to author, taped interview, 8 Sept. 1977.

11. Lester Brown with Erik Eckholm, *By Bread Alone* (New York: Praeger, 1974), pp. 5-6, 43, 61, 83. USDA, Economic Research Service, *Agricultural Outlook* (Jan.-Dec. 1977).

12. Earl O. Heady, "The Agriculture of the U.S.," *Scientific American,* 235 (Sept. 1976), 106.

13. Nicholas Wade, "Sahelian Drought: No Victory for Western Aid," *Science,* 19 July 1974, p. 236. See also John Prospero and Ruby Nees, "Dust Concentration in the Atmosphere of the Equatorial North Atlantic," *ibid.* 10 June 1977, pp. 1196-98; Michael Glantz (ed.), *The Politics of Natural Disaster* (New York: Praeger, 1976). There are 6 Sahelian nations: Senegal, Mauritania, Mali, Upper Volta, Niger, and Chad. The most recent information is that drought has returned to the area.

14. Francis Moore Lappé and Joseph Collins, *Food First: Beyond the Myth of Scarcity* (Boston: Houghton Mifflin, 1977), pp. 98-107. See also Claire Sterling, "The Making of the Sub-Saharan Wasteland," *Atlantic Monthly,* 233 (May 1974), 98-105; and "Sahel: Land of No Return?" *UNESCO Courier,* Apr. 1975 (entire issue).

15. See Boyce Rensberger's articles on the Nairobi conference, *New York Times,* 21 Aug.-11 Sept. 1977. "A Halt to Desert Advance," *UNESCO Courier,* June 1977 (entire issue). Erik Eckholm and Lester Brown, *Spreading Deserts—The Hand of Man,* Worldwatch Paper 13 (Washington, D.C.: Worldwatch Institute, 1977).

16. Useful on the climate change controversy are Reid Bryson and Thomas Murray, *Climates of Hunger* (Madison: University of Wisconsin Press, 1977); Stephen Schneider with Lynne Mesirow, *The Genesis Strategy* (New York: Plenum Press, 1976); John Gribben, *Forecasts, Famines, and Freezes* (New York: Walker, 1976); Lowell Ponte, *The Cooling* (Englewood Cliffs, N.J.: Prentice-Hall, 1976); and *Newsweek,* 23 Jan. 1978, pp. 74-76.

INDEX